FOURTH EDITION

# MUSIC
## A Way of Life
## for the Young Child

### Kathleen M. Bayless
Kent State University

### Marjorie E. Ramsey
Georgia Southwestern College

Merrill, an imprint of
Macmillan Publishing Company
New York

Collier Macmillan Canada, Inc.
Toronto

Maxwell Macmillan International Publishing Group
New York   Oxford   Singapore   Sydney

Cover photo by Mary Elenz-Tranter
Editor: Linda A. Sullivan
Production Editor: Constantina Geldis
Cover Designer: Russ Maselli

This book was set in Times Roman.

Macmillan Publishing Company
866 Third Avenue, New York, NY 10022

Collier Macmillan Canada, Inc.


**Library of Congress Cataloging-in-Publication Data**
Bayless, Kathleen M.
    Music, a way of life for the young child / Kathleen M. Bayless,
Marjorie E. Ramsey.—4th ed.
        p.   cm.
    Includes bibliographical references and index.
    ISBN 0–675–21372–X
    1. Music—Instruction and study—Juvenile. I. Ramsey, Marjorie
E., 1921–    . II. Title.
MT1.B35   1991
372.87—dc2                                          90–44437
                                                    CIP
                                                    MN


Printing:              5   6   7   8   9    Year:          3   4

# Preface

We have always sung with and to young children. We have practiced with our "special thirteen." Ultimately, our belief that music is a necessary and vital dimension in the lives of the very young led us to write the first edition of this book, then the second, the third edition, and now the fourth. It is evident that many of you agree and support our belief.

Throughout a significant part of our professional careers we have been concerned about music in the lives of very young children. For a long time little guidance was available to teachers, parents, and care givers as they sought to add musical experience for the young. Now more materials in music for the preschool child are offered, and we are seeing increased awareness and interest of many individuals and national groups.

Before you scan the Contents and enjoy the photographs and songs, we urge you to consider carefully our Statement of Beliefs, which follows this preface. The book is built on these beliefs. We want to emphasize the "why." Theory and practice go hand in hand. There is a strong developmental thread throughout the various age levels from birth to age five.

The songs, ideas, suggestions, and musical concepts are time-tested. Parents, teachers, would-be teachers, care givers, and students have aided in the compiling and trying out of the contents of this fourth edition. You will note that piano accompaniments have intentionally been arranged for ease of playing. In order to increase the number of songs in this edition, some of the accompaniments to the songs have been deleted and only the melodies are provided. Also, the keys of some of the songs have been transposed to lower keys to better accommodate the singing range of young voices and for ease of singing by the teacher. In this edition, a fingering chart for the recorder has been added. Where Autoharp chording on songs is indicated, play the indicated chord until the next chord change.

Musical concepts and activities appropriate for each age level have been included to accompany some of the songs and rhythms. It is not our intention that music experiences provided for the children should always be used to teach them something. The children's awareness and understanding of the concepts and skills presented should grow out of the natural encounters with the musical selections and activities. Using music in creative ways is encouraged. At these age levels, enjoyment of the music should be paramount. We hope that as you discover the materials, you will enjoy the musical activities whether in your home or in the large community where children gather. Live good music with young children, as we have, and become an advocate for music in their lives. Even though you feel you lack experience, just begin! Young children are not critics of your expertise with music—they enjoy, participate, and thrive as you do the same.

If you are familiar with earlier editions of *Music: A Way of Life for the Young Child,* you will notice that in this fourth edition we have expanded some sections, combined others, and reemphasized still others. Each chapter now has brief key ideas, a summary, and questions to consider. Sound language and movement thread throughout the text.

Part I is an expanded discussion of the very earliest years and musical enrichment for infancy, the ones to twos, and the twos to threes. Part II concentrates on preschool and kindergarten children's growth in musical experience. Part III emphasizes music in an integrated curriculum, with suggestions and songs suitable to the academic areas, language arts, sciences, mathematics, social studies, and related content. An expanded section on "Stories That Sing" and using music to promote whole language has been added to Chapter Six. It is here that those who work with young children can realize the opportunities for music through the day.

Chapter Seven, Music for Children with Special Needs, evolved from the first edition of this text to the present from our convictions that all children need and enjoy music. The extensive and enthusiastic response to the inclusion and expansion of this chapter has supported our beliefs.

Young children are part of a rapidly changing world—a world of shrinking distances; thus, Chapter Eight, Music: A Child's Heritage, shares the musical richness and diversity of such a world.

Selected bibliography and suggested readings offer further learning and stimulation for adults wishing to deepen their understanding of the potential of music. The appendixes offer an abundance of resources.

As before, naturalness and ease dictate the use of the pronouns *he* and *she,* and the understanding of the reader is solicited. Also interchangeable are the terms teacher and care giver.

No text is the work of a single individual. Professional colleagues, students, friends, children, and families contribute in unique ways to this book. However, particular appreciation is extended to:

- Mary Ruth McNatt, Riverdale Elementary School, Germantown, Tennessee, for her gracious sharing of time, materials, and music theme packets for young children.

- Dr. Joyce Harvey-Joder, Director, Barbara K. Lipman Early Childhood School, Memphis State University, for her suggestions.
- Staff of the Child Development Center, Kent State University, for their suggestions and support.
- Marjorie Yurtinus, kindergarten teacher, Masaryktown, Florida, for photographs.
- The Kent State University Library staff and the children's librarians at the Hudson Public Library and Kent Public Library in Ohio.

Our thanks also to the following reviewers who provided helpful suggestions: Audrey Boyd, Guilford Tech Community College; Karen S. Schafer, Vincennes University; and Eileen Mahoney, Hudson Valley Community College.

Every effort has been made to trace and acknowledge owners. Omissions are unintentional.

It is most useful in teaching music to the very young to have appropriate materials assembled in advance. We suggest you begin your collections of songs, records, poetry, and tapes immediately. Make music an indispensable part of your life and of those you teach. Enrich the quality of your days through music.

*Kathleen M. Bayless*
*Marjorie E. Ramsey*

# Statement of Beliefs

Music is a vital part of daily living. It becomes a part of life as opportunities are provided for experiences in singing, responding physically to different rhythms, creative expressions, playing instruments, and quiet listening. A well-organized musical environment provides for a wide range of musical activities and experiences adequate to meet the needs and interests of all children. It also supports and strengthens learning in the other areas brought into the unified experience. Music helps children understand other people and their cultures and gives increased opportunities for social and emotional development. Music also provides a means for the aesthetic enrichment and growth of every child.

## WE BELIEVE

### Young Children Have a Right to

- have a variety of musical experiences that will bring pleasure and enjoyment to them throughout their lives
- experience musical activities and materials that are appropriate to their age level and developmental needs
- engage in musical experiences that are based on an action art, not a performing art
- be guided to the fullest development of their musical potential
- have the opportunity for support and/or extension of content areas through the medium of music
- express themselves musically in an atmosphere of freedom and trust, where divergent and creative interpretation is encouraged

- be involved in the full gamut of musical experiences, regardless of physical, social, emotional, or intellectual limitations
- have sufficient time provided each day for the exploration of musical experiences

### Adults Working with Children Will

- provide both planned and spontaneous musical activities as a part of each child's day
- offer opportunities for listening, creating, singing, moving rhythmically, and experimenting with sound
- place emphasis on the child's enjoyment of the musical experience rather than on an expected outcome
- provide musical activities that will enhance other learning, such as acquisition of language, listening skills, auditory discrimination, and social understanding
- arrange an environment in which children will feel free to explore and engage in a variety of musical experiences that represent contributions from ethnic groups and other cultures
- recognize and plan for well-balanced musical experiences for all children, adapted to physical, social, emotional, and intellectual capabilities

### Because

- one of the main goals for music is to make children's lives richer through musical experiences that will help develop their aesthetic senses
- a balance of musical activities can contribute to the development of all children according to their individual patterns of growth and development

- music can support concepts and skills that children are developing, but enjoyment of music should hold priority
- children are natural musicians and, given the opportunity, will express themselves musically in a variety of creative ways

In 1898, Sarah E. Sprague, State Institute Conductor and Inspector of Graded Schools for Minnesota, wrote:

> Life's Song, indeed would lose its charm,
> Were there no babies to begin it;

> A doleful place this world would be,
> Were there no little people in it.

Sarah Sprague concluded,

> Home, nature and school are the three great influences in a child's life, and when these are harmoniously blended it is the "World Beautiful" realized for him, wherein he may grow, as a plant does, always toward the light.

# Contents

# I

# Music in the Earliest Years

*The first cry of the newborn is the generator not only of the spoken language and of musicality but also of movement and of musical rhythm.*

—Fridman, 1973, p. 265

# CHAPTER ONE

# Infancy

## THE YOUNG CHILD'S MUSICAL DEVELOPMENT

Today music permeates children's lives through more avenues than ever before due to record, tape, and compact disc players, radio, and television. Music, in the early years, contributes to healthy development for all children.

The child's whole world is filled with sound and music. It is everywhere. Children all over the world bring with them their ability to make and respond to music. They like to explore its many possibilities, like to create it, and are highly motivated by its fascinating sounds and rhythms. As the vast body of literature on child development was researched for the first edition of this book, we discovered that references to musical development of young children are rare. At the writing of the fourth edition the same discovery holds true. It seems strange that emphasis has not been given to this aspect when one considers how pervasive and valuable music is in our world.

Children's musical growth is similar to the rest of their development. As children grow, they are constantly gathering all sorts of sounds and movement impressions. Children who have ample opportunities to experiment with sound and movement will acquire a rich background for later musical growth and understanding. Those youngsters who have come from homes and communities where music is fostered and valued will tend to reflect similar kinds of musical interest. There are now several studies that indicate the relationship of the home musical environment and its influence on the musicality of young children (Brand, 1985; Jenkins, 1976; Lind and Hardgrove, 1978; Reynolds, 1960; Shelton, 1965). In homes where music expression has been encouraged, parents sing to children, musical instruments are played, and recordings are listened to; in these families, children's responses to music are better and of a higher quality as they grow older.

## MUSIC MAKING IN INFANCY

From the moment of birth and even before, children adapt to the sounds within their environment, relating them to their own abilities to create and explore the rhythms and tonal patterns of sound. It has been determined that in the fifth month of pregnancy, the fetus responds to sounds of all kinds. It is not unusual to hear a mother-to-be announce that her unborn baby is much more active when she strums and plays a guitar or Autoharp® held close to her body.

The unborn baby's sense of hearing is activated when music is played at the same time each day. Being careful to adjust the volume, some expectant mothers place the headset of a tape recorder on their stomachs and play classical music to the fetus. As cited by Shetler (1985, p. 27), "infants who received systematic prenatal stimulation exhibit remarkable attention behaviors, accurately imitate sounds made by adults and appear to structure vocalization much earlier than infants who did not have prenatal musical stimulation."

After birth, infants soon begin to use their resources for exploring the world about them. They search for the sound when voices are heard. From the fourth week, babies can detect who is near them by the timbre (characteristic quality) of the voice. Around three months of age they are often awakened or comforted by the sound of the mother's or care giver's voice. Typically, the baby will turn his eyes and head in the direction from which the sound is coming. Even though he cannot grasp the object, a baby will become excited, wiggle, and smile at the sound of a bell attached to a familiar puppet dancing.

At approximately four months, babies may use their feet or hands to strike a favorite toy that produces a pleasant sound when it is struck. At first this action is reflexive and is accidental in nature; but if the sound is interesting, pleasing, or perhaps amusing, infants will tend to repeat the action time and again. Around four months they also enjoy the sound of their own laughter and repeat it. According to McCall (1985, p. 106), by six months babies can hear almost as well as adults.

As described by Greenberg (1979, p. 56), there are two stages of music making during the child's first year and a half. The first stage is approximately from birth to three or four months. Crying is the baby's first sound. It does not take long for the baby to manipulate the cry by "opening and closing the mouth, thus varying the pitch, rhythm patterns, and dynamics" (Brand, 1985, p. 30). Babies will coo, gurgle, squeal, and babble during this stage. During the first year, babies will experiment in making sounds that are pleasing.

The second stage of music extends from approximately 4 months to 18 months (Greenberg, 1979, p. 58). Babbling will increase. Often the vocalizations of babies will be motivated upon hearing their parents sing or talk to them. "Between six and nine months of age, musical babbling, defined as making speech sounds on various pitches, begins and often is produced when the baby moves to music. It is frequently produced when someone sings to the infant" (p. 60).

From six to nine months, as the baby continues to grow and experiment with his voice, his sounds often take on the form of singing. At this stage of the baby's development, he is in almost constant motion and frequently will make sounds to accompany his play and motion. These sounds are often produced as the child interacts with objects in his play. Around 11 months of age jabbering begins, and by 18 months a child is speaking and ready to sing. In their own way, babies constantly communicate with those around them. Very rarely are these beginnings of musical sound and bodily movement absent from the young child.

## IMPORTANCE OF LULLABIES

Since response to sound is one of the most highly developed abilities in the newborn infant, children need to be musically nurtured from birth. Staincliffe Maternity Hospital in England soothes new infants by playing recorded music of such composers as Brahms, Handel, and Mozart. The effect on the infants "works wonders," hospital attendants say. In some hospitals a program of lullaby music is piped into rooms where mothers are feeding their babies.

Lullabies from the greatest composers and spontaneous melodies sung and hummed by loving guardians have brought comfort and sleep to countless babies. For generations, people throughout the world have sung lullabies to their own babies as they cuddled them in their arms and gently rocked them to sleep. Modern research is only beginning to discover the full importance of lullabies. Singing soft, rhythmical songs brings a sense of calmness and security to the sensitive infant. Besides soothing an infant, rocking and singing help the infant become accustomed to the "feelings" of sound motion. Without this type of gentle introduction to music, many infants will continue to react with a startle to sudden movement and loud sounds and noises. According to Friedrich (1983, p. 55), babies tend to go to sleep faster if they hear the recorded sound of a human heartbeat or other similar rhythmic sounds. Some toys with such sounds are now being marketed.

Another benefit of singing lullabies is the communication that occurs between the care giver and the baby. Often, an infant seems to be responding directly to the singer by cooing and babbling, thus encouraging the development of speech and singing.

In our technological world of today, people are accustomed to hearing music produced by top professionals. It's understandable that when comparing themselves to the professional, some people feel inadequate in making music on their own. It is not unusual for parents and teachers to become unduly concerned about the quality of their singing voices. Some will not attempt to sing to or with children. Dr. John Lind, professor emeritus at Karolinska Institute, Stockholm, Sweden, discovered that children who have parents with rather poor singing voices still grow up to love to sing and are able to sing on key (Fletcher, 1981, p. 26). It is not important that parents sing *well* but that they *do sing* to their babies. Authorities such as Lind and Hardgrove (1978, p. 10) remind us, "It is not the quality of the voice that matters, it is the connection. . . . It is not the on-key, smooth mechanical perfection that brings joy to infants as well as adults. The joy comes in the rendition, and the example of this intimate parent-to-infant message encourages the child to sing."

Although singing lullabies comes naturally to many people, some may need a few tips on sharing them with infants.

1. Build a repertoire of favorite lullabies. If possible, memorize them. This is important, as many of today's young parents have no memories of being lullabied and are not familiar with the most beautiful lullabies from around the world. There are excellent lullaby books on the market. There is also a wide variety of good lullaby recordings and tapes available. (See listing at the end of Chapter 1.) *Note:* If records or tapes are used by the parent or teacher, they should be used only as accompaniment or

to learn new songs. The parent's or teacher's voice should always be present.

2. Some infants prefer one lullaby over another; however, don't limit your singing to only music labeled *lullabies*. Try singing some of the contemporary songs and show tunes. Infants often enjoy variety and a change of pace.

3. As you securely hold and gently rock an infant, smile warmly and look directly into the infant's face and eyes. This kind of "bonding" brings contentment and security to the infant.

Infants' interest in a world of sound can be enhanced in different ways and through different qualities of tones and pitches, rhythmical movement, and songs.

## AUDITORY STIMULATION OF INFANTS

### Birth to One Year

Developing the sense of hearing is important to all future learning. Parents and others caring for infants should provide sound-stimulation toys and experiences that will promote auditory development. One such toy is a weighted apple that will reproduce a series of "ting-a-ling" sounds when it is shaken or struck. When an infant is a few weeks old, the parent can shake the musical toy so it can be heard. Later, when the infant is being changed or is lying awake in bed, the musical toy should be placed close enough so that he can produce the same sound when his hands or feet strike the apple. The infant will probably continue to repeat this behavior because it is pleasing to him. Parents should be close by to enjoy and guide this experience with their child. Between three and six months the infant will respond to sound stimulation or speech by vocalizing. Around five months infants will react and vocalize to their own names.

Those caring for infants under six months of age will find the following suggestions helpful in promoting auditory development:

1. Talk, hum, chant, or sing to the baby when you change diapers, bathe, dress, and feed the baby, and when you take him for a ride out-of-doors. Poems and nursery rhymes are good choices.

2. Soothe and calm a restless infant by singing or playing a quiet song such as "Hush Little Baby" or "Sleep Baby Sleep." Hold the baby in your arms. Sing or hum the song softly, and use a gentle rocking motion.

3. If the baby seems upset or unhappy, sing a livelier tune to catch his attention and mood. Then change to a more quiet, soothing lullaby type of song to quiet the child. To make a baby more attentive, begin by singing a soothing lullaby and then change to a more active and rhythmical one.

4. Let the baby hear the ticking of a clock (ticking sound should not be harsh). As infants and then toddlers grow older, they are fascinated by the different sounds of clocks. The cuckoo clock is one of their favorites.

5. When talking to the baby, vary the tone of your voice. A baby likes to hear sounds that keep changing. Use inflection in your voice.

6. Occasionally play selections from a good-sounding music box.

By eight months, babies will begin to approximate the pitch of sound that is sung to them. "Nine-month-old babies will slide their voices upward and downward in an effort to produce the sounds that they hear. By the age of ten months, an experienced baby can sing patterns of sounds that he hears" (Palmer, 1977, p. 22).

Babies need singing models so they can learn to sing, just as they need good speaking models to imitate for talking. When they hear others sing, they discover that there is another way of expressing themselves that is different from talking. It is important to do lots of singing to the baby, at a close range, so that the baby can see the shape and movement of the lips as the sounds are produced. Evans (1978, p. 29) reminds us, "It is important to do this because the

baby needs to understand clearly where the sound is coming from if he is to understand that he can make such sounds with his own mouth.''

One of the best ways parents and care givers can model singing is to sing about what is going on. Make up little musical phrases. It doesn't matter what notes you sing; make up the tune and rhythm spontaneously to fit the words. After a few attempts you will be surprised at how easy it is to make up these little musical episodes.

Songs and rhythms that actively involve the baby are usually liked the best by both parties. A baby will generally smile and squeal with delight when someone helps him clap his hands or move his legs up and down to a favorite nursery rhyme or lilting rhythmical tune. Watch the baby's face ''light up'' as she opens and closes the lid of a music box; how ''in control'' the baby is in starting and stopping those beautiful sounds.

The staff of the Parent-Infant-Toddler Program at the Child Development Center, Kent State University, have used music and auditory discrimination extensively in their program. Soon after the program was implemented, the staff quickly became aware that they had underestimated the enjoyment and importance to the children of the role of auditory discrimination and stimulation. They observed that infants showed continuous preferences for the auditory play materials. Some of these materials included Ticking Clock (Fisher-Price), Happy Apple (the Childcraft one in particular), musical instruments (such as bells, drums), pots, pans, spoons, toys that squeak, and action-response toys (for example, a push-pull musical cylinder). They also observed the immediate impact of the sound of a record playing in the classroom. When a staff member would begin playing a record, virtually all of the infants in the 3- to 11-month class would stop interacting and turn toward the sound of the music.

Those caring for infants older than six months will find the following additional suggestions helpful in promoting auditory development:

1. Continue to talk, hum, or sing to the baby. Talk about toys, and play games like pat-a-cake and peek-a-boo. Infants enjoy songs even more if their names are mentioned. (See songs on p. 9.)
2. Attach a mobile near the baby's crib. Many mobiles revolve and have music boxes that play delightful nursery-rhyme tunes. Other mobiles contain objects that make different sounds when struck with the hand or foot. (*Note:* When purchasing a musical mobile for an infant's crib that has objects such as attached circus animals, it is best to choose one with the animals horizontal rather than vertical. This will assure that the infant lying down can see the full view of the animals.)
3. Let the infant hear the radio and records. Occasionally, as you put the baby to bed, play a record containing

soft, soothing music. (*Caution:* Do not play music constantly. Do not play highly stimulating music when putting baby to bed.) Lullabies and music for relaxation provide good bedtime music.
4. When the infant is awake, play a record. Turn the volume up and down so differences in intensity can be heard. Also, play records that contain both loud and soft music.
5. Tie a bell to the baby's bootie or shoestring. Older infants like to shake a bell.
6. Use good-quality wind chimes that are hung inside the house or out-of-doors.
7. Provide lightweight, colorful rattles producing different sounds. (*Note:* Choose rattles with pleasing, musical sounds. Many rattles are just noisemakers.)
8. Crumple pieces of tissue or newspaper near one of the baby's ears.
9. Shake a set of keys.
10. At times, hold the telephone receiver up to the baby's ear so the voice on the other end can be heard. (Babies are usually fascinated by this.)
11. Point to the telephone when it is ringing.
12. Let the baby hear and see water running from a faucet.
13. Clap your hands. Go from loud clapping to soft clapping. Take hold of the baby's hands. Clap them together. Sing in time to the clapping.
14. Clap your hand on a low tabletop and watch the baby (supported by the table) imitate you.

15. Show the baby how a doorbell is rung. As the doorbell rings, try reproducing the sound with your voice.

16. When reading books containing pictures of animals or other objects that make sounds, try to imitate the sounds with your voice. As the baby grows older, invite participation in making the different sounds. After several repetitions the baby's response will generally become spontaneous.

17. When talking with a baby, imitate the sounds he makes and encourage him to imitate you. This is an excellent exercise.

18. Play melodies on instruments such as the piano, organ, or guitar. Hold the baby on your lap while playing the piano. Place one of his fingers on a key or string and let the baby listen to its sound. Now move the finger up and down the keys or string in scalewise fashion.

19. Give the baby a pan and lid, or a pan and wooden spoon; often such a combination of sound makers is preferred over musical toys.

20. Place the baby on your lap, facing you. Hold his wrists and rock him forward and backward in time to songs such as ''Jack and Jill'' and ''See Saw, Margery Daw.''

21. Hold the baby in your arms and dance to music on the stereo or radio. Change your movements according to the tempo and mood of the music.

22. Push-and-pull musical toys are favorites with infants. The combination of the sound and motion of the toy is very satisfying. (Be sure the musical sound is pleasing and not irritating.)

23. Infants enjoy sitting in a mechanical, wind-up swing that functions like a metronome. The even, rhythmical movement of the swing creates a soothing effect on the child.

## MUSICAL LEARNING ACTIVITIES

Infants are attentive to musical sounds and games in their environment and move gradually from receivers to participators. Parents and infant-caregivers can do much to nurture the attention and response infants give to music. The following activities have been used successfully in the Parent-Infant-Toddler Program at Kent State University.

### Fancy Footwork

*Participants*
A 3- to 8-month-old infant and an adult

*Materials*
Velcro strip ankle bells

*Explanation*
Gently shake the ankle bells in front of your baby to focus his attention. Allow time for examining. Perhaps take a moment and try once again the visual tracking episode using the Velcro bells. Now place the bells on your baby's ankles. Observe how your baby responds. Does he notice the bells? If baby becomes frustrated, remove strips. Perhaps your baby simply wants to see or touch them at first.

*Purpose*
This activity is one way of offering leg exercise to your baby in preparation for creeping and crawling. It offers opportunities to flex and extend the legs. It is also an action-response activity—''When I move my legs, the bells ring!''

*Variation*
Take a stuffed animal, hang a few bells on it, and tie it with heavy string to the crib rails so that it hangs just above baby's feet. This tempting toy is out of hands' reach, so feet become the next best thing to make the sound. Baby may kick vigorously. The bell sound will be a motivating factor in getting the baby to stretch and kick.

### Mirror, Mirrors*

*Question, answer responses may be sung*

*Participants*
A 6- to 8-month-old infant and an adult

---

*This game has been adapted from Gordon, Ira J., *Baby Learning Through Play*. New York: St. Martin's Press, 1970, pp. 27–28.

*Materials*
Hand mirror

*Explanation*
Place the baby comfortably on your lap and have him look into a hand mirror so that he can see himself. "Look, here's _____. Where's _____?" Have him point to his own image in the mirror. Do this at various times, and you will notice he will begin to recognize himself. About a year from now he will playact in front of a mirror, striking poses, making faces.

You may even add to this activity in time by pointing to parts of the body and naming them after you're sure that he recognizes the total as himself. (Parts of the body may be sung as you point to them.)

*Caution*
This is one game that takes two to play. If the glass mirror is a breakable one, do *not* leave it unattended.

## Listen–Look–Reach*

*Participants*
A six- to nine-month-old baby and an adult

*Materials*
Rattle or any small toy that makes a pleasing sound when shaken

*Explanation*
Capture baby's attention by shaking the rattle so the baby can see it. Then move the rattle to a different position and shake it again. After the baby looks and tries to reach for the rattle, move it to another position and shake it once more. To keep the baby's attention, keep the activity moving rather quickly. After several movements, stop the action and allow the baby to hold the toy and enjoy it.

*Purpose*
To give the infant the experience of responding by looking and reaching toward sound stimulation.

## Touch and Name

*Parents are encouraged to try a "Touch and Sing" adaptation as they play the game with baby*

*Participants*
A 6- to 12-month-old baby and an adult

---
*This game has been adapted by K. Bayless from one by Jane Dias, a Kent State University student.

*Explanation*
Touch different parts of your baby's body and name them. For example, "This is (supply baby's name) nose. Here is ( ) foot. Where is ( ) arm? Here it is. Here is your arm!" Now, touch your own body parts and do the same thing. "Here is Mommy's nose." If others are close by, touch their noses; for example, "Here is Daddy's nose."

*Purpose*
To develop in the baby an awareness of himself and his body image and to help the baby understand the difference between himself and others. In addition, the activity shows connections between objects or actions and words, including names and pronouns. Even though it will be a while before the baby uses these words, he will learn (through this type of experience) to recognize words and their meanings.

*Variations*
Once the child begins, through practice, to learn the names of some of the parts of the body, try turning the game around. Ask, "Where is ( ) arm? Where is Mommy's arm? Where is Daddy's arm?"

## Give and Take

*Question, answer responses may be sung*

*Participants*
A 9- to 12-month-old baby and another person. Some babies will continue to enjoy this or a variation of this game after their first year.

*Materials*
A block, small ball, or some other object like a rattle or small musical toy that can be easily held in the baby's hand.

*Explanation*
Having developed the ability to grasp, most babies now are learning to let go. This is an example of a game that many babies initiate on their own. Be enthusiastic as you play the game. Give the object to the baby and say, "Here's the ball" (or whatever the object is). Then, put your hand out as if to receive it back. When the baby places the object in your hand, take it and say, "Thank you." If the baby imitates your "thank you," respond, "You're welcome." Continue this give and take for as long as the baby enjoys it.

*Purpose*
To give the baby practice in letting go and using his hand muscles in a controlled way. This activity also serves as a form of social interchange. It is a good way to teach the use of appropriate language to accompany social interchange.

**FAVORITE SONGS AND RHYTHMS**

## PEEK-A-BOO

Words and music by K. BAYLESS

Peek - a - boo,*     Peek - a - boo,     Mom - my's†play-ing   a   game    with you.

Peek - a - boo,     Peek - a - boo,     See    if    you    can   play    it,   too.

_____

*Use appropriate actions.
†May substitute other names such as daddy's, brother's, etc.

## PAT-A-CAKE, PAT-A-CAKE

Adapted by K. BAYLESS

Pat - a - cake,   pat - a - cake,   bak - er's    man!

Bake    me    a    cake    as    fast    as    you    can.

Pat    it,    and    prick    it,    and    mark    it    with    T,     and

put    it    in    ov-en    for    Tom - my    and    me.
(may substitute child's name)

Short, rhythmical singing games also please the young child. Around 6 months of age, babies begin to enjoy playing peek-a-boo. Peek-a-boo and pat-a-cake, long-time favorites, have been set to music so that the family can play and sing these games with baby.

# ALL THE FISH

Adapted by<br>"Miss Jackie" Weissman

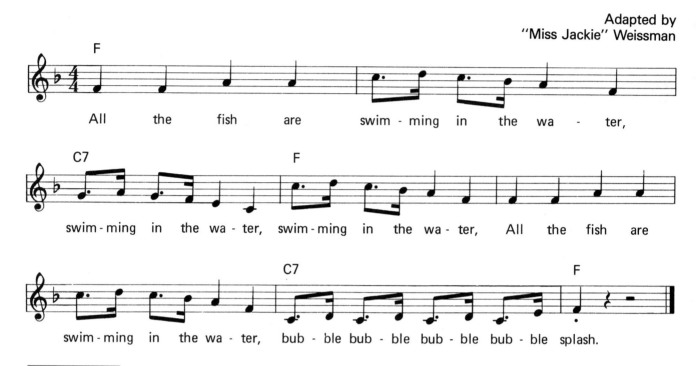

All the fish are swim - ming in the wa - ter, swim - ming in the wa - ter, swim - ming in the wa - ter, All the fish are swim - ming in the wa - ter, bub - ble bub - ble bub - ble bub - ble splash.

Reprinted by permission of "Miss Jackie" Weissman.

"All The Fish" is a favorite of children around six months of age and older. Put your hands together (palms flat touching each other) and move them around like fish swimming in the water. During the "splash" part, push them apart and pretend you are splashing someone. Make up new verses, such as "All the frogs are hopping in the water" and "All the ducks are quacking in the water."

## BABY'S FACE

Words and music by
"Miss Jackie" Weissman

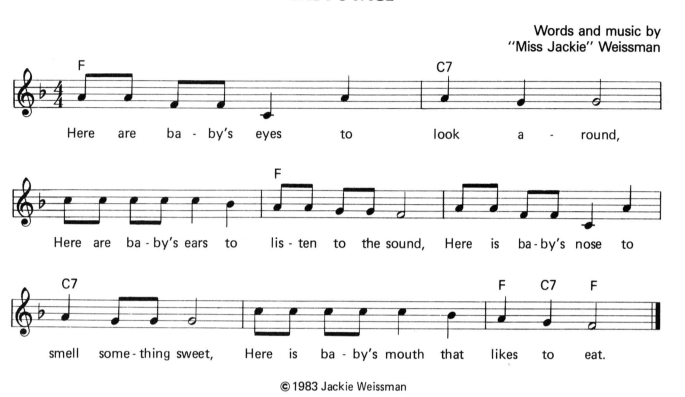

Here are ba - by's eyes to look a - round,

Here are ba - by's ears to lis - ten to the sound, Here is ba - by's nose to

smell some - thing sweet, Here is ba - by's mouth that likes to eat.

This song will help your baby identify body parts. There are many ways to play the game when you sing the song.

Sing the song to the baby and touch each body part as you name it in the song. At the end of the song when you sing the words "likes to eat," pretend you are eating and say "yum, yum, yum."

Another way to sing the song is to take the baby's hands and put them on his eyes, ears, etc.

A third way to sing the song is to use a doll or stuffed animal to touch as you sing.

The following lullabies are favorites of parents, teachers, and children.

## ROCK-A-BYE BABY

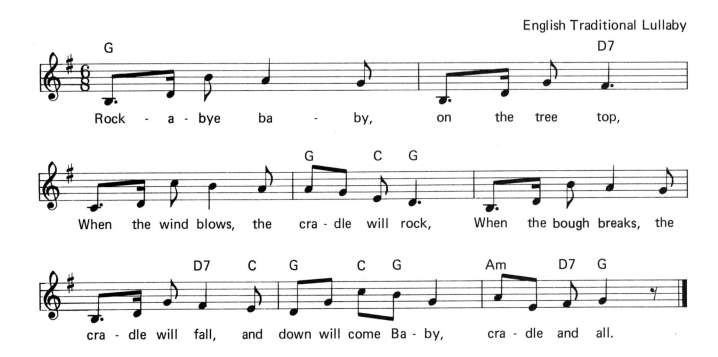

# HUSH LITTLE BABY

Alabama Folk Song

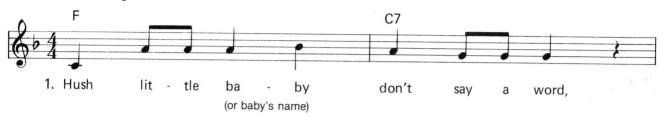

1. Hush lit - tle ba - by don't say a word,
(or baby's name)

Ma - ma's gon - na buy you a mock - ing bird.

2. If that mocking bird won't sing, Mama's gonna buy you a diamond ring.
3. If that diamond ring turns to brass, Mama's gonna buy you a looking glass.
4. If that looking glass gets broke, Mama's gonna buy you a billy goat.
5. If that billy goat won't pull, Mama's gonna buy you a cart and bull.
6. If that cart and bull turn over, Mama's gonna buy you a dog named Rover.
7. If that dog named Rover won't bark, Mama's gonna buy you a horse and cart.
8. If that horse and cart fall down, You'll be the sweetest girl* in town.

---

*The word *babe, boy,* or *children* may be substituted for *girl.*

This beloved folk song appeals to children and persons of all ages. It is a part of our cultural heritage and a song that should be passed on from one generation to the next. It is often sung as a lullaby.

## SLEEP, BABY, SLEEP

German lullaby

Sleep, ba-by, sleep! Your fa-ther tends his sheep. Your mo-ther shakes the

dream-land tree. Down falls a lit-tle dream for thee. Sleep, ba-by, sleep.

## HUSH! BE STILL

Source unknown
Lullaby as sung by GRANDMA THOMAS

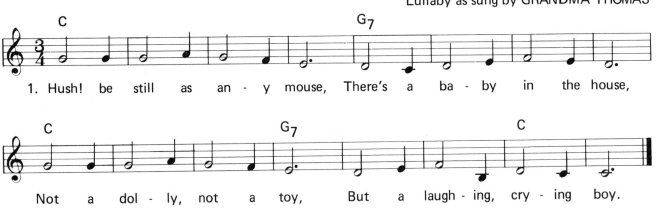

1. Hush! be still as an-y mouse, There's a ba-by in the house,

Not a dol-ly, not a toy, But a laugh-ing, cry-ing boy.

2
Hush! be still as any mouse,
There's a baby in the house,
Not a dolly, with a curl,
But a laughing, crying girl.

The following selected skills reference listing is for children birth to 36 months. It makes reference to cognitive and expressive language and gives parents and care givers ap- proximate ranges during which young children will begin to respond to sound and music.

## SELECTED SKILLS REFERENCE LIST FOR CHILDREN BIRTH TO 36 MONTHS

**Cognitive**

Responds to sounds　birth–1 month
Responds to voice　birth–2½ months
Listens to voice for 30 seconds　1–3 months
Begins to play with rattle　2½–4 months
Awakens or quiets to mother's voice　3–6 months
Localizes sound with eyes　3½–5 months
Shows interest in sounds of objects　5½–8 months
Plays "peek-a-boo"　6–10 months
Moves to rhythms　11–12 months
Matches sounds to animals　18–22 months
Enjoys nursery rhymes, nonsense rhymes, fingerplays, poetry　18–30 months
Matches sounds to pictures of animals　22–24 months

**Expressive Language**

Cry varies in pitch, length, and volume to indicate needs such as hunger and pain　1–5 months
Coos open vowels (aah), diphthongs (oy as in boy)　2–7 months
Disassociates vocalizations from bodily movement　2–3 months
Cries more rhythmically with mouth opening and closing　2½–4½ months
Responds to sound stimulation or speech by vocalizing　3–6 months
Reacts to music by cooing　5–6 months
Looks and vocalizes to own name　5–7 months
Babbles to people　5½–6½ months
Babbles with inflection similar to adult speech　7½–12 months
Babbles in response to human voice　11–15 months
Babbles monologue when left alone　11–12 months
Attempts to sing sounds to music　13–16 months
Jabbers tunefully at play　17–19 months
Imitates environmental sounds　18–21 months
Attempts to sing with words　18–23 months
Sings phrases of songs　23–27 months
Recites a few nursery rhymes　30–36 months

Selected from *Hawaii Early Learning Profile (HELP) Activity Guide* by the Enrichment Project for Handi- capped Infants, by Setsu Furuno, Katherine A. O'Reilly, Carol M. Hosaka, Takayo T. Inatsuka, Toney L. Allman, and Barbara Zeisloft. Available from VORT Corporation, Palo Alto, CA 94306.

## MUSIC SKILLS DEVELOPMENT FROM BIRTH TO FIVE YEARS

The following material was written by Marilyn Cohen and Pamela Gross and first appeared in "Let's Make Music," in the March 1982 issue of *Parents*.

It is a developmental table of when one might expect a child to begin new music skills. It's important to remember, however, that every child grows at a unique pace. While the order of these sequences is generally the same for all chil- dren, the age at which a particular child progresses from one stage to another may vary.

## LISTENING AND MOVING TO MUSIC

| | |
|---|---|
| **Birth to 4 Months** | *Awareness of music starts almost immediately.* The baby may show his early awareness by responding differently to different kinds of music; he quiets himself to a soothing lullaby and becomes more active when lively music is played. |
| **4 to 8 Months** | *Musical awareness becomes more active.* The baby now enjoys listening intently to all types of sounds in his environment. He begins showing more active awareness of musical sounds by turning his head or face toward the source of the music. |
| **10 to 18 Months** | *Expression of musical preferences begins.* The infant may begin indicating the types of music he likes best—many at this age prefer vocal to instrumental—as well as showing clear displeasure at music he does not like. He rocks or sways his hips to a familiar tune, although not necessarily in time with the music, and claps his hands to a pleasing song. |
| **18 Months to 2 Years** | *Exploration of musical sounds increases.* Sounds in her environment continue to captivate the toddler. Her developing language skills and increasing mobility allow her to seek out sounds that please her most. She may especially enjoy music on daily TV or radio programs or commercials, and may watch with fascination as a family member plays a musical instrument. |
| **2 to 3 Years** | *Dance begins.* The toddler now attempts to "dance" to music by bending his knees in a bouncing motion, turning circles, swaying, swinging his arms, and nodding his head. He especially likes a marked rhythm, so band music, nursery songs, or catchy TV jingles may be favorites. He shows an increasing ability to keep time and to follow directions in musical games, which he loves. You'll also notice that he can now pay attention for longer periods. While easily distracted in the past, he can now lie or sit down quietly and listen for several minutes at a time. |
| **$3\frac{1}{2}$ to 4 Years** | *Self-expression through music increases.* At this stage, a very significant change takes place. As the child listens, she is increasingly aware of some of the components that make up her favorite music. She may love to dramatize songs and may also enjoy trying out different ways of interpreting music (for example, experimenting with different rhythms). She shows marked improvement in keeping the beat, although she is still not always entirely accurate. (Music is now an important means for her to express and communicate ideas and emotions that may be beyond her developing language skills.) |
| **4 to 5 Years** | *Ability to discuss musical experiences expands.* By now the child can talk about what a piece of music suggests to him, and he is able to tell you in greater detail what he is hearing. This is the stage of the "active listener." With encouragement, the child's desire to listen to music will increase. |
| **5 to 6 Years** | *Actual coordinated dance movements begin.* The child's increased motor control and ability to synchronize his movements with the rhythm of the music are evident as one watches his attempts to dance. He can actually synchronize hand or foot tapping with music and can skip, hop on one foot, and make rhythmic dance movements to music. This is the time when he may begin to show an interest in dance lessons. |

# SINGING

| | |
|---|---|
| **Birth to 4 Months** | ***Crying is a baby's first "musical" sound.*** A baby's cries are her first and most important means of expressing early needs and feelings. They vary in pitch, loudness, and rhythmic patterns, making them musical in a very real sense. Gradually, she begins to experiment with other sounds; she coos, gurgles, squeals, and begins to "babble," repeating long strings of sound, such as "ba-ba-ba." |
| **6 to 18 Months** | ***Babbling increases, taking on more pronounced musical characteristics.*** As the baby continues to experiment with his voice, "babbling" becomes a favorite activity. As the infant's range of pitch, tone, and voice intensity widens, this activity comes to resemble song. Don't be surprised if at some point the baby is able to repeat the pitches you sing to him on exactly the same notes. |
| **$1\frac{1}{2}$ to 3 Years** | ***Real singing begins.*** The baby's tuneful jabbering during play now sounds more like real song. She may chant a catchy rhyme, using nonsense syllables or even her own name as she plays, but she is still unable to sing a song like "Farmer in the Dell" completely accurately. She may join you in favorite nursery rhymes or songs; she especially enjoys familiar tunes and asks you to sing them repeatedly. (Although she'll sing along with you or a family member, she's still hesitant to sing in front of other children and may balk at a solo performance in preschool.) |
| **$3\frac{1}{2}$ to 4 Years** | ***Accuracy in matching simple tunes begins.*** Now the youngster starts to approximate adult singing. He may spontaneously make up his own songs, although the words are often repetitive and the tune may closely resemble one he already knows. |
| **4 to 5 Years** | ***Singing accuracy increases.*** The child shows increased voice control and a closer approximation of pitch and rhythm. He may sing an entire song accurately. Sometimes he creates songs during play and may use these songs to tease others. He shows more responsiveness in group singing and may even enjoy taking a turn singing alone. He takes great pride in his ability to identify favorite melodies. |
| **5 Years and Over** | ***Song repertoire expands; recognition and appreciation increase.*** Most children now reproduce simple tunes accurately. The child's expanded vocal range should allow him to reach higher notes more easily, and his rhythmic accuracy is noticeably improved. He pays more attention to a song's "dynamics" and tempo and is able to add subtleties to its rendition, expressing meaning and emotion with his voice. |

# PLAYING MUSICAL INSTRUMENTS

| | |
|---|---|
| **6 to 9 Months** | ***Baby enjoys creating sounds with any object available.*** The infant's eye-hand coordination is rapidly improving. She loves to manipulate objects within reach and is fascinated with her newfound ability to make sounds with objects. She will tap, kick, or hit almost all objects with which she comes in contact, delighting in the sounds she creates. |

| | |
|---|---|
| **18 Months to 2 Years** | *Toddler seeks special objects to make sounds.* You may notice the toddler's repeated efforts to locate particular objects—pots and pans, cups, bowls, and other utensils—for his sound-making activities. He may begin to show interest in the phonograph, even if just to watch it as it plays. |
| **2 to 3½ Years** | *Interest in real musical instruments increases.* At this stage, when the youngster is beginning to show interest in listening to musical instruments and the phonograph, provide her with toys that make interesting musical sounds—toy xylophones, drums, pipes, tambourines, or maracas. Musical toys needn't be expensive. In fact, you can easily make your own coffee-can drums, bottle-cap tambourines, soup-can shakers, or pot-cover cymbals. |
| **4 to 5 Years** | *A child begins experimenting with real musical instruments.* At this stage, the youngster can identify certain sounds made by selected instruments and can play many rhythm instruments, both to accompany songs or instrumental pieces he hears and to create tunes of his own. He may also enjoy trying out some of the instruments he has seen others play. |

Marilyn A. Cohen and Pamela J. Gross are educational consultants and coauthors of *The Developmental Resource*, Grune and Stratton, Inc., 1979. Copyright © 1982 Gruner & Jahr USA Publishing. Reprinted from PARENTS Magazine by permission.

Whatever his age, your child needs to be actively involved in making music. As you become familiar with the way he is progressing through his musical development, you'll become more adept at recognizing the signals he gives you about his musical interest and inclinations and encouraging him. You don't have to be a trained musician to help him explore his musical potential in his early years. You'll find plenty of opportunity to provide him with encouragement. And whether or not he himself is destined to become a musical "great," he can still enjoy the tremendous rewards that music brings and can spend a lifetime exploring and expanding the natural music abilities that are part of all of us.

## KEY IDEAS

1. Children's musical growth is similar to the rest of their development.
2. In homes where musical expression is encouraged, children's responses to music are better and of a higher quality as they grow older.
3. Music making should begin in infancy.
4. Developing the sense of hearing is important to all future learning.
5. Babies usually like best songs and rhythms that actively involve them.

## SUMMARY

Music is basic—basic for all children from infancy through life. Those caring for the very young can provide a good beginning for music enjoyment and appreciation by singing and sharing music such as lullabies, chants, and rhymes. Begin early to explore music with children; share the variety and richness of our musical heritage. In addition to nurturing through food and love, add the nurturing quality of music.

We want to encourage your interest in the world of music and sound. Infancy is a good time for beginning with simple activities and experiences that are all around us. As you, as a care giver, become involved, so will the very young child, in terms of alertness, awareness, and enjoyment.

## QUESTIONS TO CONSIDER

1. Begin an informal two-week log of an infant you observe. Record short, precise details of the infant's activities. Are any of the activities influenced by music or rhythm?
2. Visit a day care center. How is music used as a learning experience or as an activity integrated throughout the day?
3. Try at least four of the activities suggested in the chapter with an infant. Record your observations and how you modified the activities to suit your purpose or the infant's reactions.

## REFERENCES AND SUGGESTED READINGS

Brand, Manny. "Lullabies that awaken musicality in infants." *Music Educators Journal,* March 1985, pp. 28–31.

Cohen, Marilyn A., and Gross, Pamela J. "Let's make music." *Parents,* March 1982, pp. 53–57.

Cooper, Catherine R. "Competent infants and their caregivers: The feeling is mutual." In *Understanding and nurturing infant development.* Washington, D.C.: Association for Childhood Education International, 1976.

Evans, David. *Sharing sounds.* New York: Longman Group Ltd., 1978.

Fletcher, Susan K. "The importance of being lullabied." *Baby Talk,* September 1981, p. 26.

Friedrich, Otto. "What do babies know?" *Time,* August 15, 1983, p. 55.

Fridman, Ruth. "The first cry of the newborn: Basis for the child's future musical development." *Journal of Research in Music Education,* Fall 1973, 21(3), p. 265.

Gonzales-Mena, Janet, and Eyer, Widmeyer Diane. *Infancy and caregiving.* Palo Alto, Calif.: Mayfield, 1980.

Gordon, Ira J. *Baby learning through play.* New York: St. Martin's Press, 1970.

Greenberg, Marvin. *Your children need music.* Englewood Cliffs, N.J.: Prentice–Hall, 1979.

Howle, Mary Jeanette. "Twinkle, twinkle, little star: it's more than just a nursery song." *Children Today,* July–August 1989, p. 19.

Jalongo, Mary Rench, and Collins, Mitzie. "Singing with young children!" *Young Children,* January 1985, 40(2), pp. 17–21.

Jenkins, J. M. "The relationship between maternal parents' musical experience and the musical development of two- and three-year old girls." Ph.D. diss., North Texas State University, 1976.

Lind, John, and Hardgrove, Carol. "Lullabies." *Children Today,* July–August 1978, p. 10.

Matter, Daryl E. "Musical development in young children." *Childhood Education,* May–June 1982, 58(5), pp. 305–307.

McCall, Robert B. "Can your baby hear you?" *Parents,* January 1985, p. 106.

The Music in Early Childhood Conference, Barbara Andress and Susan H. Kenney, Co-Chairs. "The young child and music: Contemporary principles in child development and music education." Reston, Va.: Music Educators National Conference, 1985.

Moomaw, Sally. *Discovering music in early childhood.* Newton, Mass.: Allyn and Bacon, 1984.

Palmer, Mary. "Music appreciation—For babies." *American Baby,* August 1977, p. 22.

Papalia, D., and Olds, S.W. *A child's world: Infancy through adolescence.* 3rd ed. New York: Macmillan, 1977.

Reynolds, G.E. "Environmental sources of musical awakening in pre-school children." Ph.D. diss., University of Illinois, 1960.

Ribble, Margaret A., M.D. *The rights of infants: Early psychological needs and their satisfactions.* 2d ed. New York: Columbia University Press, 1973.

Shelton, J.S. "The influence of home musical environment upon musical response of first grade children." Ph.D. diss., George Peabody College for Teachers, 1965.

Shetler, D.J. "Prenatal music experiences." *Music Educators Journal,* March 1985, p. 27.

Wein, Bibi. "Tiny dancers." *Omni,* May 1988, p. 122.

## SONG COLLECTIONS

1. *Let's Sing and Play to Grow,* 2d ed.
   Karen Jorgenson and Marty Richardson
   Retono Books
   1721 Wendy
   Edinburg, Tex. 78539

2. *Once A Lullaby* (1983)
   B. P. Nichol
   Greenwillow Books
   New York, N.Y.

3. *Rock–a–bye Baby Book*
   Committee for UNICEF
   *Lullabies of many lands and peoples. A music book with original words and translations.*

4. *Songs to Sing with Babies* (1983)
   ''Miss Jackie'' Weissman
   10001 El Monte
   Overland Park, Kan. 66207
   *Sixty–four pages of songs and activities to do with babies. Categories include songs for rocking and nursing, riding in the car, taking a bath, cuddling, and more. Chords for piano, guitar, and Autoharp included with the songs.*

5. *The Lullaby Songbook* (1986)
   Jane Yolen
   Harcourt Brace Jovanovich
   New York, N.Y.

## RECORDINGS FOR INFANTS AND TODDLERS*

*Baby Can Do*
Children's Book & Music Center
*Songs and activities that baby can do. Physical fitness activities for infants, identification of body parts, fingerplays, and imitation of sounds. Birth to one year.*

*Baby Face,* by Georgiana Stewart Kimbo
*Activities for infants and toddlers. Ways of turning baby's play-time into fun and meaningful learning experiences.*

*The Baby Record,* by Bob McGrath and Katherine Smithrim
Children's Book & Music Center
*Rhymes, fingerplays, action songs, and lullabies for babies.*

*Baby Song,* by Hap and Martha Palmer
Educational Activities, Inc.
*Songs about baby's world and daily experiences.*

*Golden Slumbers*
Children's Book & Music Center
*Twenty-four lullabies from around the world, sung by eight folk singers.*

*It's Toddler Time*
Children's Book & Music Center
*Activities designed for toddlers' fitness and development.*

---

*This collection contains recordings not listed in Appendix C. Current catalogs can be obtained from the record companies whose addresses are listed in that appendix.

*Let's Visit Lullaby Land*
Children's Book & Music Center
*Restful music for quiet times. Soothing; a variety of classical selections and contemporary tunes. For example, "Prayer" from* Hansel and Gretel *and "Edelweiss."*

*Little Favorites*
Children's Book & Music Center
*Sixteen classic songs for young children, such as "Hush Little Baby."*

*Loving and Learning from Birth to Three*
Children's Book & Music Center
*A sleeping/resting, play-and-learn record. Includes lullabies, children's prayers, and learning songs.*

*Lullabies from 'Round the World*
Children's Book & Music Center
*Fourteen lovely international melodies for quiet time.*

*Lullabies and Laughter,* by Pat Carfra (A & M Records of Canada Ltd.)
Children's Book & Music Center
*For babies and small children, thirty-three lullabies and play songs that make it easy to sing to the young child.*

*Lullaby from the Womb,* by Dr. Hajime Murooka, Long Play
2611 E. Franklin Ave.
Minneapolis, Minn. 55406
*Sounds from the womb plus soothing selections.*

*Lullaby Magic* DM–1 (tape)
Ellen Wohlstadter
4130 Greenbush
Sherman Oaks, Calif. 91423
*Highly recommended.*

*Lullaby Time for Little People*
Children's Book & Music Center
*Contains many of the traditional lullabies.*

*Music for 1's and 2's,* sung by Tom Glazer
Children's Book & Music Center
*Songs for the very young. A favorite recording of many.*

*My Teddy Bear and Me*
Children's Book & Music Center
*Musical play activities for infants and toddlers. Familiar melodies and simple actions especially structured to help the very young become aware of objects and spatial relationships. Also helps develop coordination and listening skills.*

*Quiet Time,* by Harrel C. Lucky
Melody House
*Music for resting, relaxing, or enjoyable listening.*

*Songs for Sleepyheads and Out-of-Beds!* by Pat Carfra
A & M Records of Canada Ltd.
*Forty-one easy-to-sing lullabies and play songs for very young children.*

*Tickly Toddle* (Songs for Very Young Children), by Hap Palmer
Children's Book & Music Center
*For use with small groups of children in day care and nursery school settings, or for use at home. The activities are simple and afford opportunities for interaction between adult and child.*

*Wee Sing Nursery Rhymes and Lullabies,* by Pamela Conn Beall and Susan Hagen Nipp
Price/Stern/Sloan Publishers, Inc. New York, N.Y.

## RESOURCES

*Creative Movement for the Developing Child*, rev. ed. (1971)
Clare Cherry
David S. Lake Publishers
6 Davis Dr.
Belmont, Calif. 94002
*More than 200 goal-oriented activities for preschoolers to grade 1, plus singing and listening materials.*

*Experiences in Music for Young Children* (1977)
M. C. Weller Pugmire
Delmar Publishers
Albany, N.Y. 12212

*Feeling Strong, Feeling Free: Movement Exploration for Young Children* (1982–83)
Molly Sullivan
National Association for the Education of Young Children
Washington, D.C. 20009
*Comprehensive booklet full of techniques, including a format for teaching movement exploration.*

*Lullaby to the Wind* (1984)
Karen Whiteside
Harper and Row
New York, N.Y.
*A quiet journey into sleep, with a little girl prancing, flying, and yawning in her sleepsuit as the wind sings a lullaby to a candle, curtains, rain, trees, and the sea, then finally to her while she snuggles in her mother's arms.Children (1982–83)*

*Musical Games, Fingerplays, and Rhythmic Activities for Early Childhood* (1983)
Marian Wirth, Verna Stassevitch, Rita Shotwell, Patricia Stemmler
Parker Publishing Co.
West Nyack, N.Y.
*132 musical singing games, chants, and fingerplays for the preschool and primary grades. Each activity spells out appropriate age levels. Tunes are notated in a range comfortable for both children and adults. This is an excellent resource, a must for the early childhood teacher.*

*Piggyback Songs for Infants and Toddlers*
Totline Press
P.O. Box 2250
Everett, Wash. 98203
*Over 170 songs sung to the tunes of childhood favorites.*

*Think of Something Quiet* (1981)
Clare Cherry
David S. Lake Publishers
6 Davis Dr.
Belmont, Calif. 94002
*Contains songs and rhymes for resting time. For preschool to grade 4.*

# CHAPTER TWO

# Music for the Ones to Twos

## NEW OPPORTUNITIES FOR ENJOYMENT AND LEARNING

As children continue to grow and to become more interested in their world, music can offer new opportunities for moving, listening, creating, singing, and playing instruments. Besides imparting to children the enjoyment and pleasure of music activities, adult guides can also teach children skills and competencies by choosing the *appropriate* activities. Selection of these activities should be made in accordance with what can be reasonably expected of children at certain stages of their development. Parents, care givers, teachers, and specialists—such as music and physical education teachers—need to work closely to plan music experiences that are suitable for young children of different ages. As McDonald (1979, p. 4) so aptly reminds us: ''They (children) need adults to assist them in awakening their awareness of what their singing voices can do, what their bodies can express rhythmically, and what their hands and fingers can produce on musical instruments. Moreover, they need adults to help them become acquainted with many kinds of music.''* It is vital that selection of music activities and experiences be based on sound child growth and development principles.

Since wide variations exist in children's maturation and experience, some selected characteristics of what can be normally expected of children at certain ages should prove helpful to persons providing musical experiences appropriate for the young.

---

*Reprinted by permission from *Music in Our Lives: The Early Years* by Dorothy T. McDonald. Copyright © 1979, National Association for the Education of Young Children, 1834 Connecticut Ave., N.W., Washington, D.C. 20009.

## SELECTED CHARACTERISTICS OF ONE- TO TWO-YEAR-OLDS

1. Jabber in response to voices; may cry when there is the sound of thunder or a loud crash
2. Enjoy listening to certain sounds, such as the fluttering of the tongue, and enjoy imitating them
3. Answer questions such as ''What does the cow say?'' by making the sound ''moo''
4. Can point to or put hands on body parts on request
5. Rock or sway hips to a familiar tune, although not necessarily in time with the music
6. Like to play peek-a-boo and hiding games
7. Continue to reproduce sounds or combinations of sounds to explain wants and needs (for example, may half-sing, half-say ''bye-bye'' when they want to go for a ride in the car)
8. Generally enjoy being held and sung to
9. Are able to sing parts of songs
10. May ''mouth'' the words of a song or whisper them while others sing
11. May choose to join a group socially but not sing
12. Will often refrain from singing any of the words to songs, such as ''Twinkle, Twinkle, Little Star,'' since they are concentrating so intently on doing the actions
13. Will strike an instrument to produce a sound. Often choose pots and pans and other utensils for sound-making activities.

## USING NURSERY RHYMES

Those who love poetry and music will find themselves reciting poetry and nursery rhymes and singing those unforgettable rhymes to the very young. Children's interest in a world of sound can be enhanced through different qualities of tones, pitches, and rhythmical movements. During these early childhood years, adults working with young children should share with them the many delightful nursery rhymes, the Mother Goose rhymes, and chants of early childhood.

It is quite natural for infants to move their bodies to certain beats of the rhymes and chants. Their inner kinesthetic sense seems to guide their ever-increasing movements. As children grow older, the appeal of rhymes seems to increase. Even though young children care little about the origin and meaning of nursery rhymes, thousands of children continue to enjoy them. The value of the rhymes lies in their delightful rhythms, repetition, good humor, nonsensical words, and imagination. Children receive much pleasure from listening to and attempting, in their own inimitable ways, to repeat the chants and rhymes while moving their bodies to the interesting rhythmic patterns that the rhymes afford.

It is desirable to say and sing these rhymes over and over again and to include the family in this sharing process. If children are provided with these experiences, they will soon spontaneously join in and participate in these fun-filled episodes. In this activity, a good foundation is being established for children's lifetime reading and musical tastes.

Who can forget the lilting, rhythmical rhymes of the following:

Bye, baby bunting,
Daddy's gone a-hunting,
To get a little rabbit skin
To wrap the baby bunting in.

This little pig went to market;
This little pig stayed at home;
This little pig had roast beef;
And this little pig had none;
This little pig said, "Wee, wee, wee!"
All the way home.
(A verse for each of the child's toes)

How many days has my baby to play?
Saturday, Sunday, Monday,
Tuesday, Wednesday, Thursday, Friday,
Saturday, Sunday, Monday.

Higgledy, piggledy, my black hen,
She lays eggs for gentlemen;
Sometimes nine, sometimes ten;
Higgledy, piggledy, my black hen.

To market, to market, to buy a fat pig,
Home again, home again, jiggity jig;
To market, to market, to buy a fat hog,
Home again, home again, jiggity jog;

To market, to market, to buy a plum bun,
Home again, home again, market is done.

Baa, baa black sheep
Have you any wool?
Yes, sir, yes, sir, three bags full.
One for my master, one for the dame,
One for the little boy that lives in the lane.

Humpty Dumpty sat on a wall,
Humpty Dumpty had a great fall;
All the king's horses and all the king's men
Couldn't put Humpty Dumpty together again.

Little Jack Horner
Sat in a corner,
Eating his Christmas pie.
He put in his thumb
And pulled out a plum
And said, "What a good boy am I!"

Pussy cat, pussy cat, where have you been?
I've been to London to visit the queen.
Pussy cat, pussy cat, what did you do there?
I frightened a little mouse under the chair.

Bow, wow, wow!
Whose dog art thou?
Little Tom Tinker's dog,
Bow, wow, wow!

Jack and Jill went up the hill
To fetch a pail of water;
Jack fell down and broke his crown,
And Jill came tumbling after.

Roses are red,
Violets are blue;
Sugar is sweet,
And so are you!

One potato, two potato,
Three potato, four;
Five potato, six potato
Seven potato, more.

Rain, rain go away;
Come again another day;
Little Johnny wants to play.

Little drops of water
Little grains of sand
Make the mighty ocean,
And the pleasant land.

Jean, Jean,
Dressed in green
Went downtown
To eat ice cream.
How many dishes did she get?
One, two, three, four, five.

## CHANTING: THE LINK BETWEEN SPEECH AND RHYTHM

Some authorities call the half-speaking, half-singing sounds a child makes as he goes about his play "chanting." Whether he is pounding with a hammer, pushing a wheel toy, or perhaps running with a balloon, one can hear his melodic fragments.

> Chanting, the most obvious link between speech and rhythm, suggests itself immediately as a most natural response. For the child, it is as instinctive as it is delightful. For him it is a part of play, a source of interesting images and sounds. Whether he chants nursery rhymes or rhymes he helps create about people and things with which he is intimate . . . he enters into the activity naturally and joyfully. With guidance, his chanting can open the door to all rhythmic and melodic experiences. Words can begin to take on color; the quality of speech begins to reflect the meanings he is trying to portray. Highs and lows—both in pitch and dynamics—can develop. And, throughout, a feeling for the various kinds of meter is acquired (Wheeler and Raebeck, 1972, p. 2).

Children love the sound of their own voices. Parents and teachers should encourage young children to improvise and should themselves serve as models. When a child chants or sings word phrases, it is sound practice for the adult to repeat them back to the child. "It is common knowledge that children all over the world sing the minor third; it has been labeled the national chant of childhood" (Shelley, 1976, p. 207).

Children often half-speak, half-sing names of people, animals, and the like, using the tones of the minor third.

Tones of the minor third

SOL  MI   Ma - ma    Dad - dy
          Cook - ie   Dog - gie

Songs or little melodies using the pentatonic scale often make use of the minor third. The scale has five tones to an octave. Found in the diatonic scale, the five-tone scale is do, re, mi, sol, la. The scale can originate on any tone. It is a scale often found in songs children make up themselves such as:

Mom - my where are you?

(*Note:* This little melody makes use of only the black keys.)

To develop further the tie-in between speaking and singing, it is advisable to sing requests and the like to children, such as the following:

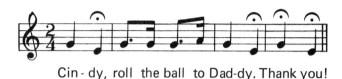

Cin - dy, roll the ball to Dad-dy. Thank you!

Mat-thew, would you like a cook - ie?

San - dy, give your cup to Mom - my.

Observe that the minor third chants just introduced constitute a two-note pattern. This is a very natural and easy way to improvise a little tune to sing to a child. We want to stress the importance and value of making up these short, fun melodies in which one sings about the everyday things the child or people around her are doing. Babies and toddlers who have had such rich and plentiful experiences, who have been talked to, played with, and sung to, will be able to join in quite accurately with words and "snatches" of melodies of familiar songs, chants, or nursery rhymes at the age when they are starting to talk.

For example, when Kathleen's two grandsons were babies, the family talked and sang a great deal to them and made up little tunes about what they were doing together with them. Throughout the day nursery rhymes were sung. The boys loved the funny songs. Two of their favorites were "The Peanut Song" and "Miss Polly," which appear on pages 61–62 of this book. Around the age of two, both Matthew and Andrew began to sing these songs in the same way. First, they laughed and clapped when Kathleen would sing the songs to them. Then she began to hear them sing the last word in each phrase or line. For example, when she would sing, "Oh, the peanut sat on the railroad track," they would join in and sing the word "track." When she held the note on the word track and gave them time to respond, she noticed that they would slide their voices up to the correct pitch for that word. She would do the same with the other words like "flutter," "again," and "butter." When singing

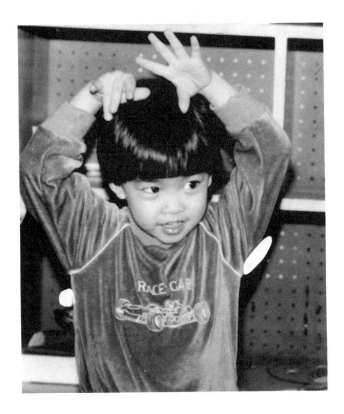

the second verse of the song, she did the same for the words "pad," "sky," "in," and "eye." As the boys grew older, they were able to pick up other words and phrases of the song and sing them. To this day they love those songs and know exactly where they appear in this book. When they were 2½ years of age, they already knew if the book was open to the correct song. They would not let Kathleen play or sing the song until the book was open to the correct page. She latched on to this ritual, since it indicated to her that locating the correct page of the song was as important to them as locating a particular picture in one of their picture books. In their own play world, the boys were pretending they were reading the song just as she was doing. This can be a first step in helping to build reading readiness in young children.

So often teachers and care givers have such narrow ideas about what constitutes music when they work with young children. They need to listen to children and observe them carefully. Children have the ability to respond to music that is brought to them. It is up to parents and teachers to provide meaningful music experiences for these active, persistent music makers.

## ELEMENTS OF MUSICAL BEGINNINGS

All growth, musical or otherwise, is an active process. From birth, for optimal musical development to occur, chil-

dren must be actively involved in making music. Some learning does take place through watching and listening to others, but the best learning takes place through trying out for oneself.

From infancy, an important element in the musical development of young children is the development of perceptual awareness. This means much more than becoming aware of all the senses, such as hearing, smelling, and touching. It is only through our senses that we learn about our environment, and it is extremely important that those caring for young children expose them to rich sensory experiences and provide the appropriate guidance. The development of a child's ability to perceive sounds, to become aware of differences and similarities, and to become involved in producing the sounds herself is of utmost importance to her future learning.

Infants around six months of age and older are fascinated by the movement and rustling of leaves and swaying branches and are soothed by the motion of riding in a buggy or car. And, in fact, infants soon become interested in the outdoor sounds of birds and animals, especially if attention is drawn to them. At times, babies try to produce similar sounds.

Auditory experiences that link the senses are particularly meaningful for young children. Our own children, Chris and Kim, now grown, often talk about the times they visited their grandparents and were awakened in the mornings by Dolly, the horse who pulled the milk wagon down the street. We first took the children out to the street to observe Dolly, and they were soon able to identify her by the senses of seeing and hearing. They learned at a very early age to know Dolly by the steady clip-clop of her shoes on the pavement and would always run to the window when they first heard her footsteps.

Kay, a mother of a preschool child, recently related that her daughter Betsy became completely fascinated at a very early age with the sounds the wind chimes made on their porch. The mother told how Betsy's eyes became "glued" to the chimes as the wind caused the small pieces of glass to clink against each other and produce the bell-like sounds. As the child grew older, Kay and Betsy began to talk about how the chimes jangled, clangled, and tangled. Eventually, the conversation about the chimes turned into a little melody. Parents and teachers like Kay will want to turn these everyday happenings into fun-filled musical experiences that make music such a natural day-by-day occurrence.

At an early age, children learn to discern differences in people's voices. It does not take infants and toddlers long to discover the difference between the soft-spoken words of love and happiness and the harsher words of disapproval. Eventually, they learn the difference between the sound of a barking dog and the purr of a cat. They will also begin to associate people, animals, and mechanical things with their respective sounds.

One should constantly be alert and prepared to promote perceptual awareness. Throughout the seasons of the year and at different times of the day, children should be taken on walks, for rides, and excursions. Care needs to be taken to point out different objects and sights and to give help in distinguishing the many different kinds of sounds in the environment. Repeat the sounds, if possible, for the child to hear. Often the child will repeat the sounds back to you. Then try repeating the sounds together.

Interesting examples of sounds and sights in the surrounding environment might be:

- the merry-go-round at a local fair
- the corn-popping machine at a stand in the park or at a local mall
- the flapping of a bird's wings
- branches waving in the breeze
- a jet airplane landing and taking off
- a bulldozer pushing logs or dirt
- the whistle of a train as it approaches a crossing
- a firecracker display on the Fourth of July
- children and adults singing Christmas carols
- the band playing in the park or at a parade
- helicopters in flight
- birds chirping
- flags flying in the breeze
- the whistle of a teakettle

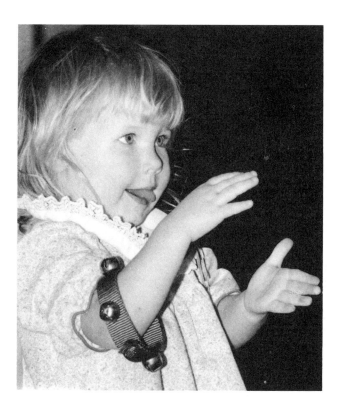

We can well remember often seeing a young father carrying his little girl or sometimes wheeling her in her buggy or stroller around our village green. When we went to the village on errands, we could see them together at different times of the day—morning, midday, sometimes after sundown. The father was always talking with his child, helping her to become aware of the many fascinating sounds, smells, and sights around her. For example, they would sit on the park bench and listen to the birds singing. They would also listen for the chimes to ring out the hour in the clock-tower on the village green. At Christmas time they would stand and look at the stuffed mouse ''running up'' the clock-tower. They could be heard singing ''Hickory, Dickory, Dock'' together. On Memorial Day they would watch and listen as the band marched down Main Street in the parade. On Sunday evenings they would sit on a blanket in the park and listen to the different bands, choral groups, and dancers that would come to present programs for the people in the village. This kind of ''planned exposure'' continued as the child grew older. One day, as we conversed with the father, he told us that he wanted his daughter to learn as much as she could about the beautiful world in which she would be growing up. He was a wise and sensitive person. Before the child became a teenager, the father died. This child will certainly have many happy memories of the time she spent with her father.

**FAVORITE SONGS AND RHYTHMS**

When not asleep, babies and toddlers are almost in constant motion. The following songs lend themselves to much movement, which is an important element in the life of the growing child. Suggestions for different kinds of actions and movements are given with each song.

# SEE MY FINGERS

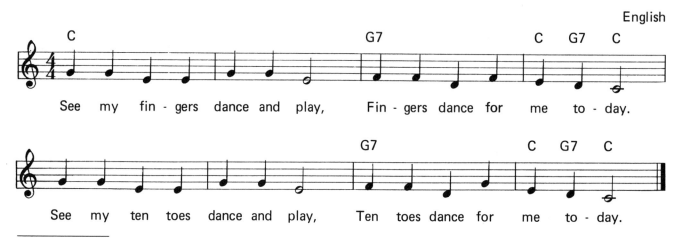

Reprinted by permission of ''Miss Jackie'' Weissman.

Singing this song will give you and the baby great pleasure. Sit the baby in your lap as you sing the song. Touch the baby's fingers when you sing about the fingers, and touch the baby's toes when you sing about the toes.

Make the fingers and toes do different things as you sing the song. Wiggle, shake, one hand or foot crossing over the other. This will help the baby develop cognitive skills. Show the baby all the different things you can do with your fingers and toes.

# LAZY MARY

Traditional

This traditional song has long been a favorite of young children. As you sing to awaken the baby, substitute the word "lazy" with the word "baby" or other words like "happy," "blue-eyed," etc. The baby's name can also be substituted for the word "Mary." For variety, change "cold and frosty morning" to the appropriate weather conditions, such as "bright and sunny morning" or "cloudy, fall morning."

Between 12 and 18 months there is great physical growth in babies, and many of them will begin to move their body parts to music quite spontaneously. At this time, episodes and rhythmic games can be created between adults and children for both enjoyment and learning. The repeat of rhythmic patterns could be initiated at this time. The patterns to be repeated should be given at a slow, simple pace.

# CLAPPING SONG

Traditional

Place the baby in a high chair or sit in front of her. Sing and clap the above song to the baby. (Repeat several times.)

If the baby doesn't respond, gently take the baby's hands in yours and clap the beats to the song again. (Repeat.)

Children above 24 months in age will be able to recognize familiar songs and many times will start clapping without much encouragement. As much as possible, adults should encourage children to tap their thighs to the beat of the music. This is an easier way of keeping the beat.

## RING AROUND THE ROSIES

Old singing game

Adapted by K. BAYLESS

This singing game is probably the most beloved action song of young children. Take the small child's hands and dance around to the music. For older children have them form a circle by holding hands and have them walk or skip around the circle. On the word "down," fall to the ground. Children delight in anticipating the falling-down action and are quick to rise on their feet and begin the game again.

## MEW, MEW, MEW - BOW, WOW, WOW

K. BAYLESS

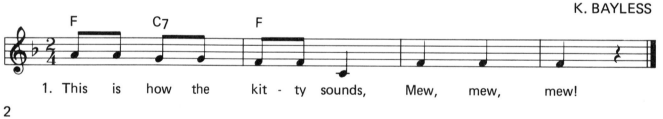

2
This is how the doggy sounds,
Bow, wow, wow!

Encourage the baby to make the sounds of the animals. Add the cow, duck, sheep, etc.

## BABY'S GROWING

K. BAYLESS

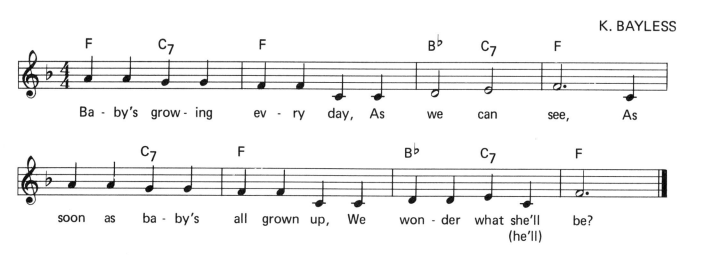

Ba - by's grow - ing ev - ry day, As we can see, As soon as ba - by's all grown up, We won - der what she'll be?
(he'll)

Help baby raise arms high above head and show how "big" he or she can be.

## DEEDLE, DEEDLE, DUMPLING

Mother Goose

Dee - dle, dee - dle, dump - ling, my son John, Went to bed with his trou - sers on. One shoe off, the oth - er shoe on, Dee - dle, dee - dle, dump - ling, my son John.

"Deedle, Deedle, Dumpling" is an age-old Mother Goose favorite and lends itself to bouncing movements. Hold the child on your lap and bounce him up and down to each "deedle, deedle, dumpling."

# TWINKLE, TWINKLE, LITTLE STAR

Traditional

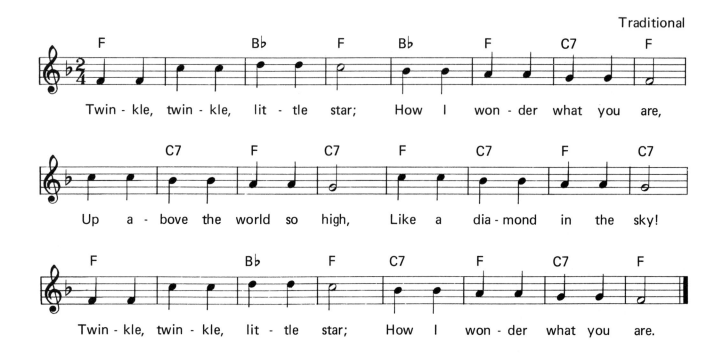

The moon and the stars are wonders to be enjoyed at an early age. Young children are particularly fascinated to look out of a window and see the yellow moon and shining stars. This is a delightful rhyme to sing at nighttime.

Show the child how to wiggle the fingers as the song is sung. In time, the child will imitate the movement. On the words "Up above the world so high," point a finger to the stars in the sky.

## HEY, DIDDLE, DIDDLE

Mother Goose

J. W. ELLIOTT

Hey, did-dle, did-dle, The cat and the fid-dle, The cow jump'd o - ver the moon; The

lit - tle dog laughed to see such sport, And the dish ran a - way with the spoon.

This Mother Goose rhyme is fun-loving and full of good humor.

Hold the child and gently sway back and forth while singing the rhyme. On the word "jump'd," take one jump. On the phrase "And the dish ran away with the spoon," take running steps in time to the music.

## HICKORY, DICKORY, DOCK*

Mother Goose

J. W. Elliott

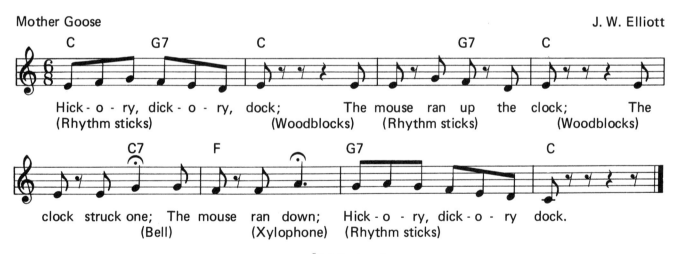

Hick - o - ry, dick - o - ry, dock; The mouse ran up the clock; The
(Rhythm sticks)                (Woodblocks)    (Rhythm sticks)        (Woodblocks)

clock struck one; The mouse ran down; Hick - o - ry, dick - o - ry dock.
(Bell)            (Xylophone)   (Rhythm sticks)

*Public domain.

"Hickory, Dickory, Dock" is a favorite Mother Goose rhyme. Adults may want to add actions to the song as they share it with children.

When children are old enough to sing the song, they may add actions to the song by running their fingers of one hand up their other arm on the words "The mouse ran up the clock." On the word "one," the children clap their hands together once. On the words "The mouse ran down," they take one hand and run the fingers down the other arm.

An adult may choose to add the rhythm instruments to the song. Children can play the instruments when they are older.

# SEE SAW, MARGERY DAW

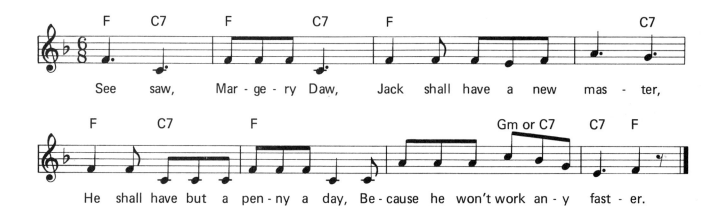

As the child matures and grows in strength and coordination, these rhymes can be expanded to include body movements.

Suggested movements for "See Saw, Margery Daw":

• Rock back and forth in a one-two rhythm.
• Stand facing the child. Take hold of hands. Swing arms to the right and then to the left throughout the song in a one-two rhythm.
• Child and adult sit on the floor facing each other, arms outstretched, hands cupped. Rock back and forth in rhythm.

## KEY IDEAS

1. Music activities should be selected according to reasonable expectation levels of children and sound growth and development principles.
2. The value of nursery rhymes lies in their rhythms, repetition, good humor, nonsensical words, and imagination.
3. Musical awareness should be built on a first-hand basis.

## SUMMARY

Sights and sounds surround us in our everyday living. Artists are very in tune to the environment and depend upon their acute awareness to express their perceptions to others through their paintings. This is also the case with music. Children need to be made aware of the sounds in their environment and of music. To be effective, this awareness must be dealt with on a firsthand basis. All of us can help children learn to appreciate the beauty of sound and music so that it can become an enjoyable, lifelong experience.

## QUESTIONS TO CONSIDER

1. What evidence can you cite from your personal experience that children love the sound of their own voices? How could chanting encourage such behavior? Give examples.
2. Devise several activities that promote perceptual awareness. Use the activities with one or two children and record your results.
3. Describe your immediate environment. What elements could be used to promote auditory awareness?

## REFERENCES AND SUGGESTED READINGS

Caplan, Frank, and Caplan, Theresa. *The second twelve months of life.* New York: Grosset & Dunlap, 1977.

Margolin, Edythe. "A world of music for young children." In *Young children: Their curriculum and learning processes.* New York: Macmillan, 1976.

McDonald, Dorothy T. *Music in our lives: The early years.* Washington, D.C.: National Association for the Education of Young Children, 1979.

Moomow, Sally. *Discovering music in early childhood.* Boston: Allyn and Bacon, 1984.

Shelley, Shirley J. "Music." In Carol Seefeldt (Ed.), *Curriculum for the preschool-primary child—A review of the research.* Columbus, Ohio: Merrill, 1976.

Wheeler, Lawrence, and Raebeck, Lois. *Orff and Kodaly adapted by the elementary school.* Dubuque, Iowa: William C. Brown, 1972.

Zeitlin, Patty. *A song is a rainbow.* Glenview, Ill.: Scott, Foresman, 1982.

## SONG COLLECTIONS

*The Raffi Singable Songbook*
Chappell
14 Birch Avenue
Toronto, Ontario, Canada
*A collection of 51 songs from Raffi's first three records for young children.*

*Nursery Songs,* arranged by Joseph Moorat
The Metropolitan Museum of Art and Thames & Hudson
New York, N.Y.
*Thirty old-time nursery songs.*

## RECORDINGS

*Golden Slumbers*
Children's Book & Music Center
*Twenty-four lullabies from around the world, sung by eight folk singers.*

*Let's Visit Lullaby Land*
Children's Book & Music Center
*Restful music for quiet times. Soothing music in a variety of classical selections and contemporary tunes—for example, "Prayer" from Hansel and Gretel, "Edelweiss," and many others.*

*Little Favorites*
Children's Book & Music Center
*Sixteen classic songs for young children, such as "Hush Little Baby."*

*Loving and Learning from Birth to Three*
Children's Book & Music Center
*A sleeping/resting, play-and-learn record. Includes lullabies, children's prayers, and learning songs for crawling, walking, talking.*

*Music for 1's and 2's,* sung by Tom Glazer
Children's Book & Music Center
*Songs for the very young. A favorite record of many.*

*My Teddy Bear and Me*
Children's Book & Music Center
*Musical play activities for infants and toddlers. Familiar melodies and simple actions especially structured to help the very young become aware of objects and spatial relationships and develop coordination and listening skills.*

*Nursery and Mother Goose Songs*
Children's Book & Music Center
*Sung by male and female voices, accompanied by simple orchestral arrangements.*

*Songs to Grow On,* Vol. 1, sung by Woody Guthrie
Children's Book & Music Center
*Woody Guthrie sings his famous chants and folksy songs, including his most popular, "Put Your Finger in the Air."*

*Tickly Toddle* (Songs for Very Young Children), by Hap Palmer
Children's Book & Music Center
*For use with small groups of children in day care and nursery school settings, or for use at home. The activities are simple and afford opportunities for interaction between adult and child.*

# CHAPTER THREE

# Music for the Twos to Threes

Where there is live music being played that has a decided marked rhythm, most two- to three-year-old children will be seen bouncing up and down and swaying and swirling their bodies to the music. When working with children of this delightful age, we find that sound and movement are almost inseparable. Since children are so sensitive to sound and movement, we will present and discuss some of the activities that they might enjoy if given the opportunity, and, at the same time, we will indicate how conceptual development can take place with these activities. Having knowledge of the characteristics of the twos to threes helps us in planning meaningful experiences for them.

## SELECTED CHARACTERISTICS OF TWO- TO THREE-YEAR-OLDS

1. Are very active and like music to which they can respond
2. Like music having marked rhythm such as band music, nursery rhymes, or catchy TV jingles
3. Can run and jump and walk on tiptoe
4. May gallop like a pony
5. Often will clap hands or tap hips to rhythm when hearing music
6. Attempt to dance to music by bending knees in a bouncing motion, turning circles, swinging arms, nodding the head
7. Usually like to have someone sing songs to them
8. Are able to sing phrases of songs
9. Show increasing ability to keep time and to follow directions in musical games
10. Can lie or sit down quietly and listen for longer periods of time
11. Enjoy going up and down steps
12. Can push and pull toys
13. Enjoy making sounds to accompany play
14. Like imaginative, dramatic play
15. Are beginning to speak in short sentences
16. Tend to play more by themselves or next to others without engaging in much conversation
17. Begin to show interest in listening to and playing real musical instruments like drums, rhythm sticks, and tambourines
18. Are beginning to become interested in radio and TV commercials set to music

## RESPONSE FROM TODDLERS TO SOUND AND MOVEMENT

Often music will elicit a particular response from the toddler. He may be seen swaying or stepping in time to an appropriate rhythm. On many occasions, as Kathleen played the piano or organ in her home and sang for her grandsons at this age, they would stand on each side of the bench, swaying back and forth to the steady, rhythmic beat. At other times they would dance around the room using their whole bodies.

One has only to watch young children as a band plays a lively march or dance to observe their response to music. If they are in a setting in which they can move, most of them will invariably begin to clap their hands and move their feet in time to the music. Their faces will light up with pleasure and delight. During the summer months, selected bands and orchestras play different types of concerts in our gazebo on the village green. The audience spreads blankets on the grass, and young and old enjoy the music during balmy summer evenings. Children are encouraged to respond to the music—to clap and to dance in the open, grassy spaces.

We shall never forget the time we saw a toddler parading back and forth on the lawn, swinging his bottle (teeth clenched on the nipple, hands unattached to the bottle) in time to the music. His bottle, hand, and legs moved in perfect synchronization. This uninhibited enjoyment continued for several minutes.

Usually, music making at this age is an individual activity. During a play period, for example, a child named Sara may be using a wooden spoon to tap on a pan; Andrew might be pushing his fire truck across the floor as he makes an authentic siren sound with his voice; Jennifer might be standing on tiptoes to reach and play the white keys on the piano. On occasion, children will form a musical group of their own and play their sound-producing instruments as they stand beside one another. It is from these spontaneous activities that we should take our cues in helping children enjoy these playful, sound-producing experiences.

Music for young children facilitates discovering sounds both inside and outside the home. As adults, we need to observe young children closely, particularly in their play, and learn more about the many ways in which they deal with sound and movement. The child at age two and over is always on the move and involved in sound-making experimentation.

As children grow and develop, one of the most important things that we can do is help them build good listening skills. Children have little motivation on their own to listen carefully unless parents and teachers encourage it. This does not imply that we must impose drill-like, structured procedures to accomplish this purpose. We need to assist children in helping them make sense out of the myriad kinds of sounds in their environment. As Evans (1978, p. 53) reminds us, "You have to be able to pay attention, to concentrate, to focus your listening on the sound you want to hear and to cut out other sounds you don't want to hear." This statement is very important to keep in mind.

For children to make sense and meaning out of the sounds they hear, sounds need to be put in context. Adults can do this quite easily by helping children relate sounds closely to everyday objects and events. It is easier to do this for children around the age of two, since children at this age are becoming more mobile and have increased ability to talk about the things they are doing. Children need to acquire language so they can talk and think about sound. With the help of understanding adults, conversations about sound can be initiated through some of the following ways.

*Adult to child*

1. "Listen, do you hear the siren? That's the police siren."
2. "The dog must be very happy. He's barking because he's excited."
3. "I wonder who's at the door? That's our doorbell ringing."

4. "I hear a lawnmower; do you? It sounds like Mr. Larson's."
5. "Look! Listen! Here comes the choo-choo train."
6. "I hear our telephone ringing. Do you hear it, too?"
7. "Do you suppose that's Daddy's car?"
8. "Daddy must be shaving. Let's go check."
9. "Is that the trash man picking up the branches?"
10. "Hear the popcorn?"
11. "Put your ear close to the kitty. Do you hear it purring?"

*Child to adult, in like nature*

1. "Doggie, Mama?"
2. "Ring the bell."
3. "Rr-rr-rr-rr."
4. "Baby crying?"
5. "Birdie singing?"
6. Repeat of a line or word from a TV commercial, such as the one for "Jello Pudding."

## BUILDING ON CHILDREN'S NATURAL MOVEMENTS

It is important to remember that children of this age need many opportunities to move—to walk, run, climb, bounce, jump—not only for the purpose of increasing their muscular

development, but also for the sake of pure enjoyment. At first, movements will be uncoordinated, but with plenty of opportunity to move and express themselves, the children will eventually gain control of their bodies, and these movements will become refined.

Children around the age of two like to bounce up and down on a bed or a sofa. As they do this, it is not uncommon to hear them singing words to accompany their movement. For example, children might be heard singing "bouncy-bounce, bouncy-bounce," keeping time with their bouncing. Some adults will scold or reprimand a child for such actions without giving redirection to this type of natural behavior. Why not provide some type of cushiony material, such as an old mattress or gym pad, for this type of activity?

Have you ever noticed how many children run in complete abandon, waving their arms like birds? Have you ever watched and listened as other youngsters keep perfect time walking down the sidewalk dragging sticks behind them? Have you watched others as they teeter back and forth from one foot to another, humming in rhythm to their teetering movements? At times, an appropriate record could be played, a song hummed or sung, or clapping provided to accompany these kinds of body movements. Join in with the children. Make it a game. Show your approval.

### Music as a Support to Movement

Music should support movement. There will be times when children will ask for musical accompaniment as they move about. A sensitive adult can encourage the child's

movements by clapping or tapping on a tom-tom or some similar instrument. When accompanying a child's movements, synchronize the accompaniment to the tempo of his movements. Throughout much of the preschool period one needs to accommodate the child's own rhythm rather than have the child conform to the beat. This can be done by first watching and listening to the child as he claps, taps, walks, tiptoes, and the like, then providing accompaniment that matches the child's own body rhythm.

> In research studies it has been found that music, phonographic or instrumental, may stimulate movement, but the children felt the desire to move first, and later asked for music. Only when the music happens to be in the child's movement tempo or he wishes to adjust his tempo to it may the two coincide . . . . It is important that the accompanist be very sensitive to the mood and the underbeat to which the child's movement relates (Chandler, 1970, pp. 9–10).

When selecting musical activities for children of this age, consider the following:

1. Large group experiences in music should be kept to a minimum. Give individual children and small groups plenty of time and space to sing, move, make sounds, and listen to music.
2. Make good use of music that promotes body movements such as jumping, running, and the like. Children of this age will respond at their own body tempo.
3. Much of children's singing at this age is spontaneous and self-initiated and appears as they engage in play activities. Provide opportunities for spontaneous play activity, particularly of the motor kind.

4. At appropriate times, enrich children's play activities and movements with your own spontaneous singing of musical phrases and short songs.

5. "Very young children are not attentive to the necessity to match pitch or tonality when singing with others. Rather they choose their own pitch range. You may match your pitch to those of the children and in this way introduce the concept of singing in unison" (McDonald, 1979, p. 14).*

6. If songs are used, choose those which appeal to the children's interests and have repetition in melody and rhythm. Also, choose songs that are short and within the children's singing range. (Children prefer singing within the range of middle C to A, a sixth above middle C. Some children prefer the range from D above middle C to B above middle C.)

7. Introduce new music material slowly. Children like to sing familiar songs. They love humorous songs.

8. "Many young children regard group singing experiences as opportunities to listen without joining in. When they do sing, they often lag behind a bit. Sometimes they begin participating by whispering the words. Often they sing only parts of songs—perhaps a repeated phrase that has caught their attention. They enjoy listening to favorite songs over and over and need many opportunities to listen before they become participants in group singing" (McDonald, 1979, p. 14).*

9. At this age, children like to experiment with instruments but should not be expected to keep "time" with the music. Introduce individual instruments one at a time so that children can become acquainted with each instrument's distinctive sound, its shape, and its name. Instruments are best used to produce certain sound effects in songs or stories or during children's play making. For example, a triangle can be used to imitate the clock striking out the number of hours in the song "Wee Willie Winkle." Children delight in jingling bells when singing "Jingle Bells."

10. "Two- and three-year-olds need opportunities to acquire a repertoire of movements [body] that they may use in creative ways in these early years, rather than drill in keeping time" (McDonald, 1979, p. 16).*

---

*Reprinted by permission from *Music in Our Lives: The Early Years* by Dorothy T. McDonald. Copyright © 1979, National Association for the Education of Young Children, 1834 Connecticut Ave. N.W., Washington, D.C. 20009.

## FAVORITE SONGS AND RHYTHMS

# TURN AROUND

K. BAYLESS

1. Can you turn a - round with me?    It's as eas - y as can be.
2. Round and round a - bout just so,    Then "ker - flop," we're bound to go.

---

Little children like to turn around in circles. This short song makes a game of it.

Hold the child's hands. Move slowly in order to avoid dizziness. On the word "ker-flop," fall to the floor or rug.

*Movement Concepts: Turning in a circle and falling*

# JUMP, JUMP, JUMP

K. BAYLESS

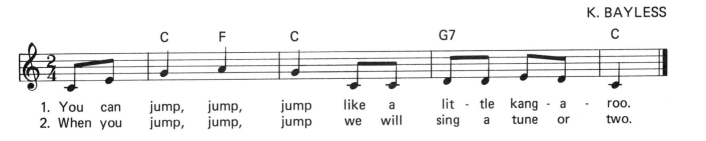

1. You can jump, jump, jump like a lit - tle kang - a - roo.
2. When you jump, jump, jump we will sing a tune or two.

---

Sing the song several times until the child gets the ''feel'' of it.

*Movement Concept: Jumping*

# SALLY, GO 'ROUND THE MOON

English Folk-Tune
Adapted by K. BAYLESS

Sal - ly, go 'round the moon, Sal - ly, go 'round the stars,

Sal - ly, go 'round the chim - ney pots, Ev - 'ry af - ter - noon. Bump!

---

This is a very popular singing game for children of this age. A circle is formed and the children walk around it. (Hands may be held or dropped at sides. A circle can be made for the children to follow by using masking tape. They could also walk around the backs of a circle of chairs to keep the circle intact.) At the word ''Bump,'' the children fall down. They get up, form the circle, and play the game again.

*Tonal and Rhythmic Concepts: Exact repetition of melody and rhythmic pattern*

*Music Concept: Staccato—note sung or played abruptly*

## SWING, SWING

K. BAYLESS

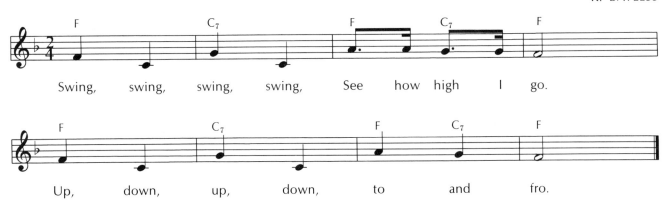

As children swing arms back and forth, up and down, you may find this short tune appropriate. Remember, do not hesitate to make up your own musical phrases to match the movement of the child. Begin with arms swinging upward.

*Movement Concept: Swinging*

*Directional Concepts: Up and down*

## ROCKING YO HO

K. BAYLESS

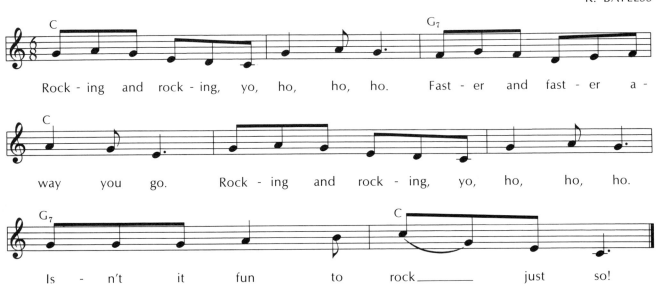

Rocking is one of the favorite movements of most two- to three-year-olds.

I composed this song while watching my grandson Matthew rock back and forth on his trusty red rocking horse, a horse that has been used by three generations. The rhythm was exactly "matched" to Matthew's rocking. Matthew was 2½ years old when this song was composed.

*Movement Concept: Rocking*

# I'M LIKE A BOUNCING BALL

Steadily

K. BAYLESS

I'm like a bounc - ing ball, I bounce with - out a fall; I bounce and bounce and bounce and bounce, Al - though I'm ver - y small.

---

This is a short song involving ''bouncing,'' another favorite movement of small children.

Bounce a rubber ball on the floor for children to see. Encourage the children to bounce their bodies like bouncing balls. Provide plenty of space for the children to move.

***Movement Concept:*** *Bouncing*

---

''Two Little Blackbirds'' and ''Where Is Thumbkin?'' are favorite fingerplays of children and have been set to music for the very young.

# TWO LITTLE BLACKBIRDS

Traditional

Arranged by K. BAYLESS

Two lit - tle black - birds sit - ting on a hill, One named Jack, And one named Jill.

Fly a - way Jack! Fly a - way Jill! Come back Jack! Come back! Jill.

Actions for ''Two Little Blackbirds'':

| | | | |
|---|---|---|---|
| Two little blackbirds | (Hold up both hands, | Fly away, Jack! | (Bend down one thumb) |
| Sitting on a hill, | thumbs erect, fingers bent) | Fly away, Jill! | (Bend down other thumb) |
| One named Jack, | (Wiggle one thumb) | Come back, Jack! | (Raise one thumb erect) |
| And one named Jill. | (Wiggle other thumb) | Come back, Jill! | (Raise other thumb erect) |

***Tonal and Rhythmic Concepts:*** *Exact repetition of melody and rhythmic pattern*

# WHERE IS THUMBKIN?

Traditional

Musical fingerplay

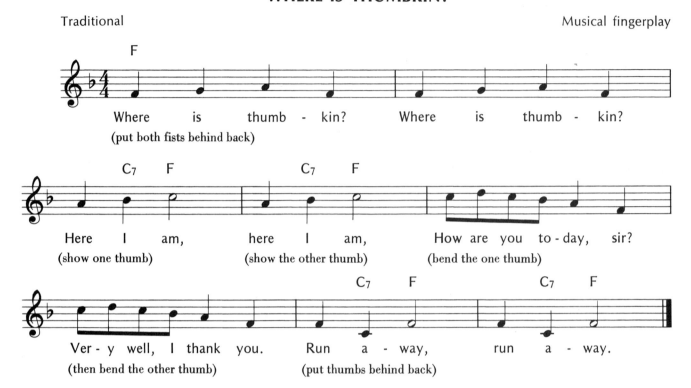

Where is thumb - kin? Where is thumb - kin?
(put both fists behind back)

Here I am, here I am, How are you to - day, sir?
(show one thumb)     (show the other thumb)     (bend the one thumb)

Ver - y well, I thank you. Run a - way, run a - way.
(then bend the other thumb)     (put thumbs behind back)

2. Where is pointer? (forefinger)
3. Where is tall man? (middle finger)
4. Where is ring man? (ring finger)
5. Where is pinkie? (little finger)

*Movement Concept: Development of small muscles*

*Music Concept: Matching measures that sound the same*

Pets are always a favorite topic of conversation with children. "The Old Gray Cat" is a song-game that young children like to dramatize. As the song is sung, listen to the words. They tell you what to do.

## THE OLD GRAY CAT

Traditional American song

Accompaniment by K. BAYLESS

The old gray cat is sleep - ing, sleep - ing, sleep - ing, The

old gray cat is sleep - ing in the house.

2. The little mice are creeping, creeping, creeping,
   The little mice are creeping through the house.
3. The little mice are nibbling . . . in the house.
4. The little mice are sleeping . . . in the house.

5. The old gray cat comes creeping . . . through the house.
6. The little mice all scamper . . . through the house.
7. The little mice are hiding . . . in the house.

### Suggestions
On verses 1, 2, 3, 4, 5, and 7, soft voices should be used. In verse 6, use louder voices.

**Rhythmic Concept:** *Adapting rhythmic movement to word meanings*

**Dynamic Concepts:** *Soft and loud*

# TEDDY BEAR, TEDDY BEAR

Traditional verse and song

Ted-dy Bear, Ted-dy Bear, turn a - round, Ted-dy Bear, Ted-dy Bear, touch the ground,

Ted- dy Bear, Ted- dy Bear, show your shoe, Ted-dy Bear, Ted-dy Bear, that will do!

2

Teddy Bear, Teddy Bear, go up stairs,
Teddy Bear, Teddy Bear, say your prayers,
Teddy Bear, Teddy Bear, switch off the light,
Teddy Bear, Teddy Bear, say "goodnight!"

---

For generations this beloved jump-rope rhyme has been a favorite of young children. Chanted in rhythmic verse or sung, this rhyme is a natural since it makes use of the descending minor third tones (Sol-Mi), (Teddy Bear, Teddy Bear). At this age, children are just beginning to develop the tie-in between their speaking and singing voices.

Pantomime the rhyme. Allow children to make suggestions for acting out the words. Substitute a child's name for "Teddy Bear." For variation, change the action.

# TWO LITTLE APPLES

Chant and Song

Traditional

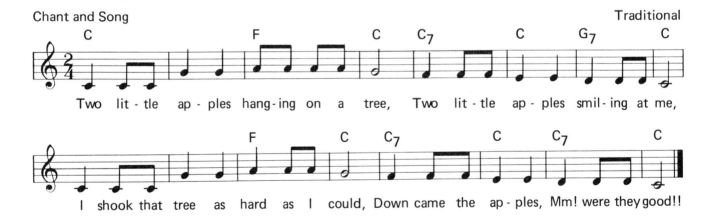

Two lit - tle ap - ples hang-ing on a tree, Two lit - tle ap - ples smil-ing at me,

I shook that tree as hard as I could, Down came the ap - ples, Mm! were they good!!

---

Chant the words of the verse with added appropriate movements.

This can also be used as a song. Extend the arms to each side. Pretend to be holding two apples, one in each hand. Shake the body (tree). Squat down and rub the tummy.

*Concept: Coordination of movement and words*

## PLANNING MUSIC ACTIVITIES FOR YOUNG CHILDREN

Giving children both opportunities and encouragement with musical experiences can lead to a lifetime of enjoyment. It is extremely important that children be given a variety of musical experiences. Some of these may be through listening, others by exploration of what their bodies can do such as singing, movement, and playing instruments. At various ages and stages, children will discover new and different ways in which music can enrich their lives.

Since most children naturally love to sing, allow them to pursue this activity as much as possible. Don't limit singing to nursery rhymes. Present "folk tunes, camp songs, songs from musicals, or songs you've learned from other sources. Children have an endless hunger to hear new songs and to repeat old favorites" (Gorka, 1989, p. 93). The benefits of singing for the toddler are many. "Singing improves vocabulary and language skills as well as auditory memory and introduces him in a very pleasant way to the dynamics of cooperative group activity" (Gorka, 1989, p. 93).

During this age, movement activities should hold high priority. Andress (1989, p. 30) reminds us that "in the area of movement, research supports the long-held belief that preschool children move at a faster overall tempo than adults and that effective teaching in terms of beat coordination involves matching the tempo of the child." This finding is many times forgotten.

In planning music activities for young children, it is imperative to keep in mind their growth and development patterns. Too often, children are asked to engage in activities beyond their understanding and ability. The musical experiences young children receive will play an important role in their total development.

## KEY IDEAS

1. For the twos to threes, music making is often an individual activity.
2. Children learn by listening and experimenting.
3. Care givers should capitalize upon the child's environment and responses as cues.

## SUMMARY

Observation and participation will provide the care giver with ample direction for music making with the twos to threes. Observation means seeing, asking questions, listening, and looking—wherever young children are. Participation means playing, singing, chanting, eating, moving—with young children wherever they are. Spontaneity and creativity should mark much of the activity at these age levels. The environment should be uncomplicated and uncluttered to promote freedom of expression.

Above all keep in mind, for the twos to threes, music is predominantly individual; music is for enjoyment and delight; music is for sharing.

## QUESTIONS TO CONSIDER

1. Select four or five unusual objects that could be used to build good listening habits. Describe an activity with each.
2. Find and record on tape several catchy, action-oriented rhythms appropriate for twos and threes. How might your tape enhance listening skills?
3. Interview the mother of a toddler and determine how the home environment is utilized to develop the perceptual awareness of the child.
4. Revisit the day care center. Select three songs from the chapter to present to the children. Summarize the results.

## REFERENCES AND SUGGESTED READINGS

Andress, Barbara. "Music for every stage." *Music Educators Journal,* October 1989, 76(2), p. 30.

Andress, Barbara. (Ed.) *Prekindergarten music education,* 1902 Association Dr., Reston, Virginia 22091, MENC Publications, 1989. (an excellent resource)

Chandler, Bessie E. "Music." In *Early learning experiences.* Dansville, N.Y.: The Instructor Publications, 1970.

Evans, David. *Sharing sounds.* New York: Longman Group Ltd., 1978.

Gorka, Julie. "The gift of music." *Parents,* March 1989, pp. 88–93.

Haines, B. Joan E., and Gerber, Linda L. *Leading young children to music.* 3rd ed. Columbus, Ohio: Merrill, 1988.

McDonald, Dorothy T. *Music in our lives: The early years.* Washington, D.C.: National Association for the Education of Young Children, 1979.

Moomaw, Sally. *Discovering music in early childhood.* Boston: Allyn and Bacon, 1984.

Ramsey, Marjorie E. (Ed.) *It's music!* Washington, D.C.: Association for Childhood Education International, 1984.

# II

# Music in the Preschool Years and Kindergarten

# CHAPTER FOUR

# Music for the Threes to Fours

Around three years of age children are beginning to take a real interest in music activities of all kinds. It is also a good time for parents and teachers to *begin* to help children understand that there is structure to music. When music is presented within a cognitive framework that is appropriate for young children, meaning and understanding should result. At this age children are almost continually in motion: walking, jumping, running, rocking, swinging, galloping, stomping, and tapping. In many instances these movements can be channeled into the dramatization of action songs or simple, musical episodes or stories. The following selected characteristics of three- to four-year-olds will be of help when selecting appropriate music activities for this age group.

## SELECTED CHARACTERISTICS OF THREE- TO FOUR-YEAR-OLDS

1. Like to gallop, jump, walk, or run in time to music
2. Can build towers with blocks
3. Are much more fluent with language; like to talk and chatter; want adults to listen and to give their undivided attention
4. Like new words; can often be influenced by such words as ''surprise'' and ''secret''; like to whisper in your ear
5. Can tell how old they are
6. Have refined notions of space: over, up on top, under, and on
7. Have more interest in detail and direction (for example, can usually find a favorite book or record from a shelf upon request)
8. Are able to tell on what street they live
9. Can count two objects, sometimes up to five or more
10. Can match colors quite ably
11. Enjoy simple versions of imaginative, dramatic play
12. Are beginning to play cooperatively and to share and take turns
13. Enjoy singing games and rhythm instruments (there continues to be a need to explore, experiment, and manipulate instruments)
14. Like to listen to stories and records
15. Are beginning to dramatize songs
16. Should be able to locate the source of a sound
17. Can remain at musical activities for a longer period of time than previously, since attention span is increasing
18. Show marked improvement in keeping the beat, although not always accurate
19. Start to approximate adult singing
20. Spontaneously make up own songs, words often repetitive and tunes may resemble familiar ones

Consider the following when planning musical activities for a child this age:

1. Encourage informal singing throughout the day.
2. Continue to improvise short action songs based upon what the child is doing.
3. Continue to sing the child's favorite songs and to add new material slowly.
4. Provide plenty of opportunities for the child to dramatize songs and ''act out'' song-stories.
5. Provide simple props such as scarves, crepe paper, feathers, hats, puppets, and instruments for the child to use with musical activities.
6. A child of this age may still lag behind a measure or two when singing. He may also mouth the words or sing only phrases or particular words of songs.

7. Introduce humorous, active songs, which hold high appeal.
8. Give increased attention to helping the child listen for and distinguish the different sounds within the environment.
9. Play simple games in which the child can find sources of different sounds.
10. Continue to introduce rhythm and melody instruments to enhance musical activities. As was indicated previously, it is best to introduce one instrument at a time. Children may show a desire to play their instruments together as when marching in a band.
11. The child is beginning to become more adept at controlling his rhythmic responses for longer periods of time (while moving his body in rhythmic patterns or playing instruments in time to music).
12. Provide increased opportunities for movement with music, such as performing locomotor movements (walking, running, jumping, etc.), nonlocomotor movements (swinging, pushing, bending, etc.), and clapping or tapping the beat of a steady rhythm.
13. Encourage the child to move and dance to music using his own creative ideas.

## CONCEPTUAL LEARNING THROUGH MOVEMENT AND MUSIC

Much movement for children this age takes place during free playtime. Often on these occasions, music accompanies the free play. If a record with inviting rhythm is played on the record player, one or more children may spontaneously decide they would like to dance. Two children may take hold of each other's hands and dance to the music. At a recent wedding reception, two children were seen holding hands and dancing together to the music of a large band for at least thirty minutes.

On another occasion, several young children were seen watching a group of dancers from a local high school singing and dancing on the village green. Spontaneously, as the spirit moved them, the children began to mirror almost every movement the dancers made. Early last fall at an outdoor ballet performance, several young girls were observed standing off to the side of a lighted stage. As the dancers began to move to the beautifully orchestrated music, the girls began to twirl and mimic the performers. This dancing continued for over half the program until the little bodies began to tire. These episodes of spontaneous, creative dancing should be encouraged. In addition to these worthwhile experiences, movement sessions, in which a small group of children are brought together in a more formal setting, encourage movement activities and stress their use and importance in the daily program.

Music concepts and concepts involving music can be taught quite easily within these sessions. They are not taught in a highly structured manner during one session but are learned gradually over a period of time. For example, songs and singing games involving movement are very appropriate to use for children at this age. Initially, some children will not want to join in these sessions, but with time will want to become a part of the group. *(Remember: Keep the group small.)*

It is well known that movement is essential to the healthy growth of young children. Music can provide an excellent medium for helping children acquire good listening skills that will gradually enhance their own creative responses. It is important to keep in mind that when children do actions to singing games and songs that require movement, they may not always sing the words. Adults should not be alarmed at this reaction, as it is considered a normal developmental process. The more vigorous the activity, the less likely children will be able to sing the words. Teaching the words to a song first, before adding the movements, will help speed up the process of becoming adept at singing and moving simultaneously.

Singing games such as "Ring Around the Rosies," "London Bridge Is Falling Down," "Looby Loo," the "Hokey Pokey," "Jack in the Box," "Jack be Nimble," etc., are ideal for initiating movements and bringing children together in a cooperative, happy experience.

Keep these things in mind when planning such sessions:

1. Have children stand or sit on a designated area (for example, on alphabet linoleum blocks formed into a circle on the floor).
2. Keep the sessions short.
3. Start with a familiar action song such as "Clap, Clap, Clap Your Hands Together" or "Look and See".
4. Perform other body movements for warm-ups such as touching different parts of the body, bending, stretching, jumping in place, etc.
5. If you are using a record, the children may not join in with the singing. They may be too involved in doing the suggested actions and movements.
6. You may ask a child to model a certain action in the song or singing game. Or a child may suggest a particular movement himself.
7. Teachers should join in the activity with enthusiasm. Children enjoy having the teacher take a turn in becoming a leader in a singing game.
8. If children do not want to become a part of the small group, do not force them. Often, they will want just to observe. It takes time to build trust between the teacher and child and between a child and the rest of the group.
9. At this age, children may find it difficult to learn and respond to the word "Freeze." A cue such as holding up a hand, or two taps on a drum could be used by the teacher instead. It is important for children to learn to stop an action or movement upon a designated cue from the teacher.

One of the finest resources on using movement with young children is *Feeling Strong, Feeling Free: Movement Exploration for Young Children* by Molly Sullivan. Published by the National Association for the Education of Young Children, Washington, D.C., it is comprehensive, suggests many techniques, and presents a format for teaching movement exploration in meaningful, productive ways.

Sounds of Thunder in the Sky is a musical activity that helps children distinguish between loud and soft tones.

### Sounds of Thunder in the Sky

Shhh! Shhh! Shhh!
Shhh! Shhh! Shhh!
Do you hear what I hear?
Way up in the sky?
It's dark and cloudy with sounds of thunder
Booming way up high.
Boom! (allow a short pause between each boom)
Boom!
Boom!

Adapted by K. BAYLESS

Children may tap their thighs or tap homemade or purchased drums as they make the "Boom" sound with their voices. Discuss the rolling and booming sound that thunder makes. Some young children are not comfortable with thunder sounds. This rhythmic verse creates a gamelike activity and allows children to become more familiar with this environmental sound.

***Music Concept:*** *Difference between loud and soft sounds*

The game Jack-in-the-Box will help children associate body movement height with high and low piano pitches.

### Jack-in-the-Box

*Materials*
Piano
1 large cardboard box (size determined by age and height of child)

*Directions*
Cut doorway on one side of the box for a child to crawl inside. The top of the box is open. Children take turns being the Jack-in-the-Box. Child squats down in the box. A low note on the piano is played three times. Pause after each time the note is played. This will help register the pitch in the child's mind. Then play a high note. Jack pops up. Children take turns being Jack. (If children have played with a mechanical Jack-in-the Box, they will catch on to the game more quickly.)

*Pitch and Movement Concepts*
Association of body movement with high and low pitches

# JACK BE NIMBLE

Nursery rhyme

Adapted by K. BAYLESS and M. RAMSEY

2

Wiggle one finger, then with two,
Let us see what you can do.
First with one, then with two,
Now we know what you can
do.†

\*If larger intervals in pitch are desired, sing C above middle C.
†Children may well offer other suggestions for movement to this lively melody.

---

Words in the first verse may be learned first and the song dramatized as the words are spoken. The phrase ''Jack jump'd high, Jack jump'd low, Jack jump'd over and burned his toe!'' will be new to many children. Talk about jumping high, jumping low, and jumping over. Have children experience these actions before singing the song. If desired, use a prop to denote the candlestick. Discuss when Jack jumps high, the melody goes higher, and we need to make our singing voices go higher. Demonstrate. When Jack jumps low, the melody goes lower, and we need to make our singing voices go lower. Demonstrate. On the words ''high'' and ''low,'' prolong the hold ⌒ (known musically as a fermata).

***Pitch Concepts:*** *High and low (pitch differences)*

***Movement Concepts:*** *Jumping and wiggling the fingers*

## PUTTING DAILY EXPERIENCES TO MUSIC

So often during a child's busy day a small incident can occur in which teachers and parents can take advantage of the situation and turn it into an enjoyable learning experience, sometimes involving music. Recently Andy, an animal lover, came rushing into the house and said a neighbor had given him a turtle for a pet. When asked what the turtle was like, Andy mentioned all the things about the turtle that he observed. These were quickly adapted to the following familiar melody.

*Turtle, Turtle*
*(Sung to the tune of "Twinkle, Twinkle Little Star")*

Turtle, turtle you walk so slow,
On four short legs which are low,
Your back is hard like a walnut shell,
And when you're frightened I can tell,
Your neck pulls in and you stand so still,
Please be my friend, I know you will.

As a supplement to many early childhood music programs, Jean Warren has compiled hundreds of songs sung to the tune of childhood favorites (like the above) and published these in six volumes: *Piggyback Songs, More Piggyback Songs, Piggyback Songs for Infants and Toddlers, Holiday Piggyback Songs, Piggyback Songs in Praise of God,* and *Piggyback Songs in Praise of Jesus.* Many of the lyrics were contributed by teachers throughout the country. (Books can be obtained from Totline Press, P.O. Box 2250, Everett, WA 98203.)

*Creative Movement for the Developing Child* (Revised) by Clare Cherry (published by David S. Lake, 19 Davis Drive, Belmont, CA 94002) is an excellent resource for parents and teachers of preschoolers. This booklet contains a wealth of ideas for developing acute sensory perception during various stages of the child's growth. The interests of the child are used as stimuli to motivate action. This resource is particularly helpful to nonmusicians.

## FAVORITE SONGS AND RHYTHMS

Have you observed how often children chant and sing about what they are doing? Often one will hear them sing their words to a familiar tune such as "Here We Go Round the Mulberry Bush." This kind of spontaneous "play with words and music" should be encouraged. Following is a song that makes use of this idea.

## THIS IS THE WAY

Adapted by K. BAYLESS

Traditional English nursery rhyme tune

Here We Go Round the Mulberry Bush

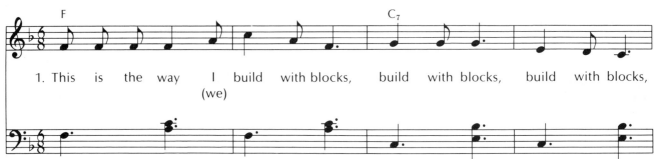

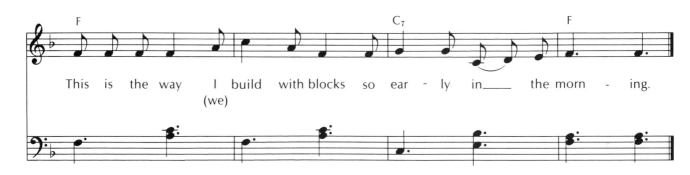

Additional suggested verses:

2. This is the way we clean our room.

3. This is the way I water the plants.

4. Tammie is wiping the tables clean.

5. Tommy is putting the trucks away.

## I'M A LITTLE TEAPOT

Traditional

Words and music by CLARENCE KELLEY and GEORGE H. SANDERS
Adapted by K. BAYLESS

*Suggestions*

This is one of the favorite songs of young children. They love to act it out and will usually learn the words and melody quickly. When they know the song well, try the following. Sing to the children the musical phrase "I'm a little teapot short and stout." Then ask them to listen carefully while you sing "When I get all steamed up then I shout." Tell them that the words are different but that the music sounds alike. Then sing it again in the same manner. This method will help sharpen children's awareness that some phrases in music are exactly alike. As they have this concept pointed out to them as they sing different songs, some children will soon be able to hear these similarities. *Caution:* Do not drill this. The ability to detect these similarities and differences will come with practice. Always keep the spirit of enjoyment as the foremost concern.

*Tonal and Rhythmic Concepts: Repeated melody and rhythmic pattern*

*Movement Concepts: Sweeping and bending*

# LOOK AND SEE

Adapted by K. BAYLESS

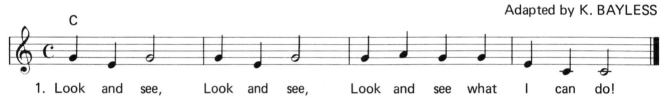

1. Look and see, Look and see, Look and see what I can do!

2
Try with me,
Try with me,
Try and see what we can do!

3
Tap with me,
Tap with me,
Tap and see what we can do!

This song encourages children to participate. Choose one child to be the leader who acts out a movement. The group follows the action of the leader. Children take turns suggesting other actions such as jumping and twisting. Until the children get used to this type of game activity, the teacher may need to make suggestions.

"Open, Shut Them" is one of the favorite musical fingerplays of children. It is an excellent song to help improve children's enunciation of words, to help them stabilize each tone as it is sung, and to help them build better listening skills. Children need to listen intently so they can follow the directions indicated by the words. The song is also used as an effective transition song in settling children for another activity.

## OPEN, SHUT THEM

LAURA PENDLETON MACCARTENEY

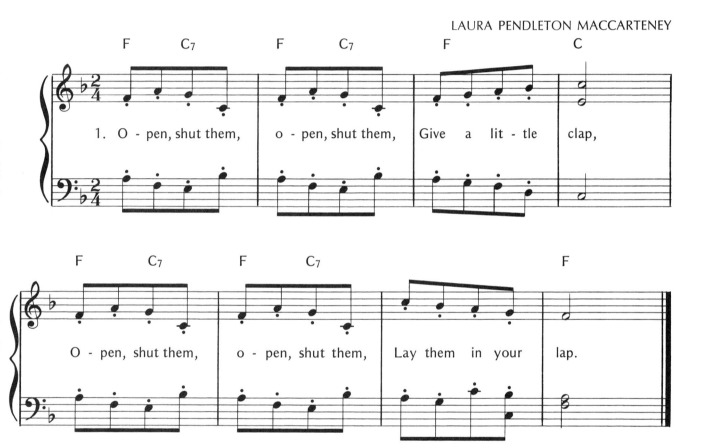

2
Creep them, creep them, creep them, creep them,
Right up to your chin,
Open wide your little mouth,
But do not let them in.

From MacCarteney, Laura Pendleton. *Songs for the Nursery School.* Florence, Ky.: Willis Music Co., 1937.

### Suggestions

The dot (.) under and over the notes is called a staccato marking.* It is an expression mark used in music. When singing or playing, each note should be detached from the other. It is not necessary to point out the marking to three- and four-year-olds. Simply demonstrate to them how the words should be sung. They will enjoy this nonlegato singing.

***Expression Concept:** Staccato singing and playing*

*Depending on the note's location, the marking will be either above or under the note.

Children will differ in their responses to types of music, rhyme, and suggested activities. Short, easy-to-sing songs such as ''Dance in a Circle'' often motivate young children to participate, thus freeing them to initiate their own creative responses. Most three- to four-year-olds will enjoy acting out and doing the movements to other songs, rhymes, and games that follow.

## DANCE IN A CIRCLE

Source unknown
Adapted by K. BAYLESS

"The Peanut Song" and "Miss Polly" are two favorite songs of young children that have been handed down through the years. Children love the fun-filled words in "The Peanut Song" and the definite rhythmic quality and rhyming words of "Miss Polly." When singing "Miss Polly," most children begin immediately to act out the words of the song. Often, when singing an action-type song with other children, the shy child begins to feel more comfortable in joining in with the others.

## THE PEANUT SONG

Traditional

1. Oh, the pea-nut sat on the rail-road track, His heart was all a-flut-ter. The choo-choo train came down the track, Toot, toot, pea-nut but-ter.

2
Oh, the bullfrog sat on a lily pad,
A-looking up at the sky.
The lily pad broke, and the frog fell in
And got water in his eye.

# MISS POLLY

Unknown

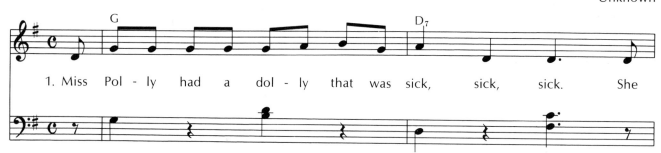

1. Miss Pol - ly had a dol - ly that was sick, sick, sick. She

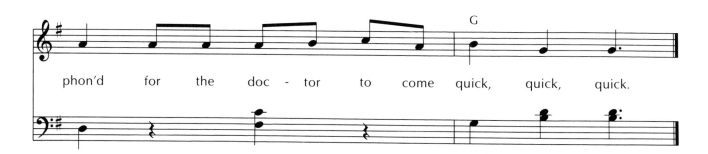

phon'd for the doc - tor to come quick, quick, quick.

2
The doctor came with his cane and hat.
He knocked on the door with a rat, tat, tat.

3
He looked at the dolly and he shook his head.
He said, "Miss Polly, put her straight to bed."

4
He wrote on the paper for a pill, pill, pill.
"I'll be back in the morning with a bill, bill, bill!"

Most children like to be asked how old they are. Some will hold up their fingers for the number of years and then will smile and answer the correct number. Note that the melody and rhythm in the song "How Old Are You?" are exactly alike in the first two measures. Sing "How old are you?" and then pause before singing it the second time. Help the children discover that the two measures sound exactly alike. It will not take children long to discover these similarities and differences in melodies and rhythms if they are guided in a developmental, sequential way.

## HOW OLD ARE YOU?

K. BAYLESS

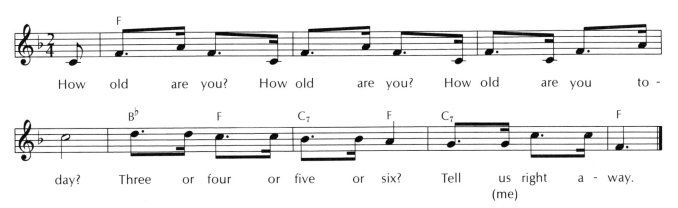

*Musical Concepts: Repetition of melody and rhythmic pattern*

Children are so proud when they can tell others their names and addresses. You will recognize that the words to "Name Your Street" have been set to the familiar tune "London Bridge Is Falling Down." Children find it much easier to sing new songs that have familiar melodies.

## NAME YOUR STREET

Traditional tune

Adapted by K. BAYLESS

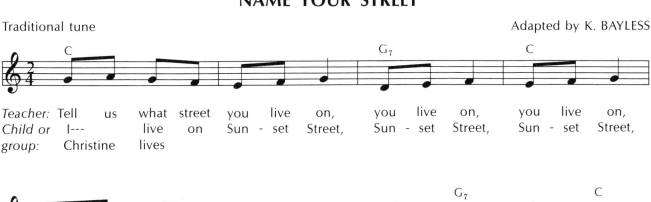

# HA, HA, THIS-A-WAY

American folk song

Arranged by K. BAYLESS

*Suggestions*

Clap on ''Ha, ha, this-a-way, Ha, ha, this-a-way, All day long.'' For young children it may be easier for them to tap the sides of their hips rather than clapping two hands together. Substitute skipping, sliding, etc., for walking. Instruments can also be used to accompany this song. For example:

''Hear us go tapping, tapping, tapping.'' (Use sticks)

''Hear us go shaking, shaking, shaking.'' (Use bells, etc.)

*Movement Concept: Exploration of many different types of rhythmic movement*

## KEY IDEAS

1. Around three years of age, children are beginning to take a real interest in music activities.
2. At this age, children are almost continually in motion. Often this motion can be channeled into productive ways of using music.
3. Children frequently chant and sing about what they are doing. This kind of play with words and music should be encouraged.
4. Teachers and parents can begin to help children understand that there is structure to music.

## SUMMARY

When music is presented within a cognitive framework that is appropriate for young children, meaning and understanding take place. Concepts are not taught in a highly structured manner but are gradually learned over a period of time. Since children of this age are almost continually in motion, they should be given opportunities to act out stories, play singing games, and use movement in meaningful ways.

## QUESTIONS TO CONSIDER

1. Select four humorous songs appropriate for threes and fours. Develop activities for each that provide conceptual awareness.
2. Using three everyday experiences common to this age level, adapt to a familiar melody, and present to a child.
3. Develop a lesson plan for presentation using three songs from the chapter. Include activities, materials, and questions you wish to raise.

## REFERENCES AND SUGGESTED READINGS

Choate, Robert A.; Berg, Richard C.; Kjelson, Lee; Peterson, Georgiana; and Troth, Eugene W. *Music for early childhood*. New York: American Book Company, 1980.

Haines, B. Joan E., and Gerber, Linda L. *Leading young children to music*. 3rd ed. Columbus, Ohio: Merrill, 1988.

Pugmire, Mary Carolyn Weller. *Experiences in music for young children*. Albany, N.Y.: Delmar, 1977.

Ramsey, Marjorie E. *It's music!* Washington, D.C.: Association for Childhood Education International, 1984.

Rinehart, Carroll A. ''The state of the art. Music: A basic for the 80's.'' *Childhood Education*, January 1980, 26(3), pp. 140–145.

Weissman, Jackie. *Hello sound*. Overland Park, Kansas, 1979.

# CHAPTER FIVE

# Music for the Fours and Fives

## BUILDING A MEANINGFUL MUSIC CURRICULUM

Since the publication of the third edition of *Music: A Way of Life for the Young Child,* today's socioeconomic conditions have encouraged even more mothers to work outside the home while their children are still young. Increasing numbers of children are being enrolled in daycare centers, nursery schools, kindergartens, corporation child-care centers, and latch-key programs throughout the country. Time spent in these programs is extending the children's day away from home. Because so many four- and five-year-old children are spending much of their day in these group settings, there is a great need to plan and develop optimal learning environments and programs for them.

Music activities have traditionally been a part of the preschool and kindergarten programs. Friedrich Froebel, "father of the kindergarten," believed in the value of musical experiences for young children and used his book, *Mother Play and Nursery Songs,* to bring this point to the attention of those who worked with children of this age. He believed that the children should be given ample opportunity to sing songs and play singing games. This thought has prevailed, and now it is considered important to make music an integral part of a child's day, as is eating or sleeping.

McDonald (1979, pp. 1–2) reminds us that young children are probably our most persistent music makers. "They create more music, explore more conscientiously, use music more consistently and spontaneously, and are more strongly motivated toward music than any other age group."

Keeping these facts in mind, capitalizing on them, and realizing that the early years are critical ones in forming favorable attitudes toward music, we suggest you review the Statement of Beliefs at the beginning of this book. We feel strongly that a music curriculum built on these beliefs can provide a solid base for establishing and carrying out the goals of a well-developed, sequential music program.

By the time children are four or five, they are ready for more planned experiences. These activities should include a balance of events, such as listening and appreciation, singing, playing instruments and sound making, creating songs and melodies, and moving about extensively. Before discussing each of these aspects, we offer descriptions of typical four- and five-year-olds.

## SELECTED CHARACTERISTICS OF FOUR-YEAR-OLDS

1. Are very active and can run up and down steps
2. Enjoy activities that require good balance, such as carrying liquids without spilling them
3. Have the ability to throw a ball overhand
4. Like to do things their own way and resist too many directions
5. Are very curious and ask many questions concerning "Why?" and "How?"
6. Talk a great deal (They like nonsense words, silly language, rhymes, and words that are repeated in poems or songs.)
7. Love to listen to stories, often will listen to two or more stories at one sitting, and have favorite stories
8. Are becoming more creative and imaginative (Sometimes they tell "tall" stories.)
9. Are beginning to understand seasons of the year—when they occur and what takes place during each season

10. Think birthdays are very important—both theirs and others
11. Are socializing more easily and ready for more group experiences
12. Can tell the street on which they live and the name of their city (Some will know their telephone numbers.)
13. On command can place a ball or rhythm instrument on, under, in front of, and in back of a chair or other object
14. Like to dramatize songs and poems, as well as stories and parts of stories
15. Should be able to carry out two simple directions in sequence

Consider the following when planning musical activities for the four-year-olds:

1. Are beginning to enjoy group singing more often
2. Show increased desire to listen to music
3. Take pride in ability to identify familiar songs
4. Some enjoy taking a turn singing alone
5. Show increased voice control and a closer approximation of pitch and rhythm
6. Some can sing an entire song with accuracy
7. Are beginning to create songs during play
8. Can talk about what a piece of music suggests
9. Like to try out instruments and accompany songs on instrumental pieces

10. Can improvise simple melodies
11. Can identify certain sounds made by different instruments

## SELECTED CHARACTERISTICS OF FIVE-YEAR-OLDS

1. Generally are conforming in nature, like to please, thrive on positive feedback, and are sensitive to praise and blame
2. Are becoming much more sociable persons
3. Like to jump and climb, still need plenty of big muscle activity (Muscle coordination is improving.)
4. Are described as "wigglers" and "bundles of endless energy"
5. Sometimes can skip on alternate feet and do quite well at galloping
6. Attempt to roller-skate, jump rope, walk on stilts, "pump" on a swing, and bounce a ball
7. Like to talk a great deal and are interested in words and their meanings (By this time most of the words that adults use are a part of the child's vocabulary.)
8. Very interested in calendars (can generally tell what day of the week it is, can name the days of the week in their proper order, are interested in holidays)
9. Know how old they are and can generally tell how old they will be in another year
10. Are very interested in all kinds of clocks but most cannot tell time
11. Like to remain close to home surroundings; are primarily interested in their home and community, not distant places; are interested in different cities and states if they know someone who lives there, such as grandparents or previous playmates
12. Understand and can carry out actions of such words as *forward* and *backward*
13. Are learning the meaning of *small, smaller,* and *smallest*
14. Are often very adept at rhyming words and performing simple mathematical computations
15. Are relatively independent and self-reliant, dependable and obedient, and protective toward younger playmates and siblings (Fowler, undated, p. 1)

Consider the following when planning musical activities for the five-year-olds:

1. Children, at this age, are refining and exploring musical skills previously learned
2. Some will be able to read words to songs
3. Can generally play instruments with accuracy
4. Girls, in particular, begin to show an interest in piano and dance lessons
5. Most five-year-olds have the ability to better synchronize movements of the body with the rhythm of the music

## LISTENING TO MUSIC

Listening (aural perception) is embodied in every phase of every activity that contributes to musical understanding and growth. It is considered to be the foundation for all musical experiences. McCall (1971, p. 7) says, "The child must learn to attend before he can assimilate and use music to his own purposes." In the preceding sections of this book, we have urged parents and teachers to help young children become more sensitive to the sounds around them and to help them translate these sounds into meaningful experiences. These efforts should be continued, since sound discrimination is vital to the musical development of the child. Unless someone has really made a point of helping a child to sharpen listening skills, the myriad sounds that must be confronted will often cause poor listening habits to be already established prior to school.

There is considerable agreement among educators and psychologists that one of the major problems of children in the elementary school is lack of good listening skills. Chosky (1981, p. 15) states, "Learning to listen is one of the most sadly neglected skills in the schools." Educators are beginning to provide suggestions for upgrading the whole area of "listening and attending."

Music activities provide an excellent means for increasing children's listening skills. "A child must listen very carefully to learn a tune or rhythm, and many children will listen more intently to a song or record than to a story or other language experience. Music activities encourage children to listen much more carefully to the sounds they hear and to form concepts about these sounds" (Moomaw, p. 2).

A very important principle to keep in mind is that children cannot develop a high level of listening skill unless attentive listening is stressed. Listening is perceiving and requires thought and reasoning. Children's minds must be "filled" with musical images in order to build on what is new and unfamiliar to them musically. This takes time and can only be developed gradually through children's active participation in diverse and varied musical experiences.

### Conditions That Promote Good Listening

1. A happy, friendly atmosphere should exist.
2. Children should be made physically comfortable. Rooms that have acoustical tile ceiling and have "soft" areas such as carpet, pillows, and drapes tend to absorb sound and make for easier and more comfortable listening.
3. Articles that might distract the children should be put away.
4. Good listening activities require much variety. They require different comprehension levels and different interests.
5. Children need to see a reason for listening (that is, they should understand what to listen for, etc.).
6. Teachers need to serve as models. It is well recognized that the example the teacher sets is by far the single most important and influential factor in conditioning children to sensitive and discriminating listening. If the teacher shows enjoyment of music and actively participates, the children will generally feel the stimulation and will respond heartily and creatively.
7. Plan listening activities according to the maturity levels, abilities, and interests of children. Gradually plan activities that encourage children to "reach" for the next level of understanding.

8. Provide an atmosphere for children to think creatively. For example, pose such questions as "What instrument would you choose to show the sound of a ticking clock?"
9. Keep the experience short enough so that discipline problems will not intrude.

"Improved listening skills facilitate finer auditory discriminations, such as hearing subtle likenesses and differences of sounds, instruments and tonal qualities" (Davis, 1980, p. 78). Since listening is involved in all the musical skills, much attention must be given to activities that can be provided by parents and teachers to improve the children's ability to listen. Thinking and reasoning should be enhanced.

### Suggested Activities

1. Adults as well as children should continue to try to cultivate awareness of sounds.
2. At times, feature listening as an activity or game, both indoors and out-of-doors.
3. Field trips offer endless ways for children to hear sounds firsthand. For example, if a train whistle blows, have the children try to match the sound with their voices.
4. Let children experiment with sounds made from their bodies by snapping their fingers, brushing with their feet, and so forth. (A detailed description of body percussion is given under the section on instruments.)
5. Make a tape of the many different kinds of environmental sounds, both those of nature and those which are man-made. Let children identify these sounds. Discuss their various tone qualities. As children gain more experience, they can begin to classify and categorize the sounds.
6. Take two containers of the same size and place different materials inside, such as rice, beans, corn, or small stones. The object is to have the children shake the containers and "match" the two that sound alike.
7. Read stories to the children about sounds. Many stories invite participation in which the children can produce the sound asked for in the story by either using their voices, parts of their bodies, or instruments that can lend the desired sound effects.
8. Arrange the children so the one speaking may be heard but not seen. Let the other children guess whose voice is being heard.
9. While playing different tones on the piano or tuned bells, play a game of having the children try to match the tones with their voices. The tones being played should not go below middle C or an octave above middle C.
10. Take a set of step bells and show the children that when the bell at the bottom of the steps is played, it produces a low sound. When the bell at the top is played, it produces a high sound. When playing the step bells, place the instrument in front of the children (to avoid confusion, we recommend that the lowest step bell should be at the children's left) so they can see and hear that when a low step bell is struck, it produces a low sound, and when a high step bell is struck, it produces a high sound. After the children have had many opportunities to hear the

differences between high and low sounds in this fashion, the instrument can then be removed from sight. Then see if the children are still able to tell which tones are high or low without seeing someone play the instrument.

11. While the children watch, strike three objects that produce different sounds. Have them close their eyes; strike one of the objects and have the children identify the one struck. At first, the sounds should be very different from each other. For example, a bell, a glass, and a wooden block can be used.

12. Have the children try to identify which of two, three, or four containers an object is shaken in. Containers can be cardboard, plastic, tin, or aluminum. Demonstrate the sounds each container makes before asking the children to turn their backs and give the response.

13. Ring bell. Children raise their hands when they hear the sound and lower them when the sound stops.

14. Have the children stand close together in a group. Demonstrate the difference between near and far sounds by producing identical sounds near the children, then from a far corner of the room, first with eyes open, then with eyes closed.

15. While the children close their eyes, produce sounds from various parts of the room. Children point in the direction of the sound.

16. Ring two bells. One has the clapper taped to a side. Which is ringing? Change hands. Hold one bell high, one low. Name direction of sound, up or down.

17. One child with eyes closed pretends to be a mother cat. Three children pretend to be her kittens. As the mother cat sleeps, the kittens run away and hide in different parts of the room. The children who play kittens should not move after they hide. The mother cat wakes up and calls the kittens. They meow; she finds them from the directions of their sounds.

## Listening Games

### Drummer

The adult or child taps on a drum a certain number of times as the children listen. A child is chosen to clap back the same number of taps. If his response is correct, he becomes the next drummer. Simple, uncomplicated beats should be used at first.

*Variation.* The adult claps hands in a given pattern. The child claps back the pattern. At first, allow the children to see the person clapping. After the game is well established, do not allow the children to see the person leading the clapping. (Clapping can be done inside an enclosure.) Instead of clapping, vary the game by tapping with the foot.

### Into the Puddle

A large circle is drawn on the floor. (Some classrooms have large circle designs molded into the floor covering.) The children find their own spaces around it. If possible, have the children space themselves an arm's length from each other so they will not bump each other as they jump into the puddle. When the teacher says, "Jump into the puddle," the children respond together. When the teacher says, "Jump out of the puddle," they return to their original places on the circle. (Children may take turns being the teacher.)

*Variation.* The teacher may tap on a drum or use a chord on the piano as the command is given.

### What Do I Hear?

A child sits on a chair in the center of a circle. Children are seated on the circle's outer rim. The child sitting on the chair holds his hands over his eyes while another youngster walks, skips, or jumps around the chair. The boy or girl doing the movement then sits down. The child on the chair must get up and repeat the same movement the other child

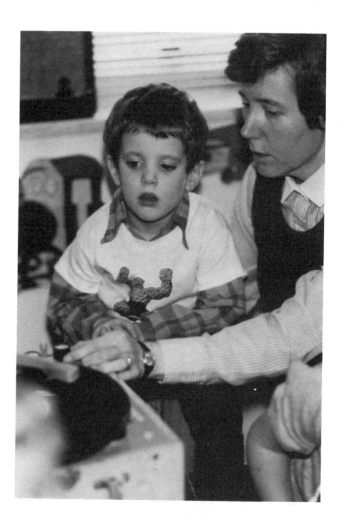

made. He then invites another boy or girl from the group to take his place.

### Name the Instrument

After children have had plenty of opportunity to see and hear different instruments, make tapes or use recordings that highlight the sounds of particular ones. Have children guess which instrument is being played.

### Tick, Tock, Where Is the Metronome?

A child is chosen to be "it" and sent outside the room. A ticking metronome is hidden somewhere in the room. "It" tries to locate the metronome. When she does, ask her to repeat the ticking the same way she hears it. This may be done by saying "tick, tock" in the same rhythm of the metronome, or by clapping, tapping on the floor, etc. Vary the ticking speed.

## Extended Listening Activities

An excellent example of an individually developed program of listening activities by Sally Roman, kindergarten teacher, can be found in Appendix D. Sally developed her listening activities program because she believed so strongly about the importance of building good listening skills. She felt her listening program was too loosely structured; therefore, she did a study of successive levels of listening and then designed a listening program, which reportedly has been most successful.

## DEVELOPING APPRECIATION OF MUSIC

### Listening to Live Performance

One of the best ways to encourage children to listen to music is to invite a guest to visit the classroom and sing or play an instrument. Children are apt to be better listeners if, at first, they can listen to a live performance. Performers could be fifth or sixth graders, junior high or high school students, parents, or other adults from the community. Seeing the instrument, while it is being played, will help children associate it with its sound. Young adult performers usually relate well to the children and often inspire them to want to play instruments when they become old enough. It is wise to discuss with the guests beforehand what aspect of the instrument would be of interest to the children. In some communities, operettas and musicals appropriate for young children are produced for their enjoyment. These help immensely to build up good listening skills while providing much enjoyment for the children.

Once children have seen a live performance, they are usually more interested in hearing music being played or sung by record. By the time children are four or five they are more ready to sit attentively for a short performance or to listen to a short recording.

## Program Music for Listening

Program music includes stories in music such as *Peter and the Wolf* by Sergei Prokofiev. This music is good for introducing and reviewing some of the instruments of the orchestra. According to Lament (1976, p. 67), program music can also be "picture music, or a composition that describes an image, conveys an idea, or creates a mood." An example of this type of music would be the *Nutcracker Suite* by Peter Tchaikovsky. Other examples would be the *Grand Canyon Suite* by Ferde Grofé and Camille Saint-Saëns's "Danse Macabre." Entire pieces or suites need not be listened to at one time. One section of a piece may be enough depending on the age, interest, and musical appreciation of the child.

## Using Background Music for Listening

Using so-called background music in the classroom to establish a mood, for example, at rest time, is sometimes controversial; however, many teachers feel that the particular expressive quality of a musical selection can create a desirable atmosphere for rest. Quiet orchestral music, lullabies, or a selection such as Saint-Saëns's "The Swan" are often chosen to be played during rest period. "Sea Gulls" by Hap Palmer has become a favorite recording to be used for quiet relaxation. The entire selection is designed to provide soothing instrumental music as a background for resting.

Sometimes children like to listen to a favorite story at this time. Recordings of poetry, nursery rhymes, and folk music are also favorites with many children. Music from other cultures is also a good choice during rest time; as the world becomes smaller due to increased international travel, trade, and cultural exchange, teachers are encouraged to use the beautiful music of other countries. Background music that contains loud tones and fast tempos is too stimulating and should be avoided at rest time. During free play time, the background music can influence the noise level of the room. Music with words or music that is loud can cause a room to be noisy and uncomfortable.

## Other Music Suggested for Appreciation

There are many good musical story records on the market today. Parents and teachers sometimes think that young children can relate to and enjoy only this type of record, but this is not necessarily true. Children who are introduced to classical music at a young age often enjoy it as much as the story type. Many children love to listen to the "Prayer" from the opera *Hansel and Gretel* (particularly after they have seen it) by Englebert Humperdinck and to parts of the *Mikado* by Gilbert and Sullivan. When our daughter Chris was four years old, her godmother gave her a recording of the *Mikado*. She learned to love the "Willow-tit-Willow" song and asked for it to be played often. After hearing parts of Beethoven's Fifth Symphony repeated, my grandson could match the music with the composer each time.

Other sources for appreciation should include selections such as Herbert's "March of the Toys," *The Grand Canyon Suite* by Grofé, selections from musicals by Rodgers and Hammerstein, music from Walt Disney, Sesame Street, and folk music of America and other countries. Young children thoroughly enjoy listening and moving to marches such as "The Stars and Stripes Forever" and others of John Philip Sousa. In addition, do not forget the value of introducing the children to such well-known national dances as Percy Grainger's delightful English Morris dances and dances from countries like Israel, Hungary, and the Far East.

Children like to listen to a composition and then make up a story about the music. Perhaps a favorite activity of young children is hearing stories set to music, such as "The Three Billy Goats Gruff" or "The Gingerbread Boy," and afterwards dramatizing them. This type of activity seems to create a real interest in music during the early years.

Since children's tastes are so diverse, it is best to have a wide variety of vocal and instrumental selections from which children can make their own choices. For an additional listing see "Listening and Appreciation" in Appendix C.

## SINGING

Singing brings much joy to children. We know that most young children love to sing and to be sung to. If one listens carefully as children go about their work and play, one will find them singing bits and pieces of created words that fit the rhythm of their movements. One might hear them chanting, "Swing, swing, swing, swing, watch me go up and down." Recently a group of five-year-olds was observed coloring with purple crayons. Suddenly one child, as she rhythmically made dots on her paper with her crayon, started to sing over and over, "Purple-durple, purple-durple, purple-purple-durple." Soon the entire group joined in the singing, picking up the little girl's rhythm and dotting their papers as she did. They had just heard the story of *Harold and the Purple Crayon*. At times, adults can sing back the chants and songs children improvise. Occasionally, these ought to be written down so children can see how songs are created and written.

As an adult sits down to play the piano or another instrument, watch the reactions of children. Usually their faces will light up as they gather around the instrument to ask for their favorite songs. At ages four and five, some of the little

voices will not be able to carry a tune. Therefore, one must be careful not to place too much emphasis on singing in tune and building musical skills at this age. Singing should not be taught formally at this time.

We believe that an enthusiastic teacher singing in the classroom provides children with a more rewarding experience than even the best singer on a recording or film. Teachers, whether or not they are naturally talented in singing, should sing with their children.

### Research and the Singing Voice

Research is beginning to help us to better understand the child's singing voice and to choose songs that will help develop it in a natural way. In general, three- and four-year-olds prefer singing in the range of middle C to A (a sixth above). Drexler found that children ages three to six could sing descending pitch intervals more easily than ascending ones (Shelley, 1976, p. 208). We have included several songs in our collection that are based on the descending scale in order to accommodate this finding.

In reference to music, it is not unusual for children to misunderstand the terms *high* and *low*. Shelley (p. 208) points out that three-year-olds will confuse high and low with big and little. Given a choice, children generally prefer a lower starting pitch and sing more easily. Children usually prefer to use a higher range when singing spontaneously but prefer a lower range for singing songs (Shelley, p. 209).

Gould, investigating the singing problems of elementary children, concluded "that kinesthetic aspects of the discovery of the singing voice by the child and his developing skill in using and controlling this new found voice are essential to improvement in singing" (Shelley, p. 211). The study established two basic principles: "The child must learn to hear his own voice in speaking and singing and to control the high and low pitches, and he must be able to sing in unison with either another voice or instrument and to learn the sound and feeling as his voice matches the pitches he hears" (Shelley, p. 211). *These two principles are extremely important and should be kept in mind when planning musical experiences for young children.*

### Suggested Singing Experiences Based on Research

Based on a review of the research pertaining to vocal development, the following list of suggestions should help adults as they plan singing experiences for young children.

1. Provide plenty of opportunity for spontaneous vocalizing throughout the day.
2. Encourage children to improvise and sing about their everyday activities at home or at school. (One kindergarten teacher we know encourages her children to sing about what they do at home in the evenings and on weekends. Some of these children sing their stories

much easier than they can say them. Many get caught up in relating these events and will chant and sing delightful musical stories.) *Suggestion:* Permit the child to hold a paper or book in his hand as if he were reading his musical story from a book.

3. Tape children's voices. Play them back. It is essential to tape individual voices so that children can hear their own. A word of caution here: Use tape recorders that reproduce voices accurately. Poor reproduction of a child's voice can distort the quality and will be inaccurate. Do not tape children's voices if they seem afraid of the experience. This could result in children withdrawing from singing. In most instances, youngsters thoroughly enjoy this activity.

4. Provide many opportunities for children to make sounds using different pitches (e.g., the sound of a mewing kitten, a barking dog, a mooing cow, a siren). These opportunities are essential in helping children to learn to control their voices.

5. Choose as many songs as possible that are written between middle C and the A above. Children should be exposed to many songs that are easy for them if their singing voices are to be encouraged. Limited-range songs should be used extensively. Scalewise songs (particularly descending ones) are good if they are not sung too rapidly. This helps develop feeling for tonality.

6. Use songs that have a limited number of pitch leaps—ones that do not wander all over the keyboard. Good examples would be such songs as "Deedle, Deedle, Dumpling" and "Twinkle, Twinkle, Little Star."

7. Vary the beginning pitch levels of songs. All too often adults find a comfortable starting pitch to fit their own voices and never change it for children. We believe that this "sameness" could be a contributing factor in children having limited singing ranges as they grow older.

8. Continue to select songs that will broaden the singing range of the children. This should be done on a very gradual basis. Many adults fail to carry through this important aspect of helping youngsters develop their singing voices.

9. On occasion, recite or say poems, nursery rhymes, or songs. Encourage children to use different voice inflections to "match" the meaning and sound. The song "If You're Happy and You Know It" has unlimited possibilities. Have the children say the words using inflection in their voices, for example, "If you're happy and you know it, toot your horn, toot, toot!" or "If you're happy and you know it, hum out loud," etc. This approach helps children find yet another way to learn to control both their speaking and singing voices.

10. Songs that make use of repeated words, musical phrases, or repeated rhythmic patterns are good choices. Some examples of these would be "Do You Know the Muffin Man?" and "Picking Up Paw Paws."

11. Encourage children to play the resonator bells or an accurate, well-tuned xylophone. Help them learn to play short phrases so they can make up words to accompany the melody or vice versa.

12. When possible, indicate melody direction (low to high, high to low) or pitch intervals by using hand signals or body movements. Have you ever considered encouraging children to sing a scalewise song as they go up or down a stairway?

Those working with young children should find the following scalewise songs helpful. Scalewise songs (singing up and down the scale) help children move their voices freely in a systematic progression.

### The Snowman

Begin at bottom of scale on middle C and sing upward.

| | |
|---|---|
| A chubby little | C |
| snowman | D |
| Had a carrot | E |
| nose. A- | F |
| long came a | G |
| bunny, And | A |
| What do you sup- | B |
| pose? | C |

Sing down the scale starting with C above middle C.

| | |
|---|---|
| That hungry little | C |
| bunny, | B |
| Looking for his | A |
| lunch, | G |
| Ate that little | F |
| snowman's nose, | E |
| Nibble, nibble, | D |
| crunch. | C |

Now start up the scale again. Begin on middle C.

Nibble (C), Nibble (D), Nibble (E), Nibble (F), Nibble (G), Nibble (A), Nibble (B), *Crunch!!!* (C)

PEARL H. WATTS
*(Source unknown)*

### Taking a Bath

Begin at top of the scale and sing downward. Begin with C above middle C.

| | |
|---|---|
| Every night I | C |
| take a bath, I | B |
| scrub and rub and | A |
| rub. | G |

| Every night I | F |
|---|---|
| take a bath, I | E |
| splash around the | D |
| tub. | C |

Repeat as above.

| Every night I | C |
|---|---|
| take a bath, | B |
| Face, nose, and | A |
| ears, | G |
| Arms and hands and | F |
| legs and feet, E- | E |
| nough to last for | D |
| years!!! | C |

M. RAMSEY

### Five Little Monkeys

Substitute "puppies," "elephants," etc., for "monkeys." Begin at the top of the scale and sing downward.

| Five little | C |
|---|---|
| monkeys | B |
| Jumping on a | A |
| bed, | G |
| One fell | F |
| off and | E |
| bumped his | D |
| head. | C |

Repeat the scale.

| Mamma called the | C |
|---|---|
| doctor, the | B |
| doctor | A |
| said, | G |
| "No more | F |
| monkeys | E |
| jumping on the | D |
| bed." | C |

Repeat using "four little monkeys," etc.

### Clap Your Hands

Start at top of scale and move downward.

| Clap, clap, | C |
|---|---|
| clap your hands, | B |
| Move them in the | A |
| breeze, | G |
| Stamp your feet, then | F |
| turn around, | E |
| Sit down, if you | D |
| please. | C |

### Autumn Leaves

Start at top of scale and move downward. Begin with C above middle C.

| Trees are bending | C |
|---|---|
| with the wind, | B |
| Leaves are falling | A |
| down, | G |
| Twirling, twirling, | F |
| swirling, swirling, | E |
| Soon they're on the | D |
| ground. | C |

K. BAYLESS

Repeat the same scale starting with C above middle C.

| I rake the leaves in- | C |
|---|---|
| to a pile, And | B |
| make it very | A |
| high, | G |
| Then I jump with | F |
| all my might, And | E |
| wheeee! I'm out of | D |
| sight. | C |

### I Know a Little Pussy

Begin at top of the scale and sing downward. Begin with C above middle C.

| I know a little pussy. Her | C |
|---|---|
| coat is silvery gray. She | B |
| lives down in the meadow, Not | A |
| very far away. She'll | G |
| always be a pussy. She'll | F |
| never be a cat. For | E |
| she's a pussy willow, Now | D |
| what do you think of that? | C |

*(Traditional)*

Now start up the scale again. Begin on middle C.

Meow (C), Meow (D), Meow (E), Meow (F), Meow (G), Meow (A), Meow (B), SCAT!!! (C)

### Whisky, Frisky

Start at the bottom of the scale and move upward. Begin with middle C.

| 1. Whisky, | C |
|---|---|
| frisky, | D |
| Hippity | E |
| hop; | F |
| Up he | G |
| goes | A |
| To the tree | B |
| top. | C |

Repeat C and go down the scale.

| 2. | Whirly, | C |
|---|---|---|
| | twirly, | B |
| | Round and | A |
| | round, | G |
| | Down he | F |
| | scampers, | E |
| | To the | D |
| | ground. | C |

Begin with middle C and go up.

| 3. | Where's his | C |
|---|---|---|
| | supper? | D |
| | In the | E |
| | shell, | F |
| | Snappity, | G |
| | crackity, | A |
| | Out it | B |
| | fell! | C |

Repeat C and go down the scale.

| 4. | Furly, | C |
|---|---|---|
| | curly, | B |
| | What a | A |

| tail! | G |
|---|---|
| Tall as a | F |
| feather, | E |
| Broad | D |
| as a | |
| sail! | C |

*(Source unknown)*

## Pumpkin, Pumpkin

Begin at top of the scale and sing downward.

| Pumpkin, | C |
|---|---|
| Pumpkin, | B |
| orange and | A |
| fat, | G |
| Turn into a | F |
| Jack-o-lantern | E |
| just like | D |
| that! | C |

*(Source Unknown)*

# I WIGGLE

LOUISE B. SCOTT

Arranged by K. BAYLESS

In singing the above song one might want to sing, "Now wiggle your fingers," etc.

# PITTER, PATTER

Very staccato

Words and music by K. BAYLESS

Pit - ter, pat - ter, pit - ter, pat - ter, rain comes fall - ing down.

Pit - ter, pat - ter, pit - ter, pat - ter, soon it's on the ground.

## Choosing Songs

It is extremely important to select song material that is appropriate for a child of a specific age level. All too often, adults do not take age into consideration when they write or choose songs for children. Careful thought should be given to the study of what children are like, what they can do, and what their interests are at certain stages of development. This should be done before writing, selecting, or presenting songs for them.

In choosing song materials, as indicated before, one should consider more than appropriate pitch range. Difficult pitch leaps and the speed at which intervals are sung can contribute to singing problems.

Choose songs where the subject matter and words are closely related to the child's understanding and interests. Four- and five-year-old children particularly enjoy action songs and singing games, contemporary and television-related songs, and songs about:

- the space age
- nature and seasons
- their own names
- birthdays and special days like Christmas, Hanukkah, and Halloween
- fun and nonsense

- school activities
- flags and patriotic days
- their families and friends
- their bodies, parts of their bodies, and clothing
- feelings, such as happiness
- animals and pets
- mechanical things

Keep in mind:

1. Short songs will probably bring more success; however, do not rule out longer ones like "Over in the Meadow" and "Puff the Magic Dragon." You will be surprised by how much children like songs of this type. They will soon learn all the verses.

2. Look for songs that contain no more than two phrases if each phrase contains melodic and word-pattern repeats.

3. Songs written using the pentatonic scale are excellent for young children. A pentatonic scale is one with five tones to an octave. An example would be the five black keys of a piano octave.

4. Question-and-answer songs such as "What Are You Wearing?" are favorites with children. Songs of this type also help develop critical thinking.

5. Folk songs are considered one of the best sources of song material for young children.

6. Patriotic songs, Christmas carols, and seasonal songs such as ''Over the River and Through the Woods'' are beloved by young and old. It is desirable for younger children to sing with older boys and girls and adults, for it provides them with an opportunity to gain the satisfaction of being a part of the larger social circle.

## Presenting New Songs

New songs can be introduced at spontaneous times when the situation seems just right or at a planned group time. They may be introduced to a small group of children who are informally gathered together or to the entire class. It is important to keep the situation as natural as possible.

Almost all children are eager to learn new songs as well as to sing their favorite ones. Children like to repeat their favorites, but interest will begin to wane if songs are overworked. Variety is necessary, and the teacher should take into consideration that the same song will not appeal to the entire group. To keep interest at a high level, teachers need to have a number of songs at their fingertips that they know well. Hildebrand (1981, p. 343) says that since it takes several hearings before children will be able to sing a song, they should be supplied with a number of songs in various stages of learning.

Whenever possible, one should memorize the words and melody of a song to use the nonverbal cues and eye contact that are so necessary when sharing a song with children. If the teacher's voice is accurate and of good quality, it is best to introduce the song without any accompaniment. It is easier for children to match their tones with the human voice than it is for them to match the melody played on an instrument. To support a teacher's voice that is somewhat shaky, or for the sake of variety, another instrument such as the piano, guitar, or Autoharp® can be used.

Some songs will need a short introduction; others will not. Sheehy (1968, p. 65) reminds us that ''songs are made to be sung, not to be talked about. . . .'' The teacher might introduce the song by showing a picture or a diorama (a three-dimensional scene showing objects and figures representative of a particular song or situation), asking a leading question, sharing a related incident, or giving some helpful background information. When presenting songs, this introduction is extremely important and must not be overlooked. Such motivation promotes interest and helps the children to understand the ''message'' of the song.

## Reluctant Singers

Do not be disturbed if all the children do not join in the singing. Once in a while you will find a child who will not sing with the others. He may sing freely at home or when he is alone but not in the school setting. His reluctance to participate may be because he is totally absorbed in watching the other children sing or because he simply is not ready to join in. These cases are rather uncommon, since most children like to sing whether or not they can carry a tune accurately. Many children of this age are still trying to find their singing voices. In dealing with the reluctant singer, encourage but do not force the child to participate. Give him time to respond. The length of time will vary depending on each child's personality and previous experiences.

Most authorities agree that children should be given an extensive range of singing experiences so they can learn how to control their singing voices. What children learn by listening to songs can have little lasting effect until it is shared by the joint singing and rhythmic interpretation of the group. In addition, emphasis should be placed on those music activities and experiences that will encourage the shy child and the ''off-key'' singer to join in the singing without fear and self-consciousness. Children can best improve the quality of their singing voices only after they have had many opportunities for singing in social groups that give meaning to their efforts. We must not forget that good attitudes about singing are as important as good singing voices.

Since children are highly motivated by action songs, we often find that those who are reticent to participate in singing will many times become involved in songs that call for action by the hands, feet, or other parts of the body. As children become involved in the physical sense, the words of the song seem to emanate and become part of the activity. Soon these children begin to take part.

Props for a song can also lend much interest. For example, in the song ''Three Blue Pigeons,'' three pigeons made of construction paper or similar material and mounted on lightweight sticks for holding and carrying while acting out the song can be the motivating factor in getting children involved. Children enjoy holding the pigeon and acting out the song, and there is also a great sense of security that goes along with having something in one's hands.

## Teaching a New Song

Knowing how to present a song effectively to young children can influence whether or not the children will like the song. Remember to sing the song slowly (not *too* slowly) and distinctly, keeping in mind the rhythmic flow.

> The teacher should not expect a response on the first day or the second. It takes time for a young child to understand and remember the words and longer still to gain a clear conception of a melody. . . . Encourage him to sing, even if he isn't singing your tune. Vocal chords need exercise, and he needs vocal expression. Drill on either words or music is harmful for preschool children. Sing the song, straight through, and let him catch what he can, even if it is only the last note. Pitch will come on the wave of rhythm (Pitcher et al., 1974, p. 47).

Smile as you sing. Rotate your head so you make facial contact with every child. Do not make the mistake of asking the children if they like the song. They may say ''No.'' When they like a song, children will generally say ''Let's sing it again!''

Sing the song through several times on the same day or on successive days. If interest is high, it will not be long before the children will begin to sing right along. This method, called the whole method, is to be encouraged. This provides children the opportunity for ''chiming in'' with a word or phrase that is easy for them to grasp and remember. Some phrases become cumulative, and soon the entire song is learned in a relatively short time. Songs that get children involved quickly and naturally we call songs that invite participation. Examples are ''Mister Rabbit'' and ''Old MacDonald Had a Farm.''

Teaching a song line by line is not good practice. This method, if used repeatedly, can destroy the entire effect of a song and cause children to dread learning a new song. This statement does not mean that a teacher should never sing a line of a song or a certain word of a song and have the children repeat it. This practice is, indeed, sometimes necessary so that children learn the pronunciation of a word correctly or fit the words and melody together as they should be. The problem arises when teachers use the ''line-to-line'' method in teaching every new song.

As new songs are repeated on successive days, it will not be long before you know if the children like the song. If, after a careful introduction, they do not seem to respond to a particular song, do not use it again for a period of time. Because there is so much good song material, do not feel upset if children do not seem to care for a particular song. One important point to keep in mind is that once in a while, when children have learned a song well, the teacher should sing along very softly or not at all so the children can hear themselves singing and strengthen their ability to carry the melody all by themselves.

It is not unusual for children of this age to have some difficulty reproducing the pitch or melody of a song. The use of echo, or answer songs, as mentioned earlier, is extremely important to continue. Scalewise songs that are not sung too rapidly are also helpful, since they contain words that stay on one sustained pitch for a period of time before moving on to the next pitch. We have included several scalewise songs in this book. In no way should a child ever be made to feel self-conscious because he cannot sing in tune! We still find students at the college level who were victims of some insensitive adults who made them so self-conscious of their singing voices that they gave up early in life and refused ever to try singing again.

It was indicated earlier that one could choose as many songs as possible that are written between middle C and the A above. As children grow older, songs having a somewhat wider range in pitches may be used (for example, middle C to D—the ninth tone above middle C). Songs that have frequent, wide pitch-leaps are not good choices. Keeping songs in a comfortable singing range such as in the keys of C, D, and F will make singing more enjoyable for both teachers and children. Songs accompanied by a guitar have recently been found to be sometimes pitched too low for children to sing; some notes are as low as G and F below middle C. Continued singing in this low range is not good for children's voices.

Singing together can be a pleasant, happy experience for teachers and children. Above all else, one should keep in mind that the joy of singing should hold the highest priority.

## INSTRUMENTS

Children are fascinated by devices and instruments that produce sound. Around one year of age, a child's attention is quickly drawn to the movement and sound of a cuckoo clock. If one tries to divert the child's attention, almost invariably the youngster will return to watch the swinging of the pendulum and to hear the sounds of the cuckoo bird.

Children are such natural inventors! As they move through the infant stage, one of their favorite activities is taking a wooden spoon and striking it against a cooking utensil or on a cup or cereal dish. We often hear parents say that their children prefer pots, pans, and spoons to commercial sound-making toys.

Have you ever watched older children jump mud puddles, landing on both feet? Have you watched them pound nails in rhythm or stomp their feet to band music? This is movement and body percussion combined. This is the ''stuff'' of which good rhythmic experiences are built.

### Body Percussion

Children delight in using different parts of their bodies to produce sounds (body percussion). They soon discover, as they shuffle their feet back and forth in rhythm, that this kind of movement makes a very interesting sound. Experimentation of this kind often helps them express how a train starts up and slows down. Encourage children to experiment in making other sounds with their bodies, such as snapping their fingers, thumping on their chests, and making sounds with their mouths such as hisses and clicks. Ask them to make the softest body percussion sound they can make; the loudest; the highest; the lowest; the heaviest. As children explore sound making through body percussion, question them as to how different things might sound. For instance, what sound would a very hot tea kettle make? A spacecraft taking off? Jet airplanes flying by? Rhythmic patterns will then become a part of the sound making. Children need time and guidance to help them explore and learn to control body percussion. It is important that instrumental patterns be reinforced in body percussion first and then extended to sound-making objects such as instruments.

## Percussion Through Sound-making Devices

Percussion, using objects, logically follows experimentation with body percussion. At this point, adults and children can begin to bring together all sorts of interesting sound-making devices. Children, guided by the teacher, can begin to sort out and classify these devices according to the kinds of sounds they produce. Collecting and experimenting with sound-making things is a very important step in introducing instruments to children. (A section on commercial and homemade musical instruments can be found in Appendix G.)

## Introducing Instruments

> Although the young child, even as a toddler, loves to play instruments for the sensorial satisfaction he derives, he is probably about four years old before he has sufficient control and perception to use them in a consciously creative way. When he does reach this level of physical and intellectual maturity, he can use many of the traditional classroom instruments to create rhythmic and dynamic accompaniments for his singing and moving. Tuned or melody instruments in pentatonic scales allow him to improvise melodies without discord and to play in consonance with others long before he acquires the skills of music reading (Haines and Gerber, 1980, p. 10).

When children are old enough to respect instruments and care for them, they should have the opportunity of using them. Both commercial and homemade instruments can be

introduced. Children enjoy making some of these instruments. Adults can make others for use with children. Whole families and classes can become involved in making some of the instruments and will enjoy sharing the sound making together. When children go through the process of making instruments, they have a much better understanding of how the sound is produced, and problem solving and creative thinking are enhanced. It is extremely important to remember that the better the tone quality of the instrument, the more satisfying and more valuable the experience can be for the child. Instruments of genuine tone quality such as resonator bells, wood and tone blocks, and xylophones are good instruments to use for sound exploration and discrimination.

It is good practice to introduce one type of instrument at a time. As the instrument is introduced, it should be explained and then passed around for children to handle and explore (Nye, 1983, p. 102). Some teachers prefer to introduce an instrument on one day and then reintroduce the same instrument on the next day before the children are permitted to explore and play it. It is important for the children to hear and see the instrument played enough times so they can distinguish its sound and know its name and how to play it. Once this is accomplished, then another type of instrument can be introduced, until children have had the opportunity to hear and explore many different types of instruments. This process takes time, and children need to be patient, but the results are rewarding. It is also wise at this point to establish a few rules for handling the instruments to prevent some of the problems that usually occur if expectations are not set. Keep the rules simple.

Once children have explored different types of instruments they can begin to use them creatively in different ways.

> The teacher should establish situations in which the child can select the instrument he believes to be the most appropriate for certain music or to accompany certain songs, poems, and stories. The formalities of the rhythm band of past years, with its required conformity, have resulted in its virtual absence from the modern school. This dictatorial type of instrumental performance is in opposition to sound theories of learning and to the creative approach wherein children are involved in exploring, questioning, designing, and performing music (Nye, 1983, p. 102).

There are many good songs and selections in which the instruments can be used for sound effects or for accompaniment. Examples would be using a wood block for the ticking of the clock or using a triangle or gong to strike the hour of one in the song "Hickory, Dickory, Dock." In the story of "Chicken Little," an instrument such as the tone block could be struck when Chicken Little thinks the sky is falling on her head. Another very effective sound is using a divided coconut shell to produce the sound of horses' hoofs.

The many nursery rhymes, folk songs, and singing games should be an integral part of every program for four- and five-year-old children. Most of these songs and rhymes have definite rhythmic qualities that motivate body percussion. Soon children will begin to see that some of the sound-making articles they collected will also fit a particular part of the music. They begin to evaluate, to listen, and to make choices and decisions about what sound or combinations of sounds go well together. This then becomes their music making, not that of the adult. If instruments are introduced in this way, children will better understand what each instrument's tone is like and how it can be played and used. Basic elements of orchestrating begin in this way. Soon children will be using instruments to accompany their songs and movements. "A great deal of musical value can come from the use of these instruments in exploring sound, discovering interesting tone qualities, and revealing concepts such as loud-soft (dynamics), high-low (pitch) and rhythm (duration)" (Nye, 1983, p. 102).

As children and adults explore sound making together, there is continued need for experimentation and problem solving. For example, children can be guided to discover that if a triangle is held tightly by the hand and then struck, it will produce a dull, "dead" sound. Children are fascinated when the front of an upright piano is removed and they are allowed to see and hear what happens when the hammers strike the different strings. They can see and hear that the high sounds on the piano correspond to the short strings and that the low, heavy sounds correspond to the long strings. Instruments like the Autoharp® and guitar are also excellent for helping children become familiar with musical concepts.

It is helpful if adults can play the piano to accompany children as they use instruments, but it is not a requisite. There are good records available for home and classroom use. Some parts of recorded classical music and folk rhythms are excellent sources to use with instruments. Some of these records introduce and explain the instruments; others tell children exactly what instruments to use and where to play them. Others encourage creativity on the part of adults and children. (A list of suggested materials to use with rhythm and melody instruments is included in Appendix C.)

There comes a time when the entire class plays instruments together. It is hoped, by this time, the instruments will have all been introduced, one at a time, to the children so they will know the sound each instrument makes and how that sound is produced. The total group experience should be the result of many individual and small group explorations. At first, if there is a sufficient number of the same instrument such as the sticks, a group of children might play the sticks together. Another group is added until the entire class is playing sticks. Select a rather short, regular beat, musical selection for a melodic and rhythmic background to accompany the sticks. Such a selection might be "Hi Ho" from the musical "Snow White" or a Sousa march. Remind the children as the instrument is passed out to them to hold it quietly in their hands or lay it on the floor in front of them. Establish rules for when to start playing the instrument, when to stop, and any other rules that will make the playing experience a happy and enjoyable one for both adults and children. As time goes on, children can help classify instruments that go well together and learn how they can be used with certain musical phrases or parts of a musical selection.

The choosing or giving out of instruments often affects children's feelings about the instruments. If given a choice, children seldom choose the rhythm sticks. This is probably because there are usually more sticks available than any other instrument. Cymbals are a favorite since there is but one pair per set. They are best used singly with padded mallets. As a general rule, the children may be given the choice of the instrument to play. This usually works well. To make sure the less aggressive child has an opportunity to experiment with the most popular instruments, the teacher, on occasion, should pass out the instruments. To satisfy the natural curiosity of children, it is a good idea to have them exchange instruments with each other so they can experience the sounds and feel of the different instruments. At times, the teacher should help children make choices. Teach children to care for their instruments in the same way the adult instruments are cared for. This would include establishing a method of placing the instruments in a box or on a shelf after using them (not thrown, tossed, or piled in helter-skelter fashion). With proper guidance, children can

quickly learn how to use and care for rhythm and melody instruments.

## ESTABLISHING A LISTENING-MUSIC CENTER

A listening-music center for children is a definite asset to any classroom, if it is carefully prepared and regulated. Certain rules must be set up and expectations carefully explained to the children.

A good center (a place set aside in the classroom for listening-music activities) could include a piano, record player, tape recorder and player, other chosen melody and rhythm instruments such as a xylophone (Orff-type), drums, resonator bells, wood block, Autoharp®, and listening equipment such as headsets. When budgets permit, a double series of Montessori bells would be an excellent addition to the center. The bells are used in training the ear to perceive differences between musical sounds. There are two sets of bells that look alike but produce successive tones of a chromatic scale. In using the bells, the task is for children to match the pair of bells that produce the same, exact pitch. One set of bells in chromatic scale order remains stationary. The child strikes the first bell, which is "Do" of the stationary series, and then finds its match from the second mixed-bell set. When the correct bell is found, it is then placed beside its match. Each note of the scale is found in this manner. After much experimentation, children are then encouraged to place the bells in correct order of the scale guided only by the sound. This reinforcement aids children greatly in helping them to sing the syllables of the scale, "Do, Re, Mi," etc. (McDonald, 1983, pp. 58–62).

Some of the instruments and listening activities within the center should be changed periodically for new interest and new challenges. Many teachers have found that the most profitable time to use the listening-music center is during children's work and playtime activity periods.

### Inviting Resource Visitors

Having musicians demonstrate instruments to children for the purpose of sound discrimination was introduced in the listening section of the book. As children's interest in instruments grows, these experiences should be continued and encouraged. In this way, children can learn firsthand what each instrument is like, how it is played, and how it sounds. The musician might encourage the children to touch the instrument and, in some cases, play it. This needs to be done under careful supervision. In instances in which the instrument's sound is produced by using the mouth, it is sound hygienic practice not to allow the children to blow into the instrument. Boys and girls will be pleased if familiar melodies and songs they know are played by the musi-

cian. If songs are familiar, children will generally chime in with singing. It is also a good idea to have the visitor play a selection that is particularly well suited to the instrument being introduced.

### Other Firsthand and Vicarious Experiences with Instruments

Many teachers make a field trip of taking their classes to the music room or the football field to provide children with the firsthand experience of seeing and hearing the band as it plays and marches across the field. We would like to encourage parents to do the same. Children also enjoy outdoor band concert programs. Every year the Cleveland Symphony Orchestra gives performances at the nearby Blossom Amphitheater. Some of the concerts are family-oriented. Parents often bring their children to these concerts. It is not uncommon to see some of the little ones rolling down the hill in time to the music or marching across the grass as the orchestra plays a stirring march on the Fourth of July. Symphony orchestras often provide children's concerts and programs for area schoolchildren in various parts of the country.

Children's TV programs have been helpful in introducing instruments in interesting ways. Appendix C lists numerous recordings on the market in which selected passages highlight a particular instrument.

## MOVEMENT

*Dancing**

A hop, a skip, and off you go!
Happy heart and merry toe,
Up-and-down and in-and-out,
This way, that way, round about!
Bend like grasses in the breeze,
Wave your arms like wind-blown trees,
Dark like swallows, glide like fish,
Dance like anything you wish . . .

ELEANOR FARJEON

### Movement for the Fours and Fives

Mimi Chenfeld (1976, p. 261) reminds us that "movement is as natural to learning as breathing is to living. We have to be taught not to move as we grow up in our inhibited, uptight society." Movement is synonymous with the growing child. Today, more than ever, we realize the great amount of learning that takes place through psychomotor activities. As indicated in earlier chapters, the young child should be free to explore and experiment with his own movements in response to stimuli. It is important that he experience these natural body movements before he is ever asked to respond to those initiated by adults.

With careful guidance, movement exploration gives children an opportunity to become aware of their own abilities and what their bodies can do. Through these experiences they often lose their self-consciousness and inhibitions. Many times, movement exploration leads to creative movements and dance. This process helps children discover new ways of using their bodies. As children's muscle coordination improves, they can begin to coordinate the rhythmic movements of their body with stimuli such as the beat of a drum, a rhythmic poem, a song, and the like.

We strongly believe that as children learn to control their body movements, they build feelings of satisfaction, self-worth, and confidence, which will grow and carry over into mastery of other areas. Undoubtedly the child will become less fearful of trying out other activities. Have you ever seen the look on a child's face who has just found the "right combination" for skipping or who has just walked across the balance beam for the first time without falling off? Success in mastery of movements such as these helps the child grow psychologically as well as physically. Prime purposes of movement programs are to help young children become more aware of what their bodies can do and to help them develop the balance and coordination needed to control all parts of their bodies. Children should have no fear of failure with experiences in movement exploration. Teachers should be constantly aware of this point as they provide guidance in this area.

Movement activities for the four- and five-year-old child vary greatly from one program to another. Ten to 15 minutes a day of marching and skipping to music or playing rhythm band instruments is not uncommon. We feel that children should have ample opportunity to move freely before they are required to respond to the steady beats of music played on a record, tape, or instrument such as the piano.

### Imaginative Teachers

Young children move and respond so naturally with an imaginative and sensitive teacher. Teachers who are willing to experiment can develop a vital, creative rhythmic program for their children. A good movement program is developed by a teacher paying close attention to children as they move—as they skip down the hall, run with the wind,

pound with their hammers, twirl around in circles, or stamp their feet in puddles. *There is no set way to begin.* One way to start would be to group children informally on the rug or gym floor. Have the children lie flat on their backs or stomachs. Can they wiggle their bodies without moving from their spaces? Can they wiggle their bodies away from their spaces? Can they move parts of their bodies that no one else can see? Can they move two, perhaps three parts of their bodies at the same time? Can they puff up their stomachs like a cake that is rising in the oven? Keeping in mind that most children are very inventive, adults can encourage them to do all kinds of "tricks" with their bodies. It is not surprising that a child can roll up into a tiny ball, make himself so rigid that no part of his body wobbles or bends, push the clouds high into the sky, or crawl into a very, very tiny box. If they are motivated by a creative teacher, it won't be long before children's ideas begin to flow. Many times the whole group will pick up another child's idea and extend it. Trying out the movements of other children often encourages the more reticent youngster to try out movements of his own. Teachers can help by speaking words of encouragement. For example, if the children are discovering different ways to move across the floor, the teacher might say, "Look, Tommy is moving sideways. Let's all try to move the same way as Tommy." After the children have tried Tommy's way, the teacher might say, "Who would like to show us another way to move across the room?" Once the children have begun to share their ideas freely, the teacher can play a very important part by expanding on the ideas that children begin. Following is an example.

On a Monday following a weekend holiday, a kindergarten boy eagerly told his teacher and classmates about a trip he had just taken with his family through Pennsylvania. He told them that at times his father suddenly had to turn on the headlights of his car because it became so dark his father could not see to drive. After considerable discussion as to what that dark place was called, a child sang out, "That dark place is called a tunnel." More children then chimed in and said, "Yes, that's what you call it, a tunnel!" The children then asked their teacher if they could darken the room and pretend that they were going through a long, dark tunnel like the ones in Pennsylvania. The teacher then asked, "What shall we use for a tunnel?" Some of the children suggested lining up a long line of tables and then crawling underneath them. Tables were quickly put together. Each child was his own automobile. Children crawled through the tunnel in orderly fashion. They had captured the mood of moving through a darkened space. More discussion followed. They began to tell what it was like to try to do things in dark places. One boy told about his father developing pictures in his darkroom. The children became so interested and asked so many questions about how a picture was developed that it was decided to enlist the

aid of the industrial arts teacher, since he had built a darkroom at the school. With the help of their teacher, the children took their own pictures and developed them. We could cite many other examples in which a creative movement idea developed into a series of expanded learning experiences.

The imaginative teacher uses word pictures extensively to help create a feeling or mood to stimulate children's thinking. For instance, when the time seems right, the teacher can begin to focus on the natural movements of a child and say, "Let's walk as if a strong north wind were pushing on our backs" or "Let's imagine we are walking through a squishy mud puddle with our boots on." If it seems appropriate, add a few simple chords on the piano or a few drum taps, making a "match" to the children's tempo. Follow the children's lead.

### Moving the Way the Music Makes You Feel

All too often children are asked to listen to a selection on a record and then are told, "Now, boys and girls, move the way the music makes you feel." Unless some feeling for the music has been built into the experience, results are often chaotic and unproductive. In like manner, children are sometimes asked to move like a particular animal such as a bear. Whether using a musical background or not, a feeling about bears should be built up before children begin to respond rhythmically. Ethelouise Carpenter, an early childhood teacher, has said, "A child cannot be what he has not experienced in some way." Naturally, concrete experiences are best for children. Sometimes the experience may need to be a vicarious one. This may come through descriptions, discussions, pictures, and video. For example, the teacher might ask the children, "How large are bears? What kind of feet do they have? How do they move through the woods? Do they move fast or slow? Can they climb trees?" Children need to really think before they respond. These kinds of descriptive discussions help children build up a feeling for what they are asked to become.

### Children Creating Their Own Movements

Children should be encouraged to create their own movements. At first these movements could be very simple ones like showing how the leaves come falling down from trees, how cats creep when they see a mouse, or how a snowman melts. Some of the very first dances are imitations and pantomimes of nature. Examples of these might be: how leaves swirl in the wind, snowflakes fall from the sky, stars twinkle, and flowers grow out of the ground. As children learn by exploration how to move their bodies, they also increase their vocabulary of skills that help them express their moods, ideas, and feelings.

## Fundamentals of Movement

Movements can be divided into three categories: locomotor movements, axial movements (nonlocomotor), and a combination of movements. Locomotor movements are those movements that propel the body through space. They are classified as walking, hopping, jumping, running, and leaping. Movements such as galloping, sliding, and skipping are variations or combinations of the locomotor movements. Axial movements are the nonlocomotor movements originating from a stationary position of the body such as bending or twisting.

In her book *Creative Movement for the Developing Child* (1971), Claire Cherry lists many different types of movements that young children enjoy and experience. With the introduction of each movement such as crawling, Cherry presents a thorough description of the movement and then gives suggestions and varied activities to help develop each skill. She feels that music motivates children to respond rhythmically and suggests using familiar melodies, such as "Twinkle, Twinkle, Little Star" and "Little Brown Jug,"

substituting appropriate words for the original in order to help describe particular movements. Preschool and kindergarten teachers would do well to develop movement activities similar to Cherry's to meet the special needs of their own children.

There are many excellent recordings (some with illustrated storybooks) that provide children with plenty of ideas for creative movement.

Many companies are producing individual story and movement records of excellent quality. Hap Palmer's and Raffi's records and tapes have become all-time favorites of thousands of America's young children. Their captivating melodies and rhythms seem to make up the kind of music children thrive on. They are caught up in the spirit of the words and rhythms. Steve Millang and Greg Scelsa (Younghart Records) have produced several volumes of *We All Live Together.* Many of their selections are excellent for movement and motor development. "Miss Jackie" Weissman has published many songs and rhythms (books and recordings). Some of her songs are included in this edition and are very adaptable for movement exploration. "Miss Jackie's" descriptions on how to teach the material are very useful and carefully written.

## Establishing the Beat

Once children have had plenty of opportunity for free movement and can move about without bumping into others, more locomotor and body movements such as walking, running, and jumping can be used. The teacher can strike up a steady beat on a drum, a tambourine, or on a piano to accompany the children's movements. As children gain more experience, the teacher can ask for response to the steady beat being played. The ability to maintain a steady beat comes easily to some children but not to others.

Research in young children's motor development and moving to music shows that the ability to maintain a steady beat by tapping is developmental according to age and does not seem to change much after age nine. Tempo is a contributing factor to accurate motor response; children, particularly those of nursery school age, are more successful in synchronizing their movement with fast speed than with slower ones (Crews, 1975, p. 61).

According to McDonald and Ramsey (1978, pp. 29–30):

One of the first spontaneous rhythmic activities among children is producing a beat (Shuter, 1968). These regular, unaccented pulsations are quite fast in tempo ($\quarternote = 120$ to $\quarternote = 176$) (Scheihing, 1952; Simons, 1964) and little attempt is made to synchronize them with those of other children. When accents appear, they are often irregular and experimental in nature. At three years of age, the ability to synchronize beat with music for a controlled duration of time begins to develop (Christianson, 1938); at age four, interest in dramatizing ideas in music appears; at age five, most children are able to march, clap, and otherwise keep time with music at relatively fast tempi (Jersild and Bienstock, 1935).

Cherry feels that after children have attained skill in walking, running, jumping, and leaping, they are ready to have more complicated experiences such as galloping and skipping. "Galloping is fairly easy for a young child to perform since it is a unilateral activity, using only one side of the body. It combines the movements of walking and leaping, and the child is quick to grasp its natural possibilities" (Cherry, 1971, p. 43). Around 3½ to 4 years of age, children begin to enjoy galloping. They are also attracted to horses at this age and often like to pretend that they are horses. For motivation, show pictures of horses, take a field trip to a farm, show a film, etc. Children will be quick to respond to discussions about their own experiences of seeing horses. Have the children gallop at different tempos: some fast, some slow. Accompany the galloping with coconut shell clappers. They make an authentic galloping sound that will please the children. You will need to use lots of "word pictures" to stimulate children as they try out new and different movements.

Skipping is much more difficult to do than galloping because it is a bilateral movement. It combines the movements of walking and hopping. The song "Hop Se Hi" on p. 92 is a good song to sing when children are attempting to learn how to skip. The words to the song can be chanted slowly as the children try out their skipping. This song has helped many children get the "feel" of how to skip. We often find that the music used for skipping (once the movement is learned) is too slow, thus causing some children to have difficulty coordinating their skipping movements with the tempo of the music. Observe the children skipping. Then adjust the music's tempo to their movements. Over the years we have found that the "Rustic Dance," written by G. R. Howell,* is one of the best selections to use with skipping. Having a piano and an accompanist for movement experiences is ideal, but certainly not necessary for successful experiences.

When children discover that they can make their bodies skip, it often becomes one of their favorite movements. "Once learned, skipping is frequently used to express a feeling of happiness and well-being" (Cherry, 1971, p. 44).

Folk songs and singing games also provide opportunities for children to move. These are particularly good for young children, since most of the songs are within their singing range. Ruth Seeger's *American Folk Songs for Children* is perhaps the best known collection of folk songs in America.

* Carl Fischer, Inc., 56 Cooper Square, New York, N.Y. 10003.

Because of their nature, most of the songs invite participation and improvisation. Three-fourths of the tunes in her collection "are accustomed to action, to being danced to, clapped to, worked to. Children listening often start clapping of their own accord, or skipping, or jumping, or kicking their feet, or trying some new motion" (Seeger, 1948, p. 24).

## Using Recordings and Props

There are many fine recordings on the market that invite movement participation. (Examples of these can be found in Appendix C.) These do not need to be records made especially for children. Some of the works of our finest composers, such as Grieg, Pierné, Saint-Saëns, Mendelssohn, Bartok, Debussy, and Stravinsky are excellent for stimulating free movement. More contemporary selections like "Raindrops Keep Falling on My Head" and "The Syncopated Clock" are also good choices for encouraging children to move their bodies freely. Tapes have also been used with good results. Teachers can put one piece of music (repeated several times) on each tape. Using this method, the desired piece of music is always at the start of the tape and can be used as long as needed. The teacher can stop or

extend the music as desired. This technique saves time and helps with classroom control.

At times, props such as scarves, long feathers, fans, strips of crepe paper fastened onto cardboard tubes, balloons, lightweight, flowing skirts, and rhythm instruments such as maracas enhance movement. Props can aid in making children less inhibited. The opportunity to hold something in their hands often gives them balance and lends variety. Keep in mind, however, that overuse of props can become very distracting and may overshadow the purpose of the activity.

As children continue to move and to sharpen their listening skills, they can begin listening for special parts in the music. As music is played, adults need to help children listen for changes of tempo, mood, and dynamics. Here again, word pictures by adults working with the children help them to interpret the many combinations of musical sounds.

### Enhancing Movement

Keep the following points in mind when planning movement activities:

1. Children need ample space for movement activities (enough for children to skip freely). Large spaces may present problems in controlling the group and may cause difficulties in hearing.
2. If a large room such as a multipurpose room or auditorium is used, prepare children in their classroom ahead of time, telling them where they are to go and what they are expected to do once they enter the room.
3. Establish boundary lines. Teachers may need to devise and make up their own.
4. Have children remove heavy clothing. Some schools require children to wear gym shoes. Authorities often advocate bare feet for certain activities. (Be aware of slippery floors.)
5. Establish signals of starting and stopping, for instance: the voice, a whistle, or a drum.
6. Have children find their own spaces. This can be done by having them spread out their arms so they do not touch their neighbors.
7. Avoid demonstrating movements.
8. Adults guiding movement activities should have access to a good-quality drum. Children generally respond well to changes in movement when signals are tapped out on a drum. Sometimes "drum language" commands attention more readily than the human voice.
9. Accept children's movements and interpretations to music.
10. Praise the timid child to encourage experimentation and freedom of movement.
11. Do not force the child to participate.
12. Make a thorough study of resources such as records, tapes, songs, poems, pictures, and films to enhance movement. Provide variety.
13. Above all, be enthusiastic and demonstrate a real interest in the activity.

### Help Children Keep Moving

Growing children need to keep moving. This is very much a part of the learning process, which continues throughout a lifetime. Keep in mind that movements expressed by children are often accompanied by their innermost feelings and ideas. Wise adults will do everything within their power to find a way in which these innermost feelings and ideas can be expressed.

The following songs have been selected as examples of songs that invite participation. Many of these songs motivate children to use different locomotor and nonlocomotor movements. Additional songs and singing games involving movement and rhythm can be found in other chapters of the book.

**FAVORITE SONGS AND RHYTHMS**

## FOLLOW, FOLLOW

GLADYS ANDREWS
Adapted by K. BAYLESS

GLADYS ANDREWS

2
This is what I can do,
See if you can do it, too.
This is what I can do,
Now I'll pass it on to you.

From Andrews, Gladys. *Creative Rhythmic Movement for Children,* ©1954, pp. 48–49. Adapted by permission of Prentice-Hall, Inc., Englewood Cliffs, N.J.

This song is one of the favorite songs of the four- and five-year-olds. A child is chosen to think of an action while the class sings the first verse. The action might be nodding the head. The child then leads the entire class ''nodding heads'' as verse two is sung. Another child is then chosen to think of the next action. The song should be sung to the tempo of the child's movements.

***Rhythmic Concepts:*** *Creative rhythmic movements*

# WHAT SHALL WE DO WHEN WE ALL GO OUT?

Traditional

What shall we do when we all go

out? All go out? All go

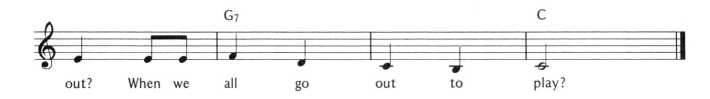

out? What shall we do when we all go

out? When we all go out to play?

---

After singing the first verse, children decide what they will do when they go out to play: "We will swing on the monkey bars," etc. Children do the actions as they sing each new verse.

(This is an excellent song for helping children understand the difference between a question and an answer.)

***Rhythmic Concepts:*** *Creative movements*

***Language Concepts:*** *Children create their own verses*

# CLAP YOUR HANDS

American folk song

Clap, clap, clap your hands, Clap your hands to - geth - er,

Clap, clap, clap your hands, Clap your hands to - geth - er.

---

This is a short, rhythmic song that is sure to invite participation from the children. It is a good perceptual-motor activity. The song has a steady beat that is easy to follow, and it also helps develop body image. The teacher begins by clapping hands and singing the song. Have children join the clapping as they listen to the song. Then ask the children to join the singing. Clap softly the first time. Increase the volume of the clapping next time (clap loudly). Suggestions for other verses might be:

2. Swing your arms
3. Blink your eyes
4. Stamp your feet
5. Wave your hands
6. Pat your knees
7. Nod your head

Have children create their own verses. Try using other movements such as: "Run, run, run to school" (home, to the park, etc.) or "Gallop, gallop, gallop in the ring."

**Dynamic Concepts:** *Loud and soft*

**Rhythmic Concepts:** *Strong, steady beats; creative body movements*

# HOP SE HI

Words and music by K. BAYLESS

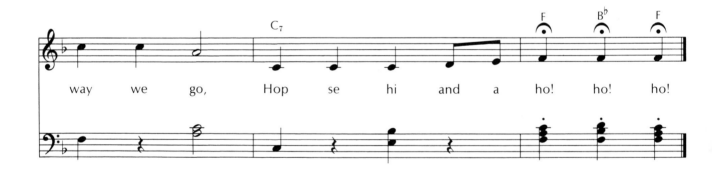

Since writing the first edition of our book, we have discovered that the song "Hop Se Hi" is an excellent one for helping children learn to skip. Start with the right foot on the words "hop se." Transfer the weight to the left foot and sing the words "hi and." Continue shifting the weight from one foot to the other. Do this slowly as the song is sung or chanted.

# SKIP SO MERRILY

Adapted and arranged
by K. BAYLESS

Children stand in a circle while one child skips around the inside. On the words "choose a partner quick as a wink," the skipping child chooses a partner and the two children skip around inside the circle. At the end of the song, the two skipping children return to their original places in the outer circle. Another child is chosen and the song is repeated. (Skipping children do not sing, as it is too difficult to skip and sing at the same time.)

*Movement Concept: Skipping*

# STAMPING LAND

Folk song from Denmark
English words by LOUISE KESSLER

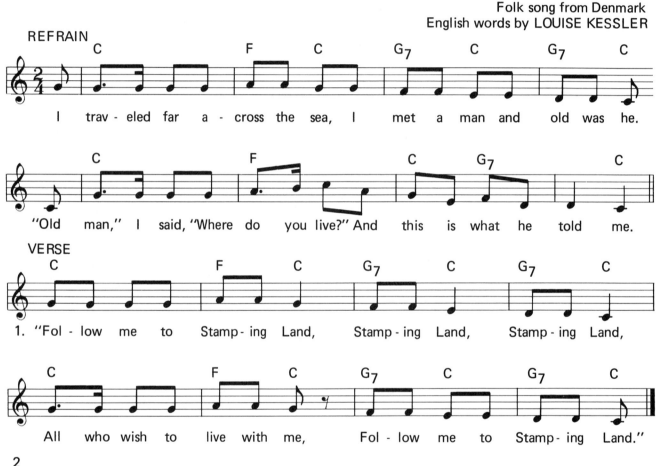

2
Follow me to Clapping Land...
3
Follow me to Tiptoe Land...

From WORLD OF MUSIC ©1988 Silver, Burdett & Ginn Inc. Used by permission.

*Rhythmic Concepts: Stamping to the beat*
*Tapping to the beat*
*Clapping to the beat*
*Jogging to the beat*

## KEY IDEAS

1. Listening is considered the foundation of all music experiences.
2. Listening is perceiving and requires thought and reasoning.
3. Regardless of natural talent, teachers should sing with children.
4. Research is beginning to help us to better understand the child's singing voice and to choose songs that help develop it in a natural way.
5. In choosing songs for children, select those in which the subject matter and words are closely related to the child's understanding and interests.
6. Knowing how to present a song effectively to the children can influence whether or not they will like the song.
7. Percussion, using objects, logically follows experimentation with body percussion.
8. When children are old enough to respect and care for instruments, they should have the opportunity to use them.
9. It is believed that as children learn to control their body movements, they build feelings of satisfaction, self-worth, and confidence that will grow and carry over into mastery of other areas.

## SUMMARY

By the time children are four or five, they are ready for more planned music experiences. These should include a balance of activities such as listening and appreciation, singing, playing instruments and sound making, creating songs and melodies, and moving about extensively.

A balance of good listening activities is important for growth in music appreciation. Children need to be exposed to, to listen to, and to try out different types of music so that they can begin to develop musical tastes and preferences. If their appreciation for music is to grow, children need to be introduced to music of enduring quality. Naturally, the music selected must be appropriate for their level of experience and understanding.

Singing together can be a pleasant, happy experience for teachers and children. The joy of singing should hold the highest priority.

Children delight in using parts of their bodies to produce sound. If children are given time to explore body percussion, reproducing rhythmic and melodic patterns with instruments should be easier for them to do.

Movement exploration gives children an opportunity to become aware of their own abilities and what their bodies can do. It is important as children are guided in this very important area of learning that they have no fear of failure as they learn to control their bodies in movement exploration.

## QUESTIONS TO CONSIDER

1. As budgetary constraints in school systems create the need to eliminate programs, music instruction is often limited or considered a frill. Develop a position statement on this issue.
2. Every teacher of young children should be a teacher of music. Defend this contention.
3. Isolate yourself in a preselected environment. In a 15-minute time span, record all sounds of which you are aware. Repeat the same activity with a group of two or three children. Compare the results. What conclusions can you draw?
4. Select four favorite songs that could be used to enhance movement. Describe the activities that invite participation.

## REFERENCES AND SUGGESTED READINGS

Anderson, William, and Lawrence, Joy E. *Integrating music into the classroom*. Belmont, Calif: Wadsworth, 1985.

Andress, Barbara. *Music experiences in early childhood*. New York: Holt, Rinehart and Winston, 1980.

Andress, B. L.; Heimann, H. M.; Rinehart, C. A.; and Talbert, E. G. *Music in early childhood*. Washington, D.C.: Music Educators National Conference, 1973.

Andrews, Gladys. *Creative rhythmic movement for children*. New York: Prentice-Hall, 1954.

Aronoff, Frances Webber. *Music and the young child*. New York: Holt, Rinehart & Winston, 1969.

Carpenter, Ethelouise. Personal communication, 1976.

Chenfeld, Mimi Brodsky, "Moving movements for wiggly kids." *Phi Delta Kappan,* November 1976, 58(3), pp. 261–263.

Cherry, Claire. *Creative movement for the developing child*. Rev. ed. Belmont, Calif.: Fearon Publishers, 1971.

————. *Think of something quiet. A guide for achieving serenity in early childhood classrooms*. Belmont, Calif.: Pitman Learning, 1981.

Chosky, Lois. *The Kodály context*. Englewood Cliffs, N.J.: Prentice-Hall, 1981.

Crews, Katherine. "Research in learning and movement." In *Music and perceptual-motor development*. New York: The Center for Applied Research in Education, 1975.

Davis, Hazel Grubbs. "Reading pressures in the kindergarten." *Childhood Education,* November/December 1980, 37(2), pp. 76–79.

Emerson, Peggy, and Leigh, Cindy. "Movement: 'Enchantment' in the life of a child." *Childhood Education,* November/December 1979, 56(2), pp. 85–87.

Evans, David. *Sharing sounds*. New York: Longman Group Ltd., 1978.

Findlay, Elsa. *Rhythm and movement: Applications of Dalcroze eurhythmics*. Evanston, Ill.: Summy-Birchard Company, 1971.

Fowler, Marie. *What to expect of the fours and fives*. Leaflet No. L. Washington, D.C.: Association for Childhood Education International, undated.

Froebel, Friedrich. *Mother play and nursery songs*. Boston: Lee & Shepard, 1878.

Greenberg, Marion. *Your children need music*. Englewood Cliffs, N.J.: Prentice-Hall, 1979.

Haines, B. Joan E., and Gerber, Linda L. *Leading young children to music*. 3rd ed. Columbus, Ohio: Merrill, 1988.

Hildebrand, Verna. *Introduction to early childhood education*. New York: Macmillan, 1981.

Hendrick, Joanne. *Total learning: Development curriculum for the young child*. 2nd ed. Columbus, Ohio: Merrill, 1986.

Jersild, A. T., and Bienstock, S. F. *Development of rhythm in young children*. New York: Columbia University Press, 1935.

Lament, Marylee McMurray. *Music in elementary education*. New York: Macmillan, 1976.

McCall, Adeline. *This is music for today—Kindergarten and nursery school*. Boston: Allyn and Bacon, 1971.

McDonald, Dorothy T. "Montessori's music for young children." *Young Children.* November 1983, 39(1), pp. 58–62.

————. *Music in our lives: The early years*. Washington, D.C.: National Association for the Education of Young Children, 1979.

McDonald, Dorothy T., and Ramsey, Jonny H. "Awakening the artist." *Young Children,* January 1978, 33(3), pp. 29–30.

Moomaw, Sally. *Discovering music in early childhood*. Boston, Mass.: Allyn and Bacon, 1984.

Nye, Robert E., and Peterson, Meg. *Teaching music with the Autoharp*. Rev. ed. Northbrook, Ill.: Music Education Group, 1982.

Nye, Vernice. *Music for young children*. Dubuque, Iowa: William C. Brown, 1983.

Pitcher, E. G.; Lasher, M. B.; Feinburg, S. G.; and Braun, L. A. *Helping young children learn*. 2nd ed. Columbus, Ohio: Merrill, 1974.

Seeger, Ruth. "Why American folk music for our children?" In *American folk songs for children*. New York: Doubleday & Co., 1948.

Sheehy, Emma D. *Children discover music and dance*. New York: Teachers College Press, 1968.

Shelley, Shirley J. "Music." In Carol Seefeldt (Ed.), *Curriculum for the preschool-primary child—A review of the research*. Columbus, Ohio: Merrill, 1976.

Sinclair, Caroline B. *Movement of the young child ages two to six.* Columbus, Ohio: Merrill, 1973.

Smith, Robert B. *Music in the child's education.* New York: The Ronald Press, 1970.

Sullivan, Molly. *Feeling strong, feeling free: Movement exploration for young children.* Washington, D.C.: National Association for the Education of Young Children, 1982.

Weikart, Phyllis S. *Teaching movement and dance.* Ypsilanti, Mich.: The High/Scope Press, 1982.

Zeitlin, Patty. *A song is a rainbow: Music, movement, and rhythm instruments in the nursery school.* Glenview, Ill.: Scott, Foresman, 1982.

Zinar, Ruth. *Music in your classroom.* West Nyack, N.Y.: Parker Publishing Company, 1983.

# III
# Music for Every Child

# CHAPTER SIX

# Music Through the Day

Music is an integral part of our contemporary American life. Think of your days. How often have you listened to music, hummed a favorite melody, or observed children caught up in rhythms of popular programs or playground activities?

We do not need to be reminded of the joy of music or its importance to our mood or well-being. We have discussed the early months and years, as well as the impact of the mother and other adults on musical development. Attitude is all important, as is opportunity. Music learning is inseparable from other learning; it is interwoven into the fabric of the child's day. We delight in singing; we sway, we clap, we tap our toes, we sing along with a companion. We sing in many places, often in the shower or as we drive. No matter what our age, music lightens the spirit.

- Music is basic.
- Music is a part of our being.
- Music is a part of our total education.
- Music is a part of romance.
- Music is a part of diplomacy.
- Music adds to our understanding of the cultures of the world.
- Music is a part of our family traditions.

Think of the many ways music can be added to the day. Young children are interested in:

- other children
- the family
- home and pets
- seasons
- travel
- holidays
- themselves
- food
- shopping

There is music to match each of these interests through humorous songs, personal songs, action songs, singing games, chants, rhymes, and holiday songs. Remember that music has an integrity of its own. Children recognize what is false, what is artificial, what does not "fit." Select only music that enhances enjoyment and appreciation. A child's natural rhythm or perhaps an inner music will be revealed.

Music can be interwoven into the pattern of daily living for children. Let us consider the possibilities for the integration of music using the boundless enthusiasm and spontaneity of children. Encourage imagination, creativity, and the action art of music rather than that of a spectator or performance.

## MUSIC AND LANGUAGE

For most young children, language unfolds naturally as part of the growth process. Maximum development comes only through careful nurturing of language opportunity by adults.

Language development is very important in the child's total development. Singing is an excellent aid in promoting good language patterns. Many songs contain repetitive sounds that can help those with speech problems. Pronunciation of the words helps distinguish initial, medial, and final consonant sounds. The child can more easily understand sentence structure in singing the phrases.

Folk songs, country music, and commercials all appeal to the young child and develop and extend vocabulary. Music activities also develop listening skills, increase the attention span, improve comprehension and memory, and encourage the use of compound words, rhymes, and images.

We know that music offers unique possibilities to expand and extend vocabulary. A rich vocabulary is a necessary skill for the young child as he grows toward adulthood. A rich language may well be our most important achievement. This gift of language must be shared. The child delights in the sharing with receptive adults. However, a word of caution: To extend fully sensory experiences and expand the use of language, the adult cannot afford to be a token listener. The young child quickly senses inattention and disinterest. The adult, too, must be imaginative and sensitive to mood and opportunity. Music is a natural and personal language. Those who work with children know that the languages of words, of music, of the body, and of gestures come naturally to most children.

Awareness is the key to language and music stimulation. Very often singing is better than talking. The adult can make simple tunes:

- ''Mary, put the box away''
- ''Tommy, you can stand up tall''
- ''Billy, let's cooperate''
- ''Mary, Mary, brush your hair''

Children are true and avid imitators. After hearing an instruction once or twice, a simple melody or a line from a book, language exhibits fluency, ease, and color. For many children, words hold a special attraction. When blended with music and movement, the enchantment expands. Remember the lyrics of Mary Poppins, the Chipmunks, the melodies of ''Mr. Rodgers'' and ''Sesame Street''—and, yes, even the commercial jingles immediately identifiable from television.

Music and language are avenues of communication. Through each, children express delight, anger, and resentment. They quickly sense love, rejection, and concern as they listen to a voice. The arts, as an emotional release for young children, are unsurpassed. Fears, discomfort, and anxiety can find outlet in song and rhythm. How much healthier than aggressive acts are the expressive arts of music and language for the young! Children delight in language play and language games and respond intuitively to the fascination of music. Even a fifteen-month-old claps and burbles on hearing the tune released from a tiny musical lamb! Infants, too, are consistent and spontaneous music makers and explorers of sound. Lullabies will produce cooing and gurgling, the precursors of language.

Nadon-Gabrion (1984) feels that language is used in the music experience for the purpose of giving directions, developing awareness and skills in rhythmic fluency, and extending the meaning and experience potential of music.

## WHOLE LANGUAGE

Much discussion today centers about psycholinguist Ken Goodman's ''whole language,'' which places a strong focus on oral language experiences and read-alouds as a means of encouraging children to use their knowledge. Fountas and Hannigan (1989) explicate the concept as one where language is language only when it is whole. Whole language programs are built on the belief that children should learn to read and write in the same natural way they learned to speak. Curriculum-related music, listening, songs, poems, and chants are used as a whole. There is community reading of songs and poems to internalize the rhythm and intonation of language. As we listen, we realize how musical speech is.

Helen Gregory (Children's Librarian, Public Library, Grosse Pointe, Michigan) shares an exciting approach that further develops whole language.

### Sing Me a Story*

We play games, jump rope, dance, relax, exercise, take showers, worship, marry, march, live, die, and are buried to music. Early experiences with simple music prepare children to enjoy more complex and subtle forms later on. Musical training deserves as much time and attention as the development of skills in color identification or animal recognition. Picture songbooks can encourage such exposure.

If we are to consider picture songbooks 'real' picture books, they must meet the following criteria generally considered in evaluating picture books:

1. High-quality illustrations in a style and medium suited to audience, subject, and lyrics. Pictures should relate directly to the song. If the text tells a story, however sketchily, the artwork should add to it. The predominant picture songbook audience is very young and tends toward literal interpretation.
2. An imaginative and well-written text. Although a well-plotted narrative is desired and is common in ballads, when that is not possible, a unifying thread may suffice. But a first-rate picture songbook is not only a 'real' picture: It should also be a first-rate song.
3. The music needn't be printed with the pictures, but it should be available for reference somewhere in the book. It is also helpful to have a simple piano accompaniment with indications of guitar chords. (Beginning guitarists appreciate diagrams as well.) . . .
4. Well-known verses ought to be included, at least in an addendum, unless there are too many to enumerate, in which case a note is in order.
5. If the language is difficult in any way, for example, regional slang, there should be a glossary.
6. If the lyrics have been translated, the original should be shown as well. Not everyone speaks English exclusively. Parents who wish to share the original version of an old song with their children may not remember the precise wording. And language students find songs a helpful supplement to their studies.
7. If there is a game that normally attends a song or if there are many variations of melody or lyric, notes are helpful.

---

*Reproduced with permission from ''Sing me a story,'' *School Library Journal* (September 1979), (R)/A Cahner's Magazine, R. R. Bowker Company.

Folk songs have a history. These notes needn't be intrusive or extensive, but they should be available for readers who want to know more . . .

8. Good pacing is a prime factor. The balance of pictures and text, important in any picture book, is more important in a picture songbook, which should flow uninterruptedly at an even rhythm, allowing readers to sing the text and turn pages at a speed that does justice to the illustrations. It might bore children to have too many lines per page and not enough happening, but it's a catastrophe when they have to stop singing in order to see the pictures. . . .

### *Stories That Sing*
(Recommended list for young children)

*Three Little Kittens* by Paul Goldone
Houghton Mifflin Company, 1986

*The Complete Story of the Three Blind Mice* by Paul Goldone
Ticknow & Fields: A Houghton Mifflin Co., 1987

*London Bridge Is Falling Down* by Peter Spier
E. P. Dutton, 1976

*Six Little Ducks* by Chris Conover
Thomas Y. Crowell Company, 1976

*Pop Goes the Weasel and Yankee Doodle* by Robert Quackenbush
J. B. Lippincott Company, 1976

*Sing a Song of Sixpence* by Tracey Campbell Pearson
E. P. Dutton, 1985

*The Balancing Act—A Counting Song* by Merle Peek
Clarion Books, 1987

*Over in the Meadow* by Paul Goldone
Prentice Hall for Young Readers, 1986

*Hush Little Baby* by Jeanette Winter
Pantheon Books, 1984

*Roll-Over: A Counting Song* by Merle Peek
Houghton Mifflin/Clarion Books, 1981

*Frog Went A-Courtin'* by John Langstaff
Harcourt Brace, 1955

*On Top of Spaghetti* by Tom Glazer
Doubleday & Company, 1963

*I Know an Old Lady Who Swallowed a Fly* by Colin and Jacqui Hawkins
G. P. Putnam's Sons, 1987

*Old MacDonald Had a Farm* by Glen Rounds
Holiday House, 1989

*The Wheels on the Bus* by Maryann Kovalski
Little, Brown and Company, 1987

*If You're Happy and You Know It—Eighteen Story Songs Set to Pictures* by Nicki Weiss
Greenwillow Books, 1987

*Cat Goes Fiddle-i-fee* by Paul Goldone
Clarion Books/Ticknow & Fields: A Houghton Mifflin Company, 1985

*Go Tell Aunt Rhody* illustrated by Aliki
Macmillan Publishing Company, 1986

*Go In and Out the Window* by the Metropolitan Museum of Art
Henry Holt & Co., 1987

*Skip to My Lou* by Robert Quackenbush
J. B. Lippincott, 1975

*Lizard's Song* by George Shannon
Greenwillow Books, 1981

*The Lady With the Alligator Purse* by Nadine Bernard Westcott
Little, Brown and Company, 1988

*Oh, A-Hunting We Will Go* by John Langstaff
Atheneum, 1974

*Peanut Butter and Jelly: A Play Rhyme* by Nadine Bernard Westcott
E. P. Dutton, 1987

*Mama Don't Allow* by Thatcher Hurd
Harper & Row, 1984

*The Thirteen Days of Halloween* by Carol Greene
Children's Press, 1983

*Over the River and Through the Wood* by Lydia Maria Child
Coward, McCann & Geoghegan, Inc., 1974

*The Friendly Beasts* by Tomie de Paolo
G. P. Putnam's Sons, 1981

*The Twelve Days of Christmas* by Jack Kent
*Parents'* Magazine Press, 1973

*We Wish You a Merry Christmas* by Tracey Campbell Pearsons
Dial Books for Young Readers, E. P. Dutton, 1983

Singing and rhyming words can play an important role in the total language program for young children. They give children an opportunity to practice the correct and distinct pronunciation of words, the stress of vowel sounds, and the rhythmic flow of syllables and words. Humorous folk songs in particular, with their nonsense syllables sung repetitiously, provide a group activity in which children use voice freely as they roll the sounds over their tongues.

In this text the songs extend language skill, as well as musical skill and enjoyment.

### MUSIC AND READING SKILLS

From experience we know that as the young child matures, so does language, and the vocabulary expands as reading becomes a natural extension. We also find the paradox of a child who ostensibly cannot read but who can "read" music and respond to familiar words and melodies. We are turning "back to basics" without realizing and acknowledging that music is a true basic, essential to development of the human personality. We know classrooms where music (and art) are frills or a reward dispensed after the real work is completed. We know of school systems in which music is an extra expense, cut from budgetary consideration when funding becomes limited. Those who know the conditions necessary for effective growth and development know that for many children, music can be the bridge between academic learning and teaching, a means of unlocking interest in formal education.

For children struggling with a new language, for those who have limited access to books, and for those for whom television plays parent or babysitter, music captures the attention. Zinar (1974) and others have noted that often a child who does poorly in regular schoolwork learns to read music, and the child who studies music seems to improve in reading and language. Researchers theorize that perhaps it is the multisensory approach—through movement, eyes, ear, and body coordination—coupled with the improvement in self-concept that makes the difference. It is the whole child who learns! Both reading and making music call for concentration, memory, and understanding of abstract concepts, and both are skills children prize and know are highly valued. It is the wise teacher/care giver who capitalizes on opportunities to spark reading.

To begin, we can set nursery rhymes or simple poetry to music, or place them in simple chants or choral verse. We feel that country songs, ballads, pop tunes, and even carefully selected commercials are legitimate when reading enjoyment and skill is the goal. Words are meanings; words open doors; words have power; words are personal; words are humorous; words tell us what we are. Words are ribbons of the future, and words set to music lead us there.

From nursery rhymes and simple poems we might progress to jingles, finger plays, short prose stories, chant stories, jump-rope chants, and even haiku, which might use music as accompaniment. Or we might select a favorite tune of the children and fit original lines to that tune. It is rhythm, fluency, and attention-holding activity we seek to build. Whatever the ability of the child, participation is guaranteed. It is the rare adult who can resist the combinations described, and sharing enjoyment with children brings an added dimension to our participation.

One potato, two potato,
Three potato, four,
Five potato, six potato,
Seven potato, MORE.
(Potatoes are extended fists.
Leader points to fist; on word
"MORE," player withdraws.)

One-ery, two-ery, zickery, seven,
Hallow bone, crack bone, ten or eleven,
Spin, spun, it must be done.
Twiddledum, twaddledum, twenty-one.

ibbity, bibbity, shindo,
My mother was washing the window.
The window got broke,
My mother got soaked,
ibbity, bibbity, shindo.

Fireman, fireman,
Number eight,
Hit his head against the gate.
The gate flew in, the gate flew out;
That's the way he put the fire out.
O-U-T spells out—
And out you go.

Yellow cornbread, red tomato
Ribbon cane, sweet potato
Round melon, ripe persimmon
Little goober-peas.

Jean, Jean,
Dressed in green,
Went downtown
To eat ice cream.
How many dishes did she eat?
One, two, three, four, five.

Or try more contemporary ideas:

### Best of All

Lollipops and gum drops,
Choc'lets, bubble gum.
Lemon drops and licorice,
Oh, yum, yum!

Lollipops and ice cream,
Choc'let cake and pie,
Butterscotch, vanilla,
O, yum, yum!

Choc'let chips and M&Ms,
Gum balls, big and small,
Jello, pudding, sundaes, rolls,
Oh, I love them all!

### Me

Today's my birthday;
I am four;
Growing bigger, too;
Cake and ice cream, gifts, and toys.
How old are you?

Today's my birthday;
I am five;
Growing taller, too;
Cookies, ice cream, cars, and boats.
How old are you?

Today's my birthday;
I am six;
Growing stronger, too;
Ice cream, chocolate, books and school.
How old are you?

All teachers and care givers of young children need a well-stocked shelf of easy books, poetry, choral verse, and jingles. From these, they can choose selections to support vocabulary activities throughout the day. Reading skills are extended by simply learning a new song. Rote memorization, proper inflection, accenting, and syllabication are strengthened. As Lapp and Flood (1983) indicate, for syllabication in particular, children can clap the beat of a song, separating the words into correct syllables, then sing part of the song, leaving out certain syllables, words, or phrases. Remember, though, that records, tapes, jingles, and the like cannot take the place of an adult who enjoys both reading and music and displays this enjoyment to children. Children want to be like the primary adult in their lives. If that adult reads, sings, and is enthusiastic about these activities, the mood and example are contagious.

No one should miss Chukovsky's delightful *From Two to Five*. Find a copy and cherish it. Few other sources can offer a better understanding of the fascination words hold for children.

Cohen and Rudolph (1977), Cowen (1983), Evans (1978), Feeney, Christensen, and Moravcik (1987), Hendrick (1984), Jalongo and Bromley (1984), and Smardo (1984) emphasize the importance of the interrelationship of music, language, and reading in the daily life of the child. The new books with beautifully illustrated songs, complete with musical scores and lyrics, are popular with children.

*Songs for the Little Ones at Home*, published in 1852, emphasizes the alphabet and music:

Come, come, my darling, I must see
How you can say your A, B, C;
Go get your book, and come to me,
And I will hear your E, F, G.

When you have said your A, B, C,
A, B, C, D, E, F, G,
H, I, J, K, L, M, N, O, P,
Q, R, S, T, U, V, W,
X, Y, Z, &—Oh dear me,
I'll try to say my A, B, C.

Sholtys (1989) offers valuable resources for teachers of non-English-speaking children. As further extension of reading and language skills, the song "Jingle Bells" could lead to winter words—winter pictures and winter poems of icicles, evergreens, snowmobiles, and others. A beginning list of sound words coupled with rhythm instruments might produce bang, boom, ring, buzz, rap, zoom, knock, clip-clap, and tick-tock—all of which children would contribute!

To further tickle the tongue and alert the ear, who could forget:

*Pufferbillies*

Down at the station, early in the morning
See the little pufferbillies lined up in a row
See the engine driver pull the little throttle
Chug, chug, Poof, poof! Off we go.

What fun to stretch the imagination of small children!

Marc Brown's *Finger Rhymes* (1980) offers delightful participation both for music and reading. "Grandma's Spectacles," "Whoops, Johnny," and "Clap Your Hands" are part of the treasure.

You will discover that music and reading are mutually supportive and beneficial to the learner. Imagination and creativity establish the bridge between the realms of music and reading.

## MUSIC, SCIENCE, AND NUMBERS

The world is mysterious to young children. Their curiosity is limitless, and the need to know is imperative. Why? is a common question in households with young children. Everything must be done and learned—telling will not suffice. (Review Taylor's excellent *A Child Goes Forth* and *When I Do, I Learn*.)

Music and science go hand in hand. This is a natural combination for children. Stars, comets, space, alien beings, space shuttles, bugs, worms, and reptiles attract children. Use these things to develop an original melody on rhyme.

Sit down with a child some Saturday morning and enter the fantasy land of the Disney channel; listen to the theme songs and jingles. The child learns these easily. Visit the malls, play NINTENDO. Sound and music surround you—and, yes, unfortunately assault the ears. Today, the telephone puts you on "hold" with music, as do the elevators. Is it not appropriate to wonder about the eagerness of the young child and the decline of interest in school as the child grows older? Could music, judiciously selected, counteract this trend?

As we think of music with which to integrate science and numbers into the child's day, the problem becomes one of selection from the wealth of resources available. Songs may be based on:

- animals
- seasons
- colors
- plants
- insects
- the child
- the body
- autumn leaves

- food
- machines
- indoors/outdoors
- senses
- travel
- tools
- growing up
- sounds

We think of rainbows and prisms, "Pop Goes the Weasel," "Curious George," "Caps for Sale," and Rimsky-Korsakov's "Flight of the Bumblebee." We recall the classics *Ask Mr. Bear, Blueberries for Sal, Make Way for Ducklings,* and *Little Bear.* You might locate the Folkways record *Songs of the Philippines* and sing "Pounding Rice." There are the sounds of nature: the music of birds, the wind in the trees, night sounds, and flowing water.

Many of us have known the following songs since childhood:

- "One, Two, Buckle My shoe"
- "Sing a Song of Sixpence"
- "This Old Man"
- "Pop Goes the Weasel"
- "Eensy, Weensy Spider"
- "Charlie Over the Ocean"
- "Back of the Crocodile"

and

Oats, Peas, Beans and Barley grows
Oats, Peas, Beans and Barley grows
Nor you nor I nor anyone knows
How oats, peas, beans and barley grows

Thus the farmer sows his seed,
Stands erect and takes his ease,
He stamps his foot and claps his hands,
And turns around
   to view his lands.

Remember how "E. T., the Extraterrestrial" enchanted us? Keep that curiosity and wonder alive as you work with young children, science, and music.

From the earliest stages, young child and adult count together and thrill to the mastery of numbers. Big, small, up, down, many, some, fat, thin, circle, square, nickel, dime, all follow a natural progression. Children quickly chant:

- "One, Two, Buckle My Shoe"
- "This Little Pig Went to Market"
- "Ten in a Bed"

- "Sing a Song of Sixpence"
- "The King Was in the Counting House"
- "Going to California"

Children grasp a feeling of power and feel a part of the adult world when numbers are understood. Roberts (1984) in *It's Music!* suggests, "The natural rhythmic count of music is utilized to stimulate the understanding of math and to drill in the basic operations of math . . . The correlation of music and math is evident in featured spots on the perennial Saturday morning television cartoons" (p. 33).

The inclusion of number in daily life may surprise you. Children notice signs, billboards, and their messages. Perhaps as adults we block them out—but young children do not! Theirs is a world of number, color, and newness. Look for numbers in your world and transfer them to the world of the child through music.

## MUSIC AND SOCIAL STUDIES

Music and social studies mesh easily. Perhaps in no other area of the curriculum is there such an abundance of songs that can add richness to the day.

The present is more important than the past or the future to the child, although reminiscing about "what you did when you were young" provokes instant interest. Events that touch the life of the child hold the most appeal. Fairs and festivals of many ethnic groups are rich with music. Refer to Chapter 8, which discusses the cultural heritages of children, for suggestions. Talk to older Americans and involve them with young children. The young child will find personal ways of knowing and celebrating through music.

Patriotic music, stirring marches, Christmas and its carols, Halloween, Easter, Valentine's Day, Hanukkah, native Americans, folk dance, and the world of work all speak to the young child and expand horizons through song. Maxim (1980) suggests that as we share the music of many cultures we are also expanding the anthropological understandings of children. Bill Martin's *Sounds of Our Heritage* is a rich resource.

Every area of social studies, history, geography, civics, economics, sociology, and anthropology can be illustrated through music. The geography of our country is revealed through song. Our historic milestones are carried from generation to generation with music as we sing "Yankee Doodle," "America the Beautiful," and "John Brown's Body." World hunger and poverty entered the consciousness of all in 1985 when favorite recording artists sang "We Are the World" and sponsored the "Live Aid" concert. While visiting China, we sang "It's a Small, Small World."

Celebrating popular local or national holidays can provide an introduction to music. Visiting museums, galleries, and private collections of articles of historic interest sparks the curiosity of children. When combined with the music of the day, these visits lend authenticity to and deepen the understanding of the concept of long ago. Each culture in U.S. society has its unique customs and music. For children to share this heritage builds pride and self-esteem. Integrating social studies and music makes sense because a natural affinity exists between the two.

We can sing of where we live.

- "Farmer in the Dell"
- "London Bridge"
- "America"
- "Home on the Range"
- "My Home's in Montana"

We can sing of our country.

- "The Stars and Stripes Forever"
- "There Are Many Flags"
- "Yankee Doodle"
- "This Land is Your Land"
- "Soldier Boy"
- "He's Got the Whole World in His Hands"
- "Down in the Valley"

The Canadian entertainers Sharon, Lois, and Bram offer delightful fare for children in *Elephant Jam* (1980, McGraw-Hill).

Songs help us learn about individuals, our likenesses and differences, our specialness and feelings. Children embrace counting songs, songs about color, musical stories, choral speaking, sea chanties, and action songs. Children enjoy participating in family concerts or inviting those with special musical talent to share the joys of music. Such possibilities exist throughout the day. Whether in art, physical education, science, or on the playground, music communicates. Our enthusiasm, participation, and flexibility will encourage children to enlarge their musical repertoire. The day is infinite, as is the child—we can never encompass all there is to know.

## SONGS

Teachers and parents requested that many of the following songs and rhythms be included in this edition. Some selections were in the first, second, and third editions; many others are new. The songs have been transposed to keys suitable for the singing range of young children and can be used with children of various age ranges.

The songs and rhythms appear in a logical order, starting at the beginning of the school year and following the seasonal changes. Suggestions for their use are included with many. Others can be used for pure enjoyment and musical value.

**FAVORITE SONGS AND RHYTHMS**

# HAPPY SCHOOL SONG

Words by Janet Lee
Used by permission

Tune: Old Mac Donald

Here we are at school to - day, Hap - py as can be!

We're here to work and here to play Hap - py as can

be!     With a "ha - ha" here, and a "ha - ha" there

Here a "ha", there a "ha," ev - 'ry where a "ha" - "ha"!

*(repeat first line)*

suggested verses:

2. with a *clap clap* or *(tap, tap)* here. . .
3. with a *shake shake* here. . .
4. with a *stomp stomp* here. . .
5. with a *hop hop* here. . .

# TODAY IS MONDAY

Source unknown

1. To - day    is    Mon - day,    To - day    is

Mon - day,    Mon - day, string - beans    all    you    hun - gry    chil - dren,

Come    and    eat    it    up. 2. To - day    is    Tues - day,    To - day    is    Tues - day,

Tues - day, spa - ghet - ti,    Mon - day    string - beans,    All    you    hun - gry    chil - dren,

1.
Come    and    eat    it    up. To - day    is

2. *Last Time*
Come    and    eat    it    up.

3. Wednesday, zoooop
4. Thursday, roast beef
5. Friday, fish
6. Saturday, chicken
7. Sunday, ice cream

*(Note:* As each verse is sung, repeat the other days of the week with their foods.)
Example of last verse:

Today is Sunday, today is Sunday
Sunday, ice cream
Saturday, chicken
Friday, fish
Thursday, roast beef

Wednesday, ZOOOOOP
Tuesday, spaghetti
Monday, string beans
All you hungry children
Come and eat it up.

---

*Concepts: Recall of words and melody, sequencing*

# MARY HAD A LITTLE LAMB

SARA JOSEPHA HALE

Traditional
Arranged by K. BAYLESS

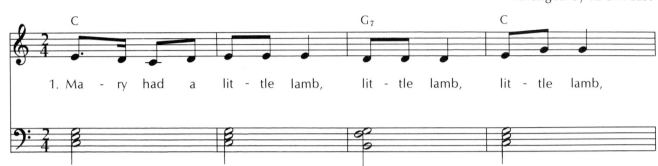

1. Ma - ry had a lit - tle lamb, lit - tle lamb, lit - tle lamb,

Ma - ry had a lit - tle lamb, Its fleece was white as snow.

2
And ev'ry where that Mary went,
Mary went, Mary went,
Ev'rywhere that Mary went,
The lamb was sure to go.

3
It followed her to school one day,
School one day, school one day,
It followed her to school one day,
Which was against the rule.

4
It made the children laugh and play
Laugh and play, laugh and play,
It made the children laugh and play,
To see a lamb in school.

# "M" IS FOR MARY

"M" is for Mary, It's eas - y you see.

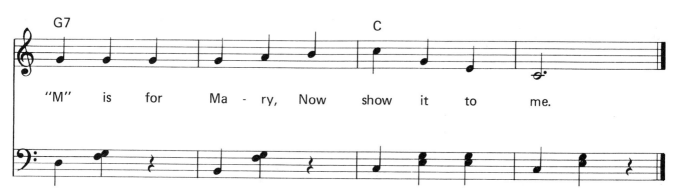

"M" is for Ma - ry, Now show it to me.

"M" is for Mary, I found it, you see,
"M" is for Mary, It's easy for me.

Presenting instructional material in a variety of ways appeals to all children, but is particularly helpful to retarded children. Chanted or sung, this little song can help vary the ways in which letters are presented and can help teach recognition of common objects and the development of a ''sight'' vocabulary.

1. Children's names on cards may be placed on a blackboard ledge. A duplicate card is shown to the child as the song is sung. The card is given to the child, and the child finds the matching card. Later only the first letter of the name is on the card the child receives. Still later, no card is given to use as a clue. The second verse is sung when the child brings back the right card.
2. The alphabet may be taught in this manner beginning with pictures of familiar objects. The initial letter or the complete object name may be on the picture card. Related groups of things may be used: fruits, vegetables, furniture, animals, etc.
3. The color names, number names, days, etc., may be presented in a similar manner.
4. Use pictures of objects needed for speech practice.

## BINGO

Scottish song                                                                    Arranged by K. BAYLESS

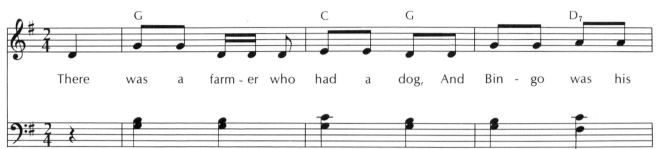

There was a farm-er who had a dog, And Bin-go was his

name - O.    B - I - N-G-O,    B - I - N-G-O,

B - I - N-G-O, And Bin-go was his name - O

**Suggestions**

Sing the song through as written. Then repeat it and clap or tap instead of singing the letter
''B'' in ''B-I-N-G-O.'' On the next repetition substitute clapping the letters ''B'' and ''I,''
etc. (This song is excellent for helping develop concentration.)

## SWEETLY SINGS THE DONKEY

Traditional

Arranged by K. BAYLESS

Sweet - ly sings the don - key at the break of day.

If you do not feed him, this is what he'll say: He -

haw! He - haw! He - haw, he - haw, he - haw!

---

***Musical Concept:*** *Adjusting voice to pitch differences* (Example: he-haw)

## WHO SEES SOMETHING RED?

Source unknown
Adapted by K. BAYLESS

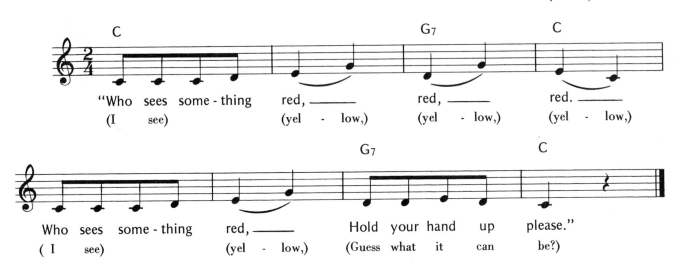

"Who sees some - thing red, _____ red, _____ red. _____
(I see) (yel - low,) (yel - low,) (yel - low,)

Who sees some - thing red, _____ Hold your hand up please."
( I see) (yel - low,) (Guess what it can be?)

*Musical Concept:* Steady, underlying beat (good for clapping or tapping)

# COLOR GAME

Words and music by K. BAYLESS

***Suggestion***

Work with children to add extra verses. For example:

If you have on brown, turn around
If you have on black, step on a crack
If you have on pink, make your eyes blink
If you have on blue, touch your shoe
If you have on white, go fly a kite

This delightful, musical playlet, ''Superbrush and the Molars,'' is often used during dental health week. Encourage the children to create their own dialogue and sound effects. Tunes A and C are in the major mode—Tune B, the minor mode. Tune C has been transposed to a lower key to acc⁄mmodate the younger voices.

*Superbrush and the Molars* by Lois Roper

Cast includes Villain (dark cape, child's play hammer, and sign saying ''Mean Old Tooth Decay''), Superbrush (red cape and large cardboard toothbrush), and five Teeth (each child holds a large, white cardboard tooth with a colored smiling face).

Teeth sing Song A, ''Happy Little Teeth.''

Tooth 1 (stepping forward): ''But here comes the bad guy.'' (Villain stalks in, stomps around, and waves hammer. He taps each Tooth lightly. As each is tapped, child turns the cardboard tooth over, hiding its smile.)

Chorus or group of children sing Song B, ''Hee, Hee, Hee.''

Teeth: ''Help!''

Teeth 2 and 3: ''Save us!''

Tooth 4: ''Look, up in the sky!''

Tooth 5: ''Is it a bird?''

Chorus or group of children: ''No!''

Everyone: ''It's Superbrush!''

Superbrush (bounds on stage, toothbrush held high): ''I'll save you!'' (He chases Villain around the stage. On the second time around, he touches the Villain with the toothbrush. Villain falls to the floor. With one foot on the victim, Superbrush raises his toothbrush.)

All sing Song C, ''Toothsome Tune.''

# A. HAPPY LITTLE TEETH

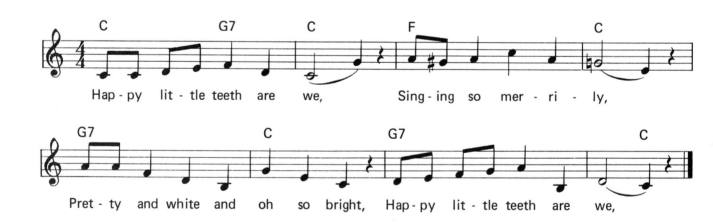

## B. HEE, HEE, HEE

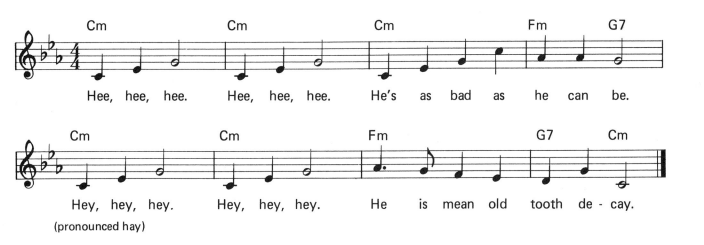

## C. TOOTHSOME TUNE

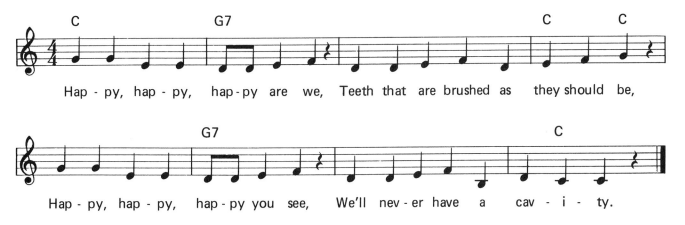

## OVER IN THE MEADOW

South Appalachian folk song

Accompaniment by K. BAYLESS

# COME BUTTER COME

Old verse

Music by K. BAYLESS's class

Come but-ter come, Come but-ter come, John-ny's at the gar-den gate,

Wait-ing for his but-ter cake, Come but-ter come. Come but-ter come.

Help the children discover that the first two measures sound exactly alike. The next two measures sound alike but have different words. The last two measures of the song sound exactly alike. *Note:* The song is fun to sing while churning cream into butter. Change Johnny's name to that of one of the children for variety.

**Musical Concept:** *Mi, re, do (3–2–1)*

# I'VE GOT THAT HAPPY FEELING

Source unknown

I've got that hap - py feel - ing here in my heart,

Here in my heart, Here in my heart. I've got that hap - py feel - ing

here in my heart, Here in my heart to stay.

2. I've got that happy feeling here in my feet (march in place).
3. I've got that happy feeling here in my hands (clap hands).
4. I've got that happy feeling all over me.

(Have children create other verses.)

# IF YOU'RE HAPPY

Traditional

Arranged by K. BAYLESS

2. If you're happy and you know it, stamp your feet.
3. If you're happy and you know it, nod your head.

4. If you're happy and you know it, swing around.
5. If you're happy and you know it, shout out loud!

**Suggestion**
Have children create their own verses.

# THE WHISPER SONG

Arranged by MARION WINTERS

By JOAN and ROGER BRADFIELD

# BROWNIE SMILE SONG

HARRIET E. HEYWOOD

Melody by Ms. Heywood's Brownie
Girl Scout troop

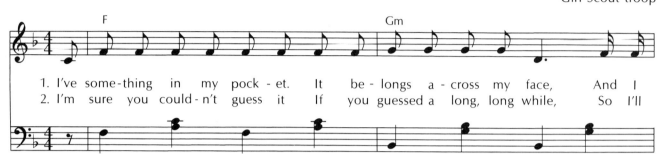

1. I've some-thing in my pock - et. It be - longs a - cross my face,     And I
2. I'm sure you could - n't guess it     If you guessed a long, long while,     So I'll

keep     it     ver - y     close     at     hand     in     a     most     con - ve - nient     place.
take     it     out     and     put     it     on--     It's     a     great     big     Brown - ie     Smile!

(May substitute "happy" for "Brownie")

Written for the Children of the Presbyterian Pre-School Center

# THE STOP LIGHT SONG

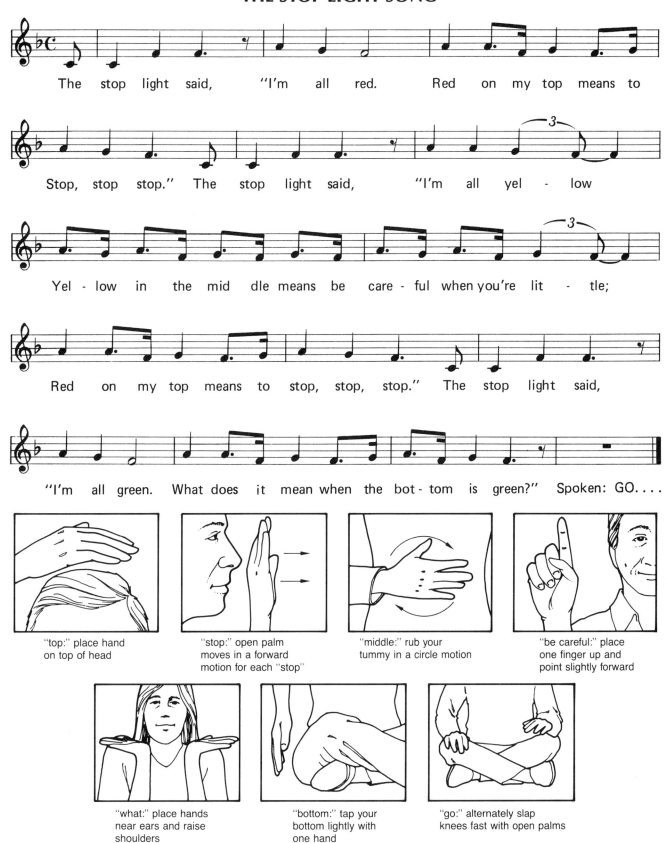

The stop light said, "I'm all red. Red on my top means to Stop, stop stop." The stop light said, "I'm all yel - low

Yel - low in the mid dle means be care - ful when you're lit - tle;

Red on my top means to stop, stop, stop." The stop light said,

"I'm all green. What does it mean when the bot - tom is green?" Spoken: GO....

"top:" place hand on top of head

"stop:" open palm moves in a forward motion for each "stop"

"middle:" rub your tummy in a circle motion

"be careful:" place one finger up and point slightly forward

"what:" place hands near ears and raise shoulders

"bottom:" tap your bottom lightly with one hand

"go:" alternately slap knees fast with open palms

By Bonnie Wendt Draeger. © 1985 from Paradiddles 1985 Music/Arts Review, P.O. Box 1348, Columbus, Indiana. Used by permission.

123

# AUTUMN LEAVES

German folk tune
Words by Helen Myers Cornwell

VERSE

F                    C7                              F

*1. Now the sum - mer is o - ver, There are leaves all a - round.

F                    C7                              F

Au - tumn leaves, red and yel - low, Soft - ly fall to the ground.

REFRAIN

F                    C7                              F

La lee la la la la la, La lee la la lee lie,

F                    C7                              F

Au - tumn leaves of all col - ors, Tell - ing sum - mer good - by.

2
Now the summer is over,
And the leaves start to whirl.
Autumn leaves turn and tumble,
Chilly winds make them swirl. *Refrain*

3
Now the summer is over,
See the leaves ev'rywhere.
Autumn leaves make a carpet
Under trees dark and bare. *Refrain*

*Transpose to key of C for ease of singing.

## JACK-O'-LANTERN

German folk tune

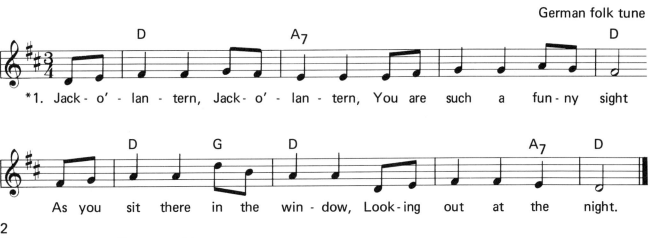

*1. Jack - o'- lan - tern, Jack - o'- lan - tern, You are such a fun - ny sight

As you sit there in the win - dow, Look - ing out at the night.

2
You were once a yellow pumpkin
Growing on a sturdy vine;
Now you are a Jack - o'- lantern,
See the candles that shine!

From WORLD OF MUSIC. © 1988 Silver Burdett & Ginn Inc. Used by permission.

*Transpose to key of C for ease of singing.

## JACK-O'-LANTERN

Words and music by K. BAYLESS

Happily

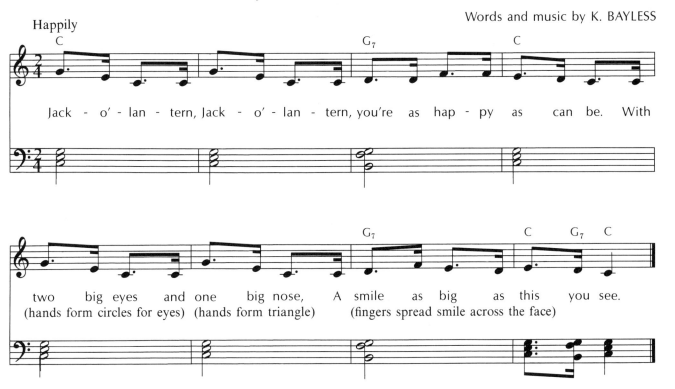

Jack - o'- lan - tern, Jack - o'- lan - tern, you're as hap - py as can be. With

two big eyes and one big nose, A smile as big as this you see.
(hands form circles for eyes) (hands form triangle) (fingers spread smile across the face)

*Five Little Pumpkins*
(To the tune of "Baa, Baa, Black Sheep")

Five little pumpkins sitting on a gate,
The first one said, "Oh, my, it's getting late!"
The second one said, "There are witches in the air!"
The third one said, "But we don't care."
The fourth one said, "Let's run and run and run."
The fifth one said, "I'm ready for some fun!"
"Ooooo," went the wind and out went the light,
And the five little pumpkins rolled out of sight.

                                        SOURCE UNKNOWN

*Halloween*
(To the tune of "The Farmer in the Dell")

1. The witch rides tonight, the witch rides tonight,
   Hi, ho, it's Halloween, the witch rides tonight.

2. The witch takes a cat, the witch takes a cat,
   Hi, ho, it's Halloween, the witch takes a cat.

3. The cat takes a bat, the cat takes a bat,
   Hi, ho, it's Halloween, the cat takes a bat.

4. The bat takes the ghost, the bat takes the ghost,
   Hi, ho, it's Halloween, the bat takes the ghost.

5. The ghost dances fast, the ghost dances fast,
   Hi, ho, it's Halloween, the ghost dances fast.

6. The ghost runs away, the ghost runs away,
   Hi, ho, it's Halloween, the ghost runs away.

# HAVE YOU SEEN THE GHOST OF JOHN?

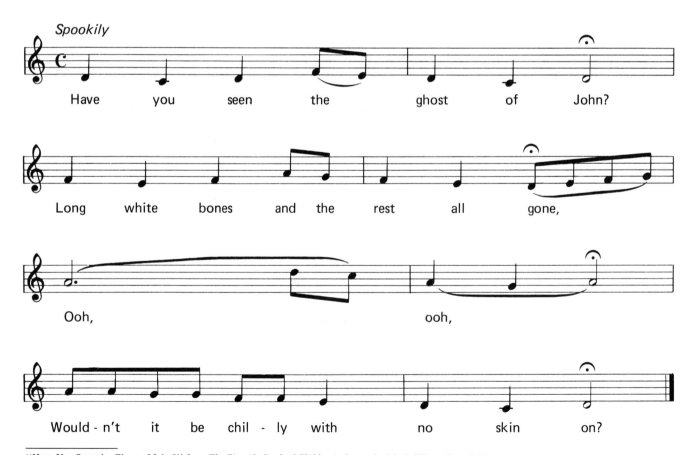

"Have You Seen the Ghost of John?" from *The Fireside Book of Children's Songs*, by Marie Winn. Copyright
© 1966 by Marie Winn and Allan Miller. Reprinted by permission of Simon & Schuster, Inc.

# HIYAH, HIYAH

Words and music by K. BAYLESS

Hi - yah, hi - yah, Hi - yah, hi - yah, beat up - on our drums.

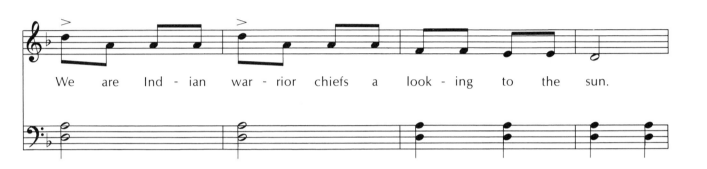

We are Ind - ian war - rior chiefs a look - ing to the sun.

Boom, boom, boom, boom, Beat - ing on our drums.

*Left-hand chords may be played an octave lower.

# GOBBLE, GOBBLE, QUACK, QUACK

Source unknown
Arranged by K. BAYLESS

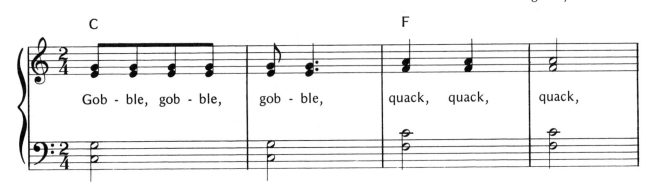

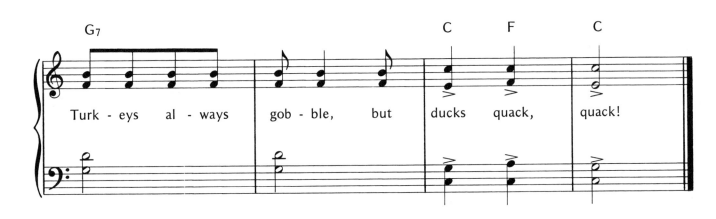

# MR. TURKEY

Words and music by K. BAYLESS

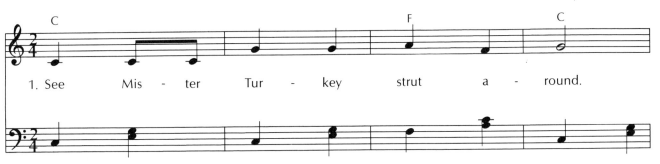

1. See Mis - ter Tur - key strut a - round.

Gob - ble, gob - ble, gob - ble, gob - ble is his fun - ny sound.

2
See Mister Turkey, he's so fat.
Wibble, wobble, wibble, wobble, round he goes like that.

# FIVE FAT TURKEYS

Traditional

Five fat tur - keys are we, We

slept all night in the tree, When the cook came a - round we

could - n't be found, So that's why we're here you see.

129

# OVER THE RIVER

Traditional American song

1. O - ver the riv - er and  through the wood, To  Grand- fa - ther's house we
2. O - ver the riv - er and  through the wood, Trot  fast,  my  dap - ple

go,_____ The  horse knows the  way  to  car - ry  the sleigh  Through the
gray! _____ Spring  o - ver  the ground  like a  hunt - ing hound,  For

white  and drift - ed  snow.  O - ver  the  riv - er  and
this is Thanks - giv - ing  day!  O - ver  the  riv - er  and

through  the  wood,  Oh  how  the  wind  does  blow! _____  It
through  the  wood,  Now  Grand - mother's  face  I  spy! _____  Hur -

stings  the  toes  and  bites  the  nose, As  o - ver the ground we  go. _____
rah for the  fun,  Is the pud - ding done? Hur - rah for the pump - kin  pie! _____

# THE NORTH WIND

M. RAMSEY

K. BAYLESS

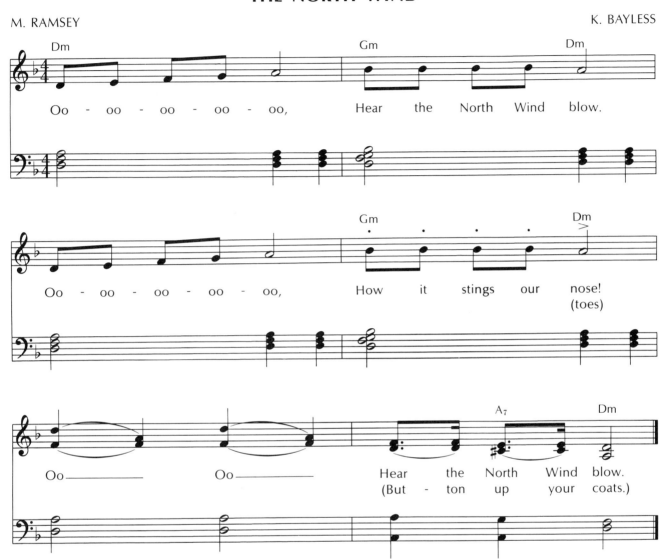

# SANTA'S HELPERS

Children's song

Arranged by K. BAYLESS

(First line use rhythm sticks.)

Tap, tap, tap, tap, Go our lit-tle ham-mers.

Ring, ring, ring, ring, Go our lit-tle bells.

(Second line use bell instruments.)

We are San-ta's help-ers, Tap-a-tap-a-tap-tap.

(Rhythm sticks)

We are San-ta's help-ers Mak-ing Christ-mas toys.

(Rhythm sticks and bell instruments)

# SIX LITTLE SNOWMEN

Source unknown

**2**
Five little snowmen all made of snow
Five little snowmen standing in a row
Out came the sun and shined all day
One little snowman melted away, etc.

*Snow*
(To tune of ''Row, Row, Row Your Boat'')

Look, look, see the snow,
   See it falling down;
Swirling, swirling, swirling, swirling
   All around the town.

Look, look, see the snow,
   Cold and very white;
Swirling, swirling, swirling, swirling
   What a pretty sight!

*Our Snowman*
(Sung to the tune of ''This Old Man'')

Our snowman
Stands so tall.
We just made him from snowballs
With a big black hat to shade him from the sun.
Making him was so much fun!!

(SOURCE UNKNOWN)

# UP ON THE HOUSETOP

Words and music by Benjamin Hanby

Arranged by K. BAYLESS

click, click, click Down through the chim - ney with good Saint Nick.

2
First comes the stocking of little Nell.
Oh, dear Santa, fill it well;
Give her a dolly that laughs and cries,
One that can open and shut its eyes.
*Chorus*

3
Look in the stocking of little Bill.
Oh, just see what a glorious fill!
Here is a hammer and lots of tacks,
Whistle and ball and a whip that cracks.
*Chorus*

# WE WISH YOU A MERRY CHRISTMAS

English carol

Arranged by K. BAYLESS

We wish you a mer-ry Christ-mas, We wish you a mer-ry Christ-mas, We wish you a mer-ry Christ-mas, And a hap-py New Year!

2
Now bring us some figgy pudding,
Now bring us some figgy pudding,
Now bring us some figgy pudding,
And bring it out here.

3
For we love our figgy pudding,
For we love our figgy pudding,
For we love our figgy pudding,
So bring some out here.

4
We won't go until we get some,
We won't go until we get some,
We won't go until we get some,
So bring some out here.

# BATTLE HYMN OF THE REPUBLIC

JULIA WARD HOWE

Music attributed to WILLIAM STEFFE
Arranged by K. BAYLESS

Glo - ry, glo - ry, hal - le - lu - ia! Glo - ry, glo - ry, hal - le - lu - ia! Glo - ry, glo - ry, hal - le - lu - ia, His truth is march - ing on!

# AMERICA, WE LOVE YOU

Words and music by K. BAYLESS

A - mer - i - ca, A - mer - i - ca, We are so proud of you. We'll give a cheer for our coun - try's flag, The red, white, and the blue!

Spoken cheer optional:   America, America, *We - love - you* !!!

## A VALENTINE WISH

Words and music by K. BAYLESS

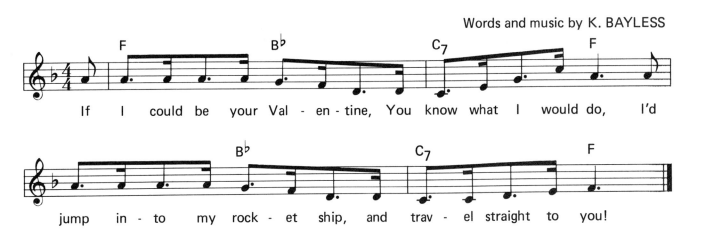

If I could be your Val - en - tine, You know what I would do, I'd

jump in - to my rock - et ship, and trav - el straight to you!

## ONE RED VALENTINE

Source unknown
Adapted by K. BAYLESS

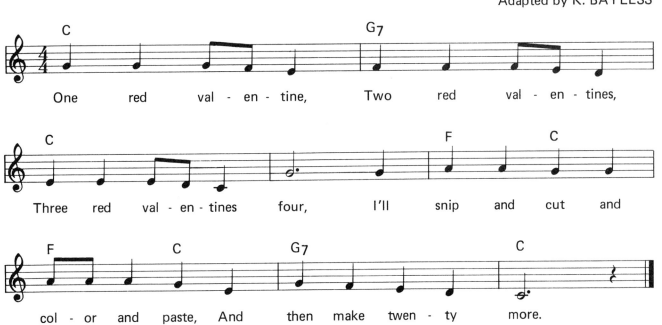

One red val - en - tine, Two red val - en - tines,

Three red val - en - tines four, I'll snip and cut and

col - or and paste, And then make twen - ty more.

# LOVE SOMEBODY

American folk song

1. Love some-bod - y, yes I do; Love some-bod - y, yes I do;
Love some-bod - y, yes I do; Love some-bod - y, but I won't tell who.

2. Love somebody, yes I do;
   Love somebody, yes I do;
   Love somebody, yes I do;
   Love somebody, but you can't guess who.

## A TISKET, A TASKET

Traditional
Adapted by K. BAYLESS

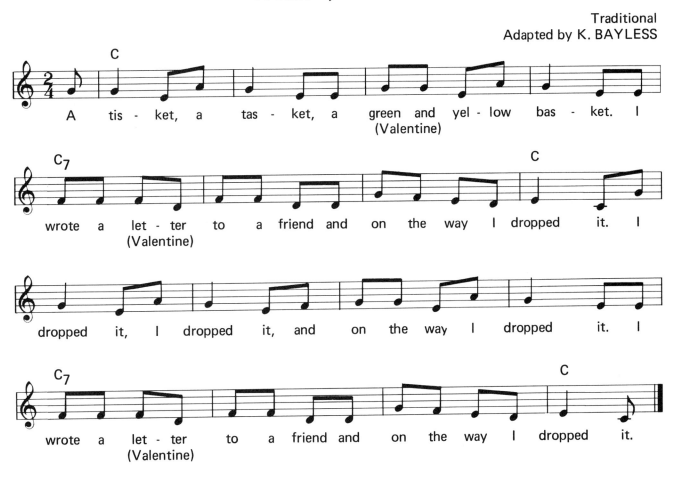

This favorite, play-party game can be adapted in many ways. For Valentine's Day use a Valentine basket and have the child who is "It" drop a Valentine behind a child in the circle. The game proceeds like "Duck, Duck, Goose."

*Musical Concept: Sol-mi minor third—The international chant of childhood*

# GROUNDHOG

Words and music by "Miss Jackie" Weissman
Used by permission

1. Ground-hog Ground-hog come on out and play. It's a beau - ti - ful beau - ti - ful
2. Ground-hog Ground-hog come on out and play. It's a gloo - my gloo - my

Feb - ru - a - ry day. The sun is shin - ing and the
Feb - ru - a - ry day. The air feels chil - ly and the

sky is blue. Won't you come on out? I want to play with you.
sky is gray. Won't you come on out? I want to play to - day.

Reprinted by permission of "Miss Jackie" Weissman.

Act out the following:

After verse 1: The groundhog climbs slowly out of his hole. He looks around and sees his shadow. "Help, help," he cries, "I see my shadow. I must go back into the ground for six more weeks of winter."

After verse 2: Ground hog climbs slowly out of his hole. He looks around but he doesn't see his shadow. "Oh, I'm so happy. I don't see my shadow. Spring will soon be here."

Encourage children to be conscious of their own shadows when out in the sun. Do a lesson on shadows using artificial lighting.

## THE EASTER BUNNY IS COMING SOON

Words and music by K. BAYLESS

The Eas - ter Bun-ny is com - ing soon to spread his cheer. He's

bring-ing lots__ of Eas - ter eggs a-gain this year. Yel - low and blue and pink and green,

such a sight you've nev-er seen, Mak-ing child-ren laugh and sing On Eas - ter in the morn - ing.

# SPRING IS HERE

K. BAYLESS

Have children sing marked notes staccato.

***Musical Concept:*** *Sol-mi minor third*

***Maypole Dance***

Skip around the pole to the dance. Repeat music, turn and skip opposite way.

Repeat music:   First two measures: girls skip into pole and bow

Third and fourth measures: girls skip out from pole and bow

Fifth and sixth measures: boys skip into pole and bow

Seventh and eighth measures: boys skip out from pole and bow

Repeat entire dance, all skipping around the pole lifting ribbons high at the end and then dropping them.

*Note:* For younger children simplify the dance by having them skip around the circle.

(This dance has been included by request from teachers.)

## MAYPOLE DANCE

Source unknown
Adapted by K. BAYLESS

Sing a song of May - time, Win - ter's gone a - way,

All a - round the May - pole, We will dance to - day.

DANCE

## HOT POTATO

Traditional rhyme set to music
K. BAYLESS

One, po - ta - to, two po - ta - to, Three po - ta - to four,

Five po - ta - to, six po - ta - to, seven po - ta - to, more!

"Hot Potato" and "I Caught a Fish" are excellent examples of rhymes that can be sung. The scalewise progression makes them easy to sing. Older children love to jump rope while teachers and students sing or chant these very rhythmic rhymes.

## I CAUGHT A FISH

Traditional rhyme set to music
K. BAYLESS

One, two, three, four, five, I caught a fish a - live,
Six, seven, eight, nine, ten, I let him go a - gain.

Why did you let him go? Be - cause he bit my fing - er so!

# ONE ELEPHANT

Singing game

Chilean folk song
Arranged and adapted by K. BAYLESS

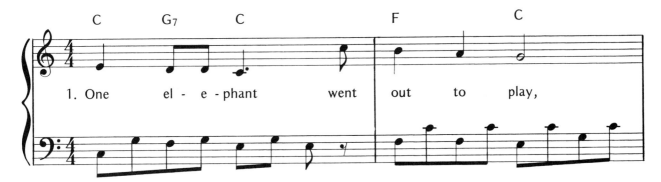

1. One el - e - phant went out to play,

All on a spi - ders web one day. He had such e -
(They)

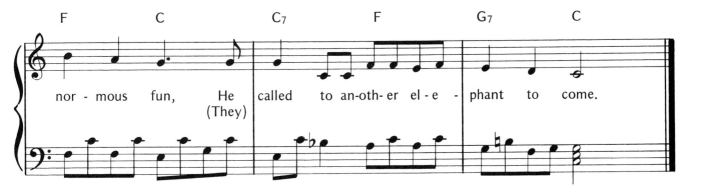

nor - mous fun, He called to an-oth- er el - e - phant to come.
(They)

2. Two elephants went out to play

3. Three elephants went out to play, etc.

---

### Suggestions

After each verse is sung, have the children call out in singing fashion for the next elephant to come. Have them sing "éléphant" (French word for elephant). Sing the syllables of the word "éléphant" as follows:

él - é - phant

One could also use the words for elephant in Spanish, Italian, or another language. Children love calling out the next elephant in different languages.

# JOHNNY WORKS WITH ONE HAMMER*

Folk song

Arranged by K. BAYLESS

2
Johnny works with two hammers,
two hammers, two hammers,
Johnny works with two hammers,
Then he works with three.

3
Johnny works with three hammers,
three hammers, three hammers,
Johnny works with three hammers,
Then he works with four.

4
Johnny works with four hammers,
four hammers, four hammers,
Johnny works with four hammers,
Then he works with five.

5
Johnny works with five hammers,
five hammers, five hammers,
Johnny works with five hammers,
Then he goes to sleep.

From *Finger Play* by Mary Miller and Paula Zajan. Copyright 1955, G. Schirmer, Inc. Used by permission.

*Actions*

Verse 1: Pound on right knee with right fist in time with music.
Verse 2: Add left fist; pound on left knee.
Verse 3: Add right foot; tap on floor.
Verse 4: Add left foot; tap on floor.
Verse 5: Add head; nod up and down. On words "goes to sleep," stop pounding, drop
  head, or lie down on floor and rest.

# THIS OLD MAN

English singing game

This old man, he played one, He played nick-nack on my thumb,

Nick-nack, pad-dy whack, Give a dog a bone, This old man came roll-ing home.

**2**
This old man, he played two,
He played nick-nack on my shoe;
Nick-nack, paddy whack, Give a dog a bone,
This old man came rolling home.

**3**
This old man, he played three,
He played nick-nack on my knee;
Nick-nack, paddy whack, Give a dog a bone,
This old man came rolling home.

**4**
This old man, he played four,
He played nick-nack on my door; (Point to forehead.)

**5**
This old man, he played five,
He played nick-nack on my hive; (Fight the bees.)

**6**
This old man, he played six,
He played nick-nack on my sticks; (Hold up index fingers.)

**7**
This old man he played sev'n,
He played nick-nack up in heav'n; (Fly like angels.)

**8**
This old man, he played eight,
He played nick-nack on my pate; (Point to top of head.)

**9**
This old man, he played nine,
He played nick-nack on my spine; (Tap between shoulders.)

**10**
This old man, he played ten,
He played nick-nack once again;
Nick-nack, paddy whack, Give a dog a bone,
Now we'll all go running home.

# THREE BLUE PIGEONS

American folk song

Arranged by K. BAYLESS

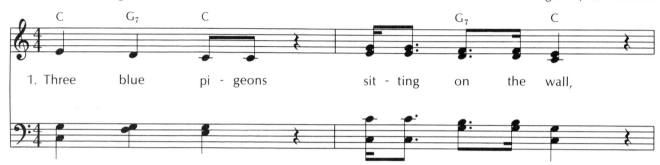

1. Three   blue   pi - geons   sit - ting   on   the   wall,

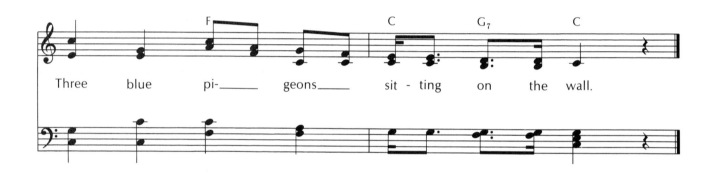

Three   blue   pi-_____ geons_____   sit - ting   on   the   wall.

*Spoken:*   One pigeon flew away. Whee-ee-ee-ee-ee!!

2
Two blue pigeons sitting on the wall,
Two blue pigeons sitting on the wall.
*Spoken:*   Another one flew away. (or) The second one
         flew away. Whee-ee-ee-ee-ee!!

3
One blue pigeon sitting on the wall,
One blue pigeon sitting on the wall.
*Spoken:*   Another one flew away. (or) The third one flew
         away. Whee-ee-ee-ee-ee!!

4
No blue pigeons sitting on the wall,
No blue pigeons sitting on the wall.
*Spoken:*   One flew back. (or) The first one flew back.
         Whee-ee-ee-ee-ee!!

5
One blue pigeon sitting on the wall,
One blue pigeon sitting on the wall.
*Spoken:*   Another flew back. (or) The second one flew
         back. Whee-ee-ee-ee-ee!!

6
Two blue pigeons sitting on the wall.
Two blue pigeons sitting on the wall.
*Spoken:*   Another flew back. (or) The third one flew back.
         Whe-ee-ee-ee-ee!!

7
Three blue pigeons sitting on the wall,
Three blue pigeons sitting on the wall.
*Spoken:*   And now the pigeons *are all home!!*

***Suggestion***
Have the children be the pigeons or use puppet pigeons on sticks to dramatize the song.

# FIVE LITTLE CHICKADEES

Old counting song

Five   lit - tle   chick - a - dees   peep - ing   at   the   door,

One   flew   a - way   and   then   there   were   four.   Chick - a - dee,   chick - a - dee,

hap - py   and   gay,   chick - a - dee,   chick - a - dee,   fly   a - way.

2
Four little chickadees sitting on a tree,
One flew away, and there were three,
(Refrain)

3
Three little chickadees looking at you,
One flew away, and then there were two,
(Refrain)

4
Two little chickadees sitting in the sun,
One flew away, and then there was one,
(Refrain)

5
One little chickadee left all alone,
He flew away, and then there were none,
(Refrain)

---

This is an excellent song to dramatize. Children can be the chickadees or make chickadee puppets.

*Movement Concept: Flying*

# FIVE LITTLE DUCKS WENT SWIMMING ONE DAY

Source Unknown

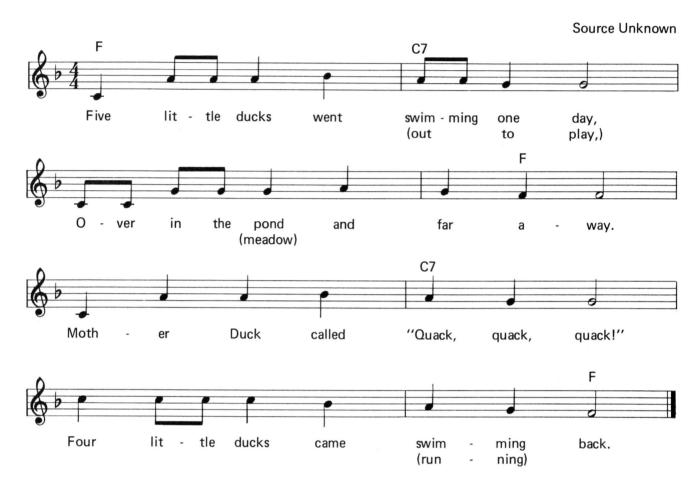

Continue singing the song until no little ducks come swimming (running) back.

Then, Father Duck said, "Quack, quack, quack" *(in a strong voice)*
    And 5 little ducks came swimming (running) back!

## SIX LITTLE DUCKS

Folk song from Maryland

Arranged by K. BAYLESS

1. Six lit-tle ducks that I once knew, Fat ones, skin-ny ones, fair ones too. But the

one lit-tle duck with a feath-er on his back, He led the oth-ers with a

quack, quack, quack! quack, quack, quack! quack, quack, quack! He led the oth-ers with a quack, quack, quack!

2
Down to the river they would go,
Wibble, wabble, wibble, wabble to and fro.
*Refrain*

3
Home from the river they would come,
Wibble, wabble, wibble, wabble, ho, hum, hum.
*Refrain*

By permission of Cooperative Recreation Service.

# ROLL OVER

Traditional American song

There were ten in the bed, And the lit - tle one said, "Roll
nine, etc.

o - ver, roll o - ver." So they all rolled o - ver and

**1.–8.**  one fell out. There were  **9.**  one fell out. There was

one in the bed, And the lit - tle one said, "Good - night!"

# LITTLE FISH

D.R.G. and B.W.C.

W.E.S.

Lit - tle fish goes out to play, He wig - gles his fins, then swims a - way; He swims and swims in the wa - ter bright, He o - pens his mouth and takes a bite! Mmmmmmm! Tastes good!

This may be done without music as a finger play and choral speaking activity. When the children have learned it, they will enjoy singing the melody as they do the motions.

Put your left hand out, palm down, fingers together, thumb sticking out. Put your right hand on top of the left, palm down, thumb out. (See the fish with fins at his sides.) Wiggle your thumbs and make the fish swim by moving hands up and down in unison. Now make the fish swim and wiggle his fins at the same time. Open his mouth. Keep the hands together but drop the left hand fingers and raise the right hand fingers. Rub tummy.

# MY DOG RAGS

Unknown

**Hand Motions**

On words "flip-flop," flip left hand over head, then right hand over head.

On words "wig-wag," put hands together in back of you. Flip them to the left and then to the right of the body.

On words "zig-zag," bend over, hands on hips. Bend the body to the left and then to the right.

# OLD MACDONALD HAD A FARM

Traditional

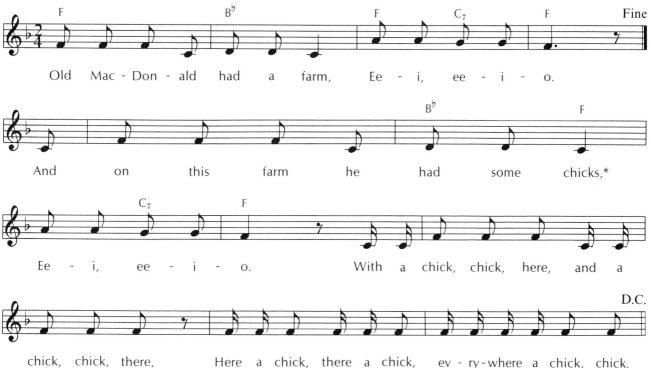

Old Mac - Don - ald had a farm, Ee - i, ee - i - o.

And on this farm he had some chicks,*

Ee - i, ee - i - o. With a chick, chick, here, and a

chick, chick, there, Here a chick, there a chick, ev - ry-where a chick, chick.

With other verses, add ducks, pigs, cows, etc.

Most children like to sing the traditional song "Old MacDonald Had a Farm." It is usually one of the first ones they like to memorize. They are "tickled" and excited as they hear their own voices produce the animal sounds in strict adherence to the interesting rhythmic pattern ("with a chick, chick, here, and a chick, chick, there," etc.). Throughout the years, this song has been adapted for many purposes. One of the ways it has been used is to help children learn their short and long vowel sounds. It is an enjoyable way for them to memorize the sounds. Once they learn it in the song, the children can easily recall a sound by associating it with the animal. The vowels are substituted for the animal sounds. For example:

### Short Vowel Version
(Sing the following to the tune of "Old MacDonald")

Old MacDonald had a farm, Ee-i, ee-i-o.
And on this farm he had a *cat*, Ee-i, ee-i-o.
With a ă-ă here, And a ă-ă there, Here a ă, There a ă, Everywhere a ă-ă.
Old MacDonald had a *cat*, Ee-i, ee-i-o.

Other verses: a *hen*—ĕ
      a *pig*—ĭ
      an *ox*—ŏ
      a *duck*—ŭ

### Long Vowel Version
(Sing the song as above but substitute animals having the long vowel sounds)

For example: some *tapirs*—ā
           some *sheep*—ē
           some *mice*—ī
           some *goats*—ō
           some *mules*—ū

*Note:* Zoo animals could be used instead of farm animals.

# I HAD A CAT

Kentucky folk song
Adapted by K. BAYLESS

1. I had a cat and the cat pleased me, I fed my cat un-der yon-der tree. (1. Refrain) Cat goes fid-dle-i-fee.

(2. Refrain) Hen goes chim-my chuck, Cat goes fid-dle-i-fee.

(3. Refrain) Duck goes quack, quack, Hen goes chim-my chuck, Cat goes fid-dle-i-fee.

2. I had a hen and the hen pleased me, I fed my hen by yonder tree.
3. I had a duck and the duck pleased me, I fed my duck by yonder tree.

---

This is a cumulative song. Children add to each verse by renaming in reverse order what has been sung before.

**Musical Concept:** *Mi-re-do (3–2–1) intervals (''yonder tree'' and ''cat goes fiddle-i-fee'')*

**Concept:** *Sequencing and memorization.*

# BARNYARD FAMILY

American folk song

Arranged by K. BAYLESS

1. I have a lit-tle roost-er by the barn - yard gate, And that lit-tle roost-er is my play-mate, And that lit-tle roost-er goes cock - a-doo-dle-doo, Doo-doo,____ doo-doo,____ doo-doo-dle doo.

2
I have a little hen by the barnyard gate,
And that little hen is my playmate,
And that little hen goes cluck, a-cluck-a-cluck,
Cluck-cluck, cluck-cluck, cluck-cluck-a-cluck.

3
I have a little duck by the barnyard gate,
And that little duck is my playmate,
And that little duck goes quack-a-quack-a-quack,
Quack-quack, quack-quack, quack-quack-a-quack, etc.

# CROCODILE SONG

Old song

Source unknown
Adapted by K. BAYLESS

She sailed a - way on a bright and sun - ny day, on the
back of a croc - o - dile. "You see," said she, "He's as
tame as he can be as I float him down the Nile." The
Croc winked his eye as she waved a mer - ry bye,
Wear - ing a hap - py smile. At the end of the ride, the
la - dy was in - side, And the smile was on the croc - o - dile. (Clap - Clap).

## Motions

Move one hand over the other arm in an up-and-down motion representing a sailing movement. Stroke one arm with the other hand so as to tame the crocodile. Wink the eye and wave good-bye. Smile. On the words "At the end of the ride, the lady was inside, and the smile was on the crocodile," open and shut hands (palms together) like a crocodile's mouth. Give two loud claps at the end of the song.

# MAMMA KANGAROO

M. RAMSEY

K. BAYLESS

I am Mam-ma Kang-a-roo, Like to see me jump? I can take a great big leap up a-bove this hump. I am Mam-ma Kang-a-roo, Peek in-to my pock-et____. This is ba-by Kang-a-roo, Sleep-ing in my pock-et____.

*The Animals in the Zoo*
(To the tune of "Here We Go Round the Mulberry Bush")

Look at the animals in the zoo, in the zoo, in the zoo,
See the different things they do, and we can do
   them too.

The elephant walks and swings his trunk, swings his
   trunk, swings his trunk,
The elephant walks and swings his trunk, and we can do
   it too.

The tall giraffe can stretch her neck, stretch her neck,
   stretch her neck,
The tall giraffe can stretch her neck, and we can do
   it too.

Monkeys swing on limbs of trees, limbs of trees, limbs of
   trees,

Monkeys swing on limbs of trees, and we can do it too.

Camels march like soldiers brave, soldiers brave, soldiers
   brave,
Camels march like soldiers brave, and we can do it too.

Bears stamp their heavy feet, heavy feet, heavy feet,
Bears stamp their heavy feet, and we can do it too.

The kangaroos go jump, jump, jump; jump, jump, jump;
   jump, jump, jump.
The kangaroos go jump, jump, jump, and we can do
   it too.

(As the song is sung, have children do the actions. Encourage them to add other verses.)

159

## FROGGIE WENT A-COURTIN'

American folk song

Arranged by K. BAYLESS

2

He rode right up to Miss Mouse's door, uh huh, uh huh.
He rode right up to Miss Mouse's door, uh huh.
He rode right up to Miss Mouse's door,
Where he'd been many times before, uh huh, uh huh.

3

He took Miss Mousey on his knee, uh huh, uh huh.
He took Miss Mousey on his knee, uh huh.
He took Miss Mousey on his knee,
And said, "Miss Mousey will you marry me?" uh huh, uh huh.

4

"Without my Uncle Rat's consent, uh huh, uh huh. . .
I wouldn't marry the President," uh huh, uh huh.

5

"Where shall the wedding supper be?" uh huh, uh huh. . .
"Way down yonder in the hollow tree," uh huh, uh huh.

6

"What shall the wedding supper be?" uh huh, uh huh. . .
"Two green beans and a black-eyed pea," uh huh, uh huh.

7

First one in was a bumblebee, uh huh, uh huh. . .
Who danced a jig with a two-legged flea, uh huh, uh huh.

8

They all sailed off across the lake, uh huh, uh huh. . .
Got swallowed up by a big black snake, uh huh, uh huh.

9

There's corn and cheese upon the shelf, uh huh, uh huh. . .
If you want more verses just sing them yourself, uh huh, uh huh.

# MISTER RABBIT

Southern folk song

Arranged by K. BAYLESS

1. "Mis - ter Rab - bit, Mis - ter Rab - bit, your ears might - y

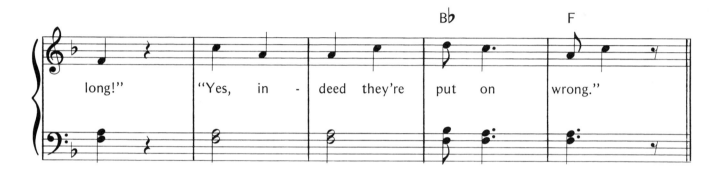

long!" "Yes, in - deed they're put on wrong."

Ev - 'ry lit - tle soul must shine, shine, shine.

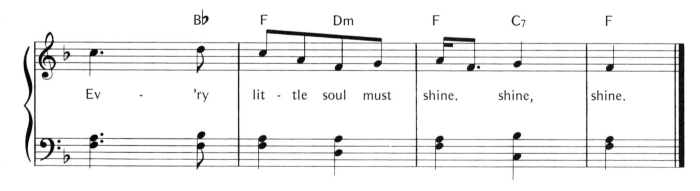

Ev - 'ry lit - tle soul must shine. shine, shine.

2
"Mister Rabbit, Mister Rabbit, your coat's mighty gray!"
"Yes, indeed, 'twas made that way."
Ev'ry little soul must shine, shine, shine.
Ev'ry little soul must shine, shine, shine.

3
"Mister Rabbit, Mister Rabbit, your tail's mighty white!"
"Yes, indeed, I'm going out of sight."
Ev'ry little soul must shine, shine, shine.
Ev'ry little soul must shine, shine, shine.

## JACK JUMPS UP, JACK STOOPS DOWN

Source unknown
Adapted by K. BAYLESS

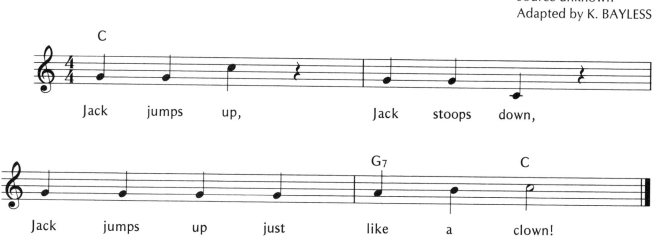

Jack jumps up, Jack stoops down,

Jack jumps up just like a clown!

---

*Movement Concepts:* *Jumping (springing with the legs); up-down*

## MONKEY SEE, MONKEY DO

Traditional

If you clap, clap, clap your hands, The mon - key

claps, claps, claps his hands, Mon - key sees and

mon - key do, The mon - key does the same as you.

(Add other verses like, "If you stamp, stamp, stamp your feet," etc.)

---

This is a good song to help develop listening skills and skill in following directions.

*Musical Concept:* *Identical melodies in the first two phrases*

# BOW, BELINDA

Traditional
Adapted

American game song
Arranged by K. BAYLESS

1. Bow, bow, Oh, Be-lin - da. Bow, bow, Oh Be-lin - da.

Bow, bow, Oh Be-lin - da. Please bow, Be-lin - da.

2
One hand out, oh Belinda,
  *or* right hand out, oh Belinda,
One hand out, oh Belinda,
One hand out, oh Belinda,
One hand out before you.

3
Another hand out, oh Belinda,
  *or* two hands out, oh Belinda,
  *or* left hand out, oh Belinda,
Another hand out, oh Belinda,
Another hand out, oh Belinda,
Both hands out before you.

# HOKEY POKEY

Traditional U.S. game song

Arranged by K. BAYLESS

1. You put your right foot in, you put your right foot out, you put your right foot in and you shake it all a-bout. You do the Hok - ey Pok - ey, and you turn your-self a-round, That's what it's all a - bout.

2. You put your left foot in,
3. You put your right arm in,
4. You put your left arm in,
5. You put your whole self in,

# GOING ON A PICNIC

1.-2. Go - ing on a pic - nic, Leav - ing right a - way;

If it does - n't rain we'll stay all day.  1. Did you bring the hot dogs?
                                                                    sal - ad?

Yes, I brought the hot dogs! Read - y for a pic - nic? Here we go!
              sal - ad!

2. Did you bring the ice cream?
Yes, I brought the ice cream!
Did you bring the melon?
Yes, I brought the melon!
Ready for a picnic?
Here we go!

# PEASE PORRIDGE HOT

Traditional

K. BAYLESS

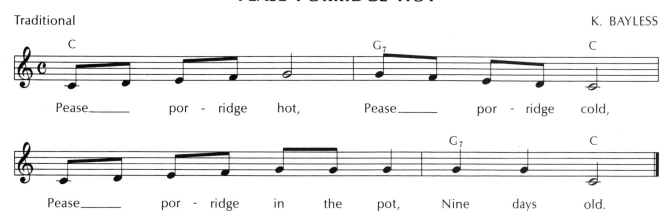

Pease_____ por - ridge hot, Pease_____ por - ridge cold,

Pease_____ por - ridge in the pot, Nine days old.

---

### Actions

Pease[1] porridge[2] hot,[3]
Pease[1] porridge[2] cold,[3]
Pease[1] porridge[2] in the[4] pot,[2]
Nine[5] days[2] old.[3]

Some[1] like it[2] hot,[3]
Some[1] like it[2] cold,[3]
Some[1] like it[2] in the[4] pot,[2]
Nine[5] days[2] old.[3]

On (1) clap hands on lap.
On (2) clap hands together.
On (3) clap hands with partner's hands.
On (4) clap right hands together.
On (5) clap left hands together.

# THE BUS SONG

Play song

Arranged by K. BAYLESS

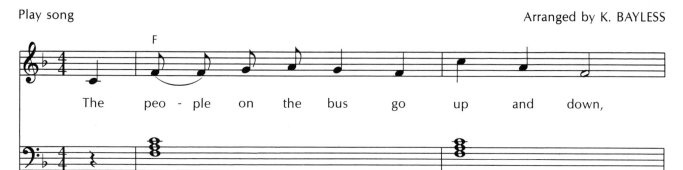

The peo-ple on the bus go up and down,

Up and down, up and down. The peo-ple on the bus go

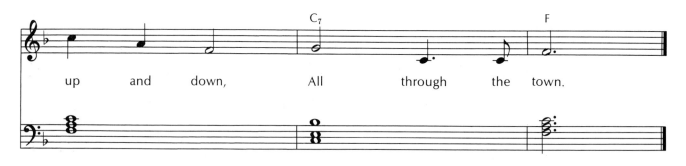

up and down, All through the town.

2

The wheels on the bus go round and round,
 Round and round, round and round.
The wheels on the bus go round and round,
 All through the town.

3

The horn on the bus goes toot, toot, toot,
 Toot, toot, toot, toot, toot, toot.
The horn on the bus goes toot, toot, toot,
 All through the town.

4

The money in the box goes ding, ding, ding,
 Ding, ding, ding, ding, ding, ding.
The money in the box goes ding, ding, ding,
 All through the town.

5

The wiper on the glass goes swish, swish, swish,
 Swish, swish, swish, swish, swish, swish.
The wiper on the glass goes swish, swish, swish,
 All through the town.

6

The driver on the bus says, "Move on back,
 Move on back, move on back."
The driver on the bus says, "Move on back,"
 All through the town.

7

The lights on the bus go flash, flash, flash,
 Flash, flash, flash, flash, flash, flash.
The lights on the bus go flash, flash, flash,
 All through the town.

8
The brakes on the bus go squeak, squeak, squeak,
    Squeak, squeak, squeak, squeak, squeak, squeak.
The brakes on the bus go squeak, squeak, squeak,
    All through the town.

9
The signal on the bus goes click, click, click,
    Click, click, click, click, click, click
The signal on the bus goes click, click, click,
    All through the town.

10
The children on the bus just like to sing,
    Like to sing, like to sing.
The children on the bus just like to sing,
    All through the town.

"The Bus Song" originally entitled "The Bus" from *Singing on Our Way* of OUR SINGING WORLD series,
© Copyright, 1959, 1957, 1949, by Ginn and Company. Used with permission. Verses 7–10 by Kathleen M.
Bayless.

# THE POPCORN SONG

Source unknown

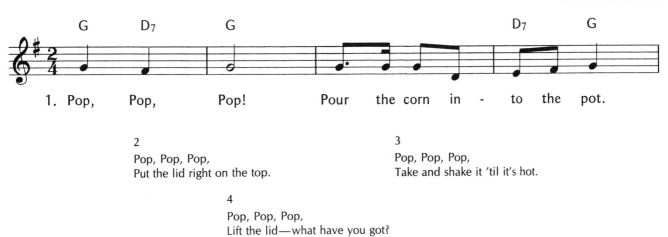

2
Pop, Pop, Pop,
Put the lid right on the top.

3
Pop, Pop, Pop,
Take and shake it 'til it's hot.

4
Pop, Pop, Pop,
Lift the lid—what have you got?

POPCORN!!!!!!!!!!! (Children clap hands.)

Children do the actions as the song is sung.

# WIGGLES

M. RAMSEY

K. BAYLESS

I can wig - gle my fing - ers, I can wig - gle my toes,

I can wig - gle my el - bows, I can wig - gle my bones,

I can wig - gle my tum - my, I can wig - gle my head, But

oh, I would much rath - er Wig - gle my nose in - stead.

## MAKING MUSIC WORK FOR YOU: THE MULTIPURPOSE MELODY

Music is gradually being recognized as an expressive and effective artistic partner for a multitude of learning experiences. Here you will find five applications for the simple folk melody "Circle Left," or "Do-oh, Do-oh." The first two contain specific suggestions for developing positive self-concepts and a heightened sense of pride and accomplishment in children. Additional applications include suggestions for language development, safety concepts, and attentive listening experiences through music. The many creative ways in which this melody can be used has led to its success as a "multipurpose" melody. Other multipurpose melodies require only creative initiative on the part of parents and teachers to discover their limitless educational applications.

Children need to succeed and to feel good about themselves. There are ways to foster these feelings and meet these goals through music. Showing love and care during a group music experience can be accomplished with the same hugs and personalized attention the caring, creative teacher uses all day. This is difficult at best from the piano bench.

Sitting among the children and singing unaccompanied or with a hand-held instrument provides a more personal experience than one initiated from the piano. No longer dependent upon the piano or record player, the confident teacher can adapt music throughout the day as a spontaneous vehicle for a myriad of learning situations.

### Application #1

Children need to have positive experiences in making choices and decisions. The lyrics to "Do-oh, Do-oh" can be changed to provide a movement exercise that includes many opportunities for such choices and decisions.

"Shake those 'simmons down"

## CIRCLE LEFT

used by permission

Cir - cle left   Do - oh, do - oh   Cir - cle left   Do - oh, do - oh

Cir - cle left,   Do - oh, do - oh   Shake those 'sim - mons down.

*From *Experience Games Through Music*, 1973, by Margaret Wharram and Sister Fleurette Sweeney. Used by permission. Adaptations of "Circle Left" by Linda Boyte White. Copyright © 1983 by Bonnie Wendt Draeger and Linda Boyte White, Paradiddles Music/Arts Newsletter, Columbus, Indiana. Used by permission.

The lyrics can be adapted as follows:

<u>Tap your hands</u>, do-oh, do-oh
<u>Tap your hands</u>, do-oh, do-oh
<u>Tap your hands</u>, do-oh, do-oh
Shake those 'simmons down.

The children are then given chances to select new motions for the underscored section. It is important to remember that *no idea* is wrong. Encourage each child to suggest a motion. Several children are likely to suggest the identical action, and *that is fine*. The object is to let them know their ideas are acceptable. The child whose idea is rejected because ''We've already done that'' will be reticent to offer an answer next time, fearing that the answer may not be correct. Guiding children through the process of making decisions and choices takes some time; however, once children feel free to create and offer ideas, they gain an eagerness and willingness to be guided through all kinds of new and varied learning experiences.

## Application #2

Teachers and parents can give a child positive recognition and attention by simply substituting her name in place of ''do-oh'':

Move your feet, just like Megan
Move your feet, just like Megan
Move your feet, just like Megan
Shake those 'simmons down.

Here the class has sung Megan's name three times, and children love to hear their names sung. A child's name is a very special possession belonging especially to her, one that no one can take away. In all applications *eye contact* is of the utmost importance. In this adaptation, only by watching Megan closely can the class copy the exact movement of Megan's feet. Megan, in turn has become a leader, her idea is accepted by the class, and she has had a positive experience, all in a few seconds' time. (*Note:* Not every child is ready to contribute an idea. Some may prefer to wait until another time. More harm is done by forcing a child to participate than by simply letting him absorb the experience. Do continue to offer him chances to share his ideas at another time or in another way. Mary Helen Richards* suggests beginning with the outgoing children first, allowing time for the shy child to ''try the song on'' before being approached for a suggestion.)

## Application #3

Music provides a wonderful vehicle for underscoring and complementing existing educational concepts. For example, a Halloween safety song is easily remembered by children already familiar with ''Do-oh'':

Carry your flashlight, do-oh, do-oh
Carry your flashlight, do-oh, do-oh
Carry your flashlight, do-oh, do-oh
Shake those 'simmons down.

---

*With sincere appreciation to Mary Helen Richards for permission to reprint ''Do-oh, Do-oh'' as well as techniques from Education Through Music (ETM).

Other verses included: ''Take along a grown-up . . .'' and ''Check my candy . . .''. Remember always to conclude with ''Shake those 'simmons down,'' using that phrase as a constant within the variations. It also acts as a control and spells the completion of the song, signaling the cessation of all prior actions.

## Application #4

A small child needs many opportunities for language development. Often a song will remain in the subconscious long after the spoken word has been forgotten.

Place infants or toddlers on a changing table or in your lap. Sing ''Touch your nose, do-oh, do-oh.'' On the final phrase, ''shake those 'simmons down,'' hands or legs can be wiggled or moved back and forth. Children need gentle and loving touches to grow, and this action fulfills both their need for touch and their need for language development. After the child has mastered nose, ears, eyes, and mouth, continue to teach elbow, wrist, knee, and so on.

## Application #5

Children enjoy a respite from spoken instructions. ''Do-oh, do-oh'' is a wonderful instructional exercise in listening attentively for home and classroom. Adapt lyrics to fit your needs. Several suggestions include

Line up Kyle, do-oh, do-oh
Line up Eric, do-oh, do-oh
Line up Matthew, do-oh, do-oh
And don't forget Meg.

Pick up your toys, do-oh, do-oh . . .

Time for a snack now, do-oh, do-oh. . . .

The uses for ''Do-oh, Do-oh'' are truly limitless. Once you gain confidence in using this melody, you will be ready to make other melodies work for you as well.

## PLANNING MUSICAL EXPERIENCES FOR YOUNG CHILDREN

The following plans have been developed as an aid for those teaching music to children. You will note that the concept to be taught is stated first, followed by anticipated learnings, materials, and possible approaches. These plans are merely guides and can be used either where music might be taught separately or as a part of the child's day. It is not necessary to use the quoted material of the teacher. Each person should feel free to introduce and carry out the lesson as it applies to a particular group of children.

### Body Senses and Body Parts Awareness

#### Concept

Children can become more aware of body senses and body parts through songs and movement.

#### Learnings

The children will

1. Identify some of the body senses and body parts
2. Sing about some of the functions of the body senses and body parts
3. Become more aware and appreciative of their bodies and what they can do

#### Materials

1. Songs: "All About Me," "The Hokey-Pokey."
2. Records: *Getting to Know Myself* (Songs: "Touch," "Turn Around") by Hap Palmer; *It's a Happy Feeling* (Song: "Spare Parts") by Tom Thumb Records; and *Walter the Waltzing Worm* (Song: "What a Miracle") by Hap Palmer.

#### Approach

Discuss the importance of the body senses. Name parts of the body involving the senses, such as the eyes, ears, nose, and mouth. Ask the children, "Why are these so important to us?" Show children pictures involving the body senses. Discuss.

#### Procedure

1. Sing the song "All About Me."
2. Have the children perform the appropriate movements to the song.

3. Ask the children to name and discuss other body parts and their functions. For example: the sense of touch (fingers can feel); the sense of taste (the tongue can taste).
4. Sing the songs and perform the movements from the suggested recordings. (This may be extended over several days.)

## ALL ABOUT ME

Source Unknown

1. I clap (tap) with my hands, I march with my feet, I sing with my mouth, And I chew with my teeth!

2. I hear with my ears, I smell with my nose, I see with my eyes, And I dance on my toes!

### "Jack-in-the-Box"

#### Concept

The power of springs to make sudden and bouncy movements

#### Learnings

The children will

1. Discover that a mechanical spring, after being compressed and released suddenly, will produce a bouncy movement
2. Duplicate the same kind of springing action with their bodies
3. Discover that the muscles in their legs serve as springs to their bodies

#### Materials

1. Jack-in-the-box toy that plays the tune "Pop Goes the Weasel"
2. A spiral gravy mixer, a "Slinky," or other objects having springs
3. Scalewise song: "Jack-in-the-Box" by Scott and Wood

#### Approach

Show the children the jack-in-the-box toy. Allow one of them to turn the handle and play the tune (Jack pops up at the end of the song).

*Teacher or parent:* "What do you think makes Jack pop up? Let's find out."

#### Procedure

1. Permit each child to push Jack down in the box with his hand and then let him jump up again. (Do not put lid down each time because that will take up too much time.) Each child can feel the springing movement. "What do you think is inside Jack that makes him pop up?" Some child will probably guess that Jack has something inside his body that makes him spring up.
2. Show the children different kinds of springs. A gravy mixer composed of a spiral spring on a handle (which takes lumps out of gravy) is a good example to use. Children can push down on the handle and let loose suddenly. They can then see the springing action.
3. Sing the song "Jack-in-the-box."
4. Have children pretend that they are jacks-in-the-box.
5. Have them spring up on the words, "Yes! I will!"

#### Follow-up

1. "What did you do to make your body spring up like a jack-in-the-box?"
2. "Why did some of you go higher than the other boys and girls?"

#### Enrichment

Poem:

Do you have something well hidden from view
That helps you jump when you tell it to?
Sometimes it helps you jump so high
You think you'll almost reach the sky!

# JACK-IN-THE-BOX

LOUISE B. SCOTT

LUCILLE F. WOOD
Adapted by K. BAYLESS

"Jack-in-the-Box," from SINGING FUN by Louise Binder Scott and Lucille Wood, copyright 1954 by Bowmar Publishing Corp. and used with their permission.

## "Pairs"

### Concepts

1. Pairs
2. Set of two

### Learnings

The children will

1. Identify a set of two and discover that a pair is a set of two things
2. Apply the concept of pairs and discover that a pair is two similar items
3. Apply the story of *One Mitten Lewis* to their own experiences

### Materials

1. Book: *One Mitten Lewis* by Helen Kay, published by Lathrop, Lee, and Shepard
2. Song: "Pairs," The Upstarts, Inc. Arranged and adapted by K. Bayless
3. Felt characters from the story of *One Mitten Lewis*
4. Feltboard
5. Paired felt mittens (different sizes and colors)
6. Paired items in a box: earrings, shoes, child-size mittens, socks, scissors, etc.

### Approach

*Teacher or Parent:* "I have a story to tell you about a little boy whose name is Lewis. Lewis had a big problem. Perhaps some of you have had the same kind of problem that Lewis had. Let's find out."

### Procedure

1. Tell the story of *One Mitten Lewis*, placing the felt characters on the feltboard as the story is told.
2. After telling the story, discuss with the children some of their experiences of losing mittens.
3. Ask the children how many mittens it takes to cover both hands.
4. Tell the children there is a special word to describe two mittens that are alike and that it is used in a song they are going to learn. "Listen to the song while I sing it for you."

5. Sing the song. Encourage the children to participate in singing the song after you have sung it a few times.
6. Ask the children if they can think of another pair of something.
7. Continue to add new verses.
8. Remove feltboard figures. Take the small felt mittens from the box and place them in random fashion on the feltboard.
9. Choose children to come to the feltboard and find two mittens that make a pair.
10. Continue to do this until all the mittens are matched in pairs.

*Evaluation*

The children will demonstrate their understanding of a pair and a set of two by:

1. Recalling pairs of things they are familiar with
2. Matching the felt mittens

The children may recall experiences of losing their own mittens and will understand how other people feel when they have lost something that belongs to them.

*Enrichment*
Poem: "The Mitten Song" by Marie Louise Allen

# PAIRS

Words and music by NANCY MACK
Arranged by K. BAYLESS

1. Pairs are things that go to-geth-er___ Go to-geth-er in twos.

Pairs are things that go to-geth-er___ Just like a pair of shoes.

2. Eyes are things that go together    3. Twins are things that go together    4. Mittens are things that go together

Used by permission of Upstarts, Inc., from the publication "Wake Up Beautiful World," Mack and Blum (copyright 1974).
*If octave jump is too great, substitute (F) for (C).

### "Ten Little Frogs"

#### Concept
Numbers as they apply to objects

#### Learnings
After hearing the song, the children will

1. Identify the numerals 5, 4, 3, 2, and 1 as they correlate them with objects or persons
2. Subtract 1 from each number as the song is sung
3. Imitate frogs by jumping into a pool

#### Materials

1. Song: "Ten Little Frogs" by Scott and Wood, which contains ten frogs; in this lesson the number is reduced to five for use with younger children. *For variation:* Teacher or children can remove a felt frog from a feltboard each time the song is sung.
2. 5 felt frogs, 1 felt log, 1 felt pool, 1 feltboard

#### Approach
*Teacher:* "I am going to sing a song for you about frogs. When I finish, let's see if you can tell us how many frogs there are altogether in the song."

#### Procedure

1. Sing the song.
2. Ask children how many frogs are in the song.
3. "If we used children instead of frogs to act out the song, how many children would we need?"
4. Discuss with the children what could be used for a make-believe log, a make-believe pool.
5. Ask for five "frog" volunteers.
6. Tell the children they may sing with you this time. Many of them will not join in. At first, they will be too absorbed in the action and in trying to remember what number comes next as each verse is sung. (*Suggestion:* At the end of each verse, count the number of remaining frogs on the log. Do this until children get accustomed to "taking away" one frog each time.) Encourage those who are not frogs to help sing.

Songs using the subtraction concept should not be used until children have had many experiences with songs using the addition concept.

#### Evaluation

1. Did the children enjoy singing the song and acting it out?
2. Could the children remember to reduce a number each time the song was sung?

# TEN LITTLE FROGS

LOUISE B. SCOTT                                      Adapted by K. BAYLESS

1. Ten lit - tle speck-led frogs, Sat on a speck-led log, Catch-ing some
2. Nine, etc.

most de - li-cious bugs, yum, yum. One jumped in - to the pool,

where it was nice and cool, Then there were nine green speck-led frogs, glub, glub.

Last verse
One little speckled frog, Sat on a speckled log,
Catching some most delicious bugs, yum, yum.
He jumped into the pool, Where it was nice and cool,
Then there were no green speckled frogs, glub, glub.

**"Head, Shoulders, Knees, and Toes"**

*Concept*

Learning to name and identify parts of the body

*Learnings*

The children will

1. Identify and name parts of their bodies as each part is mentioned in the song
2. Relate the parts of a doll's body to their own
3. Experience fast and slow tempi

*Materials*

1. Feltboard
2. Doll character, miniature boy or girl, plus body parts made of felt
3. Song: "Head, Shoulders, Knees, and Toes"—action song

*Procedure*

1. Make up a short descriptive story about a doll or boy or girl figure, naming the parts of the body as you assemble them on the feltboard. (Body parts mentioned in the song are head, shoulders, knees, toes, eyes, ears, mouth, and nose.)

2. Sing the song, pointing to the doll's body parts as they are mentioned in the song.
3. Block the board and remove one part of the body. Have the children guess the part that is missing and name it. Continue to take turns. A child may help remove a body part.
4. Sing the song again, and have the children point to their own body parts.
5. As the children become familiar with the song, increase the tempo. They will enjoy singing the song faster and faster as they point to their body parts mentioned in the song.

*Evaluation*

Were the children able to identify the parts of their bodies mentioned in the song? Were they able to name each part?

*Enrichment*

Poem:

I look in the mirror and guess what I see,
My head, my ears, they're part of me.
And every day I wiggle my toes,
And sometimes you'll find me wiggling my nose.

Song: "Boa Constrictor"—Peter, Paul, and Mommy record
Song: "Head-Shoulders, Baby."

# HEAD, SHOULDERS, KNEES, AND TOES

Action song

Head, shoul-ders, knees, and toes, knees and toes. Head, shoul-ders, knees, and toes, knees and toes and Eyes and ears and mouth and nose, Head shoul-ders, knees and toes, knees and toes.

# HEAD-SHOULDERS, BABY

Action song

1. Head shoul - ders, Ba - by, one, two, three, Head shoul - ders, Ba - by, one, two, three, Head shoul - ders, Head shoul - ders, Head shoul - ders, Ba - by, one, two, three.

Tap head and shoulders in syncopated rhythm and tap or clap on ''one, two, three.'' Add other body parts in sequence such as shoulders, hips; hips, knees; knees, ankles; ankles, toes. If desired, then reverse the actions. For the last verse, sing ''That's the end, Baby, one, two, three.''

**"Mister Wind"** *(rhythmic movement)*

*Concepts*

Wind:

1. Is air set in motion
2. Has the power to carry and push things
3. Can be felt and heard but not seen

*Learnings*

The children will

1. Discover that wind is air set in motion, has the power to carry and push things, and can be felt and heard but not seen

2. Use their imaginations to create their own movements stimulated by discussions about the wind

*Materials*

1. Pictures showing ''winds'' of different strengths at work and play. Include flying kites, wind blowing against an umbrella, storms, sailboats sailing in the water, branches of trees bending in the wind, etc.
2. Poem: ''Who Has Seen the Wind?'' by Christina G. Rossetti
3. Rhythmic participation record: *My Playmate the Wind*, Young People's Records. (This record, which is presently out of production, is a valuable resource.)
4. Song: ''Mister Wind'' by K. Bayless and M. Ramsey

*Approach*

*Teacher or Parent:* Read or say the poem "Who Has Seen the Wind?"

*Procedure*

1. Show and discuss pictures of wind scattering milkweed seeds, a flag flying in the wind, leaves blowing to the ground, storms, kites flying in the sky, etc.
2. Have children blow on their hands. Help them discover that by using their mouths they are making a small wind.
3. Play activity record, *My Playmate the Wind*. Have children find their own spaces and move to the words and music.
4. At another time, permit children to find their own spaces and create their own movements stimulated by "word pictures," music, visuals, poems, records, etc., about the wind.

*Teacher or Parent:*

1. "Pretend that you are a tree. Your arms are the branches. How would you move your branches if the wind were blowing slowly and gently? If it were blowing very hard?
2. Now pretend you are holding onto an umbrella. Suddenly a gust of wind comes along. How would you hold your umbrella so it wouldn't get away from you?
3. The wind is strong and pushing hard on your back. How would you walk?
4. If you were a kite, use your arms and hands to show how the wind might blow you about in the sky."

*Evaluation*

1. Were the children able to create their own rhythmic movements illustrating the effect of wind on people and things?

## MISTER WIND

Words and music by K. BAYLESS

1. Mis - ter Wind, you seem to be So mys - te - ri - ous to me. I can feel and hear you too, But see - ing you I can - not do.

2
You are like a funny clown,
Twirling up and sometimes down,
But you help me fly my kite,
So Mister Wind, you are all right!!

2. Did the children give examples of feeling and hearing the wind?

### Enrichment
Poems

- ''Wind Song''—Lilian Moore
- ''The Wind''—Robert Louis Stevenson
- ''Clouds''—Christina G. Rossetti
- ''The North Wind Doth Blow''—Unknown
- ''To A Red Kite''—Lilian Moore

Songs

- ''The North Wind''—K. Bayless
- ''The Autumn Leaves''—Words and music by A. Harwood, *The Spectrum of Music*

Records

- *Rustle of Spring*—Christian Sinding
- *Autumn Leaves*—Mercer et al.

## Toy Symphony

### Concept
Children becoming appreciative and discriminating listeners by exposure to good music throughout the early years

### Learnings
The children will:

1. Have the opportunity to listen to and appreciate an appropriate piece of musical literature
2. Enjoy the unusual ''toy'' sounds produced with traditional orchestral instruments
3. Experience hearing music that is full of gaiety and happiness
4. Become acquainted with the word *composer*

### Materials

1. Record player
2. Record: *Toy Symphony* by Franz Josef Haydn

### Approach
*Teacher or Parent:*  ''Today we are going to listen to some music that is played by an orchestra.'' (If children are hearing the word *orchestra* for the first time, explain what the word means.) ''You will be surprised when you hear some of the sounds the instruments make.''

### Procedure

1. Play the recording. Expect the children to smile and laugh at some of the unusual ''toy'' sounds.

2. If the children are not too young, play it again so they can begin to identify some of the ''toy'' sounds.
3. Help them understand that certain kinds of music, like this piece, are written to make people feel happy and joyful.
4. Explain to the children that the composer (explain the word *composer*) wrote the music for people to enjoy, particularly for boys and girls like themselves.

### Evaluation

1. Were the children able to identify some of the ''toy'' sounds?
2. Could they recognize parts of the music that delighted them?

### Enrichment

1. *Visuals:* Show illustrations of instruments that were highlighted in the selection.
2. *Resource visitor:* Invite a resource visitor to the room to play some of the instruments. Show children how a musician plays some of the unusual sounds heard in the selection.
3. *Musical recording:* Use *March of the Toys* by Victor Herbert, played by the Philadelphia Orchestra, Eugene Ormandy conducting.

## Loud and Soft

### Concept
Musical tones played soft or loud (dynamics)

### Learnings
The children will

1. Understand that music can be played using different dynamics, such as soft and loud
2. Be able to recognize and distinguish parts of music that are played soft and loud
3. Understand the following words: *concerts* and *orchestra conductor*
4. Gain an appreciation for fine music

### Materials

1. Record player
2. Record: *Symphony No. 94 in G Major* by Franz Josef Haydn, *Surprise Symphony,* second movement
3. Piano
4. Tape recorder (Previous to the lesson, tape sounds that are played softly and then loudly. For example, play a drum softly. Wait a few seconds and then play it loudly. Tape other sounds in the same manner.)

### Approach

Play the tape. Have children distinguish when the drum is played softly and when it is played loudly. Do the same with chords on the piano. Ask the children to touch their heads with their hands when the sound is soft. Ask them to raise their hands very high when the sound is loud.

### Procedure

1. Tell the story of why Mr. Haydn wrote the music. (It is not certain that this story is factual.) "Mr. Haydn was a very famous composer. He also conducted an orchestra that played concerts for people. These concerts were often attended by the King. Sometimes the King would fall asleep and snore while the music was being played. This made Mr. Haydn very unhappy. So he decided to write some music that would make the King wake up. Let's listen to the music and find out how Mr. Haydn did it."
2. Play Haydn's *Symphony No. 94 in G Major.* (Play only the part where the theme begins softly and ends with a loud, abrupt chord.)
3. Play it again. Discuss which part is soft, which is loud. Have the children clap once on the very loud, surprise chord.

### Evaluation

1. Were the children able to identify the soft part and the very loud chord?
2. Did they remember to clap once on the loud, surprise chord?
3. Could they explain the following words: *concerts* and *orchestra conductor?*

### Enrichment

#### I Love Music

Sometimes the music gets so loud
I feel my heart just pound
And then it gets so very soft
I hardly hear a sound.

I like to open and close my eyes
While pretty music plays,
Right away my feet join in
They tap, tap, tap this way.

Then before I know it
My hands are clapping too,
My whole self seems to feel it
I love it so, don't you?

BETH FRAZIER

## Skating Movement

### Concept

Sliding feet alternately and smoothly over the floor (ice-skating motion)

### Learnings

The children will:

1. Make movements with their bodies as if they were skating on ice
2. Have the opportunity of hearing music in ¾ rhythm and adjusting their gliding movements to the rhythm
3. Be careful to use their own spaces and not bump into their neighbors
4. Hear that the first beat in ¾ rhythm is accented more than the second and third beats

### Materials

1. Record player
2. Record: *The Skater's Waltz* by Emil Waldteufel
3. Pair of ice skates

### Approach

*Visual:* Show picture of children skating on ice. Have children tell what is happening in the picture.

### Procedure

1. Hold up a pair of ice skates. Discuss such things as: "Why are ice skates difficult to stand on?" "What is the name of the part of the ice skate you stand on?" (blade)
2. *Teacher or parent:* "We are going to pretend that we are skating on ice. Instead of using real ice skates we are going to use pretend ones. Before we skate we are going to listen to some skating music."
3. Play the record.
4. After hearing the selection, have children glide to the music in skating fashion. The waltz has such a pronounced rhythm that it should not take the children long to be able to glide smoothly in rhythm.

### Humor

#### Concept

Children can develop an appreciation for humor through an acquaintance with nonsense songs and rhymes.

#### Learnings

The children will

1. Develop an appreciation for good humor and nonsensical rhymes
2. Have an opportunity to sing and move to nonsense songs
3. Discuss why absurd situations are funny and if they could really take place
4. Create additional, absurd verses to the song "Old Joe Clarke"

#### Materials

1. Songs: "Mares Eat Oats," "One Elephant Went Out to Play," "Old Joe Clarke"

#### Approach

Sing or read some of the suggested songs or a funny poem. Absurd, funny pictures can also be shown. Discussion can follow as to why the situations are humorous. Ask the question "Could this really happen?"

#### Procedure

1. Sing the song "Old Joe Clarke." (Only the first half of the song is used as the melody to the second part is much too high for young voices to sing.)
2. Permit the children to dance and move to the music.
3. After singing the second verse, discuss the absurdity of it.
4. Sing and move to the first verse as each additional verse is created.

#### Evaluation

1. Did the children enjoy the humor found in the songs and rhymes?
2. Were the children able to determine the absurdity in the verse?

(*Note:* Authorities say that it is vital, in the lives of children, to help them develop an appreciation for good humor.)

## OLD JOE CLARKE

American folk song
Adapted by K. BAYLESS

1. Round and round, old Joe Clarke, Round and round I say,

Round and round, old Joe Clarke, I ain't got long to stay.
(don't have)

2. Old Joe Clarke he had a house, Sixteen stories high,
Ev'ry story in that house Was full of chicken pie.

## KEY IDEAS

1. Music is basic to the young child's day.
2. Enjoyment and appreciation are primary goals for including music in the young child's day.
3. The use of music enhances the flow of language as well as fluency and extension of language.
4. Research evidence indicates that there is a relationship between music and the development of reading skills.
5. Through careful selection of songs, science concepts can be extended and clarified.
6. Number learning can now be enjoyed through use of nursery rhymes and songs, jingles, and poetry.
7. Every area of the social studies curriculum can be expanded and illustrated through the use of songs.
8. Musical opportunities abound throughout the day and the curriculum. Seek them out.
9. Adults establish a musical environment through enthusiasm, participation, and flexibility.

## SUMMARY

Music is a part of the daily lives of all children. Teachers and care givers have virtually unlimited opportunity to seek out music resources to enhance the study of language, science, numbers, and social studies.

Research evidence supports the use of music to develop language, expand vocabulary, and enhance reading skills. Music naturally attracts the attention of children and leads to increased fluency in communication as they sing favorite melodies.

Adults working with young children should seek out a wealth of music resources to incorporate into activities for children in their daily lives. Begin a collection of a broad variety of songs, chants, and poetry, and a collection of tapes, records, and texts.

## QUESTIONS TO CONSIDER

1. Give examples of songs illustrative of the basic concepts presented in the opening paragraphs of the chapter.
2. Music offers unique possibilities to expand and extend vocabulary. Select six songs that present unusual vocabulary appealing to children.
3. Describe how the following song from an 1852 songbook could expand vocabulary and enhance listening skills, perceptual awareness, and movement.

### *Country Music**

| | |
|---|---|
| The cock is crowing; | The brook is babbling; |
| The cows are lowing; | The geese are grubling; |
| The ducks are quacking; | The barn-door creaking; |
| The dogs are barking; | Sally is churning; |
| The mule is braying; | The grindstone turning; |
| The horse is neighing; | John is sawing; |
| The sheep are baa-ing; | Willie hurrahing; |
| The boys are ha-ha-ing. | The peacock screeching; |
| The birds are singing; | And Carrie teaching; |
| The bells are ringing; | Amid all the noise. |

*Ward, Mary O. *Songs for Little Ones at Home*. American Tract Society: New York, 1852, pp. 63–64.

4. Select at least two songs that might be used to integrate music and math, music and science, music and social studies, music and reading skills, music and art.
5. Prepare a bulletin board featuring music and one of the curriculum areas.
6. Describe what in your opinion is the best example of children's television programming incorporating music.
7. List your ten favorite children's songs. What children's book could extend each one?

## REFERENCES AND SUGGESTED READINGS

Cohen, Dorothy H., and Rudolph, Marguerita. *Kindergarten and early schooling.* Englewood Cliffs, N. J.: Prentice-Hall, 1977.

Cowen, John E. (ed.) *Teaching reading through the arts.* Newark, N. J.: International Reading Association, 1983.

Duke, C. R. "Integrating reading, writing and thinking skills into the music class," *The Journal of Reading,* November 1987, 31(2), pp. 152–157.

Duntschin, J. W. "Music across the curriculum: More than just circle time." *Day Care Early Education,* Winter 1987, 15(2), pp. 22–25.

Evans, David. *Sharing sounds.* London: Longman Ltd, 1978.

Feeney, Stephanie; Christensen, Doris; and Moravcik, Eva. *Who am I in the lives of children?* 3rd ed. Columbus, Ohio: Merrill, 1987.

Fountas, Irene C., and Hannigan, Irene L. "Making sense of whole language: The pursuit of informed teaching." *Childhood Education,* Spring 1989, 65(3), pp. 133–137.

Hall, W. Vann. "Bob Dorough: Academic hipster mixes math and music." *Music Educators Journal,* November 1985, 72(3), pp. 28–30.

Hendrick, Joanne. *Total learning: Development curriculum for the young child.* 2nd ed. Columbus, Ohio: Merrill, 1986.

Hitz, Randy. "Creative problem solving through music activities." *Young Children,* January 1987, 42(2), pp. 12–17.

Jalongo, M. R., and Bromley, K. "Developing linguistic competence through song picture books." *The Reading Teacher,* May 1984, 37(9), pp. 840–845.

Lapp, Diane, and Flood, James. *Teaching reading to every child,* 2nd ed. New York: Macmillan, 1983.

Martin, Bill, Jr. *Sounds of our heritage.* New York: Holt, Rinehart and Winston, 1976.

Maxim, George W. "Music." In *The very young: Guiding children from infancy through the early years,* pp. 405–417. Belmont, Calif.: Wadsworth, 1980.

Nadon-Gabrion, Catherine. "Language, a bridge to learning in movement and music." *Theory into Practice: Teaching the Arts,* Autumn 1984, 23(4), pp. 335–339.

Phoenix, C. Y. "Music motivators: Rappin'; rhymin'; and rhythm." *Learning,* October 1986, 86(2), p. 80.

Piper, D. "Language growth in the multiethnic classroom." *Language Arts,* January 1986, 63(3), pp. 23–36.

Roberts, John A. "Music is everyday." In *It's music!,* Marjorie E. Ramsey (ed.). Wheaton, Md.: Association for Childhood Education International, 1984.

Shehan, P. K. "World music: Window to cross-cultural understanding." *Music Educators Journal,* November 1988, 75(3), pp. 22–26.

Sholtys, Kathryn Cullen. "A new language, a new life." *Young Children,* March 1989, 44(3), pp. 76–77.

Smardo, Frances A. "Using children's literature as a prelude of finale to music experiences with young children," *The Reading Teacher,* April 1984, 37(8), pp. 700–705.

Smith, John A. "Enhancing reading instruction with music." *The Reading Teacher,* February 1984, 37(6), pp. 550–551.

Starkey, M. A. "Do-re-mi in art." *School Arts,* May 1986, 85(9), pp. 23–36.

Taylor, Barbara J. *A child goes forth,* 5th ed. Provo, Utah: Brigham Young University Press, 1980.
_____.*When I do, I learn,* 5th ed. Provo, Utah: Brigham Young University Press, 1980.

Winshon, P. M. "Facilitating oral languages competence: The natural ingredients." *Childhood Education,* December 1986, 63(2), pp. 91–94.

Zinar, Ruth. *Music in your classroom.* West Nyack, N. Y.: Parker Publishing Company, 1983.

# CHAPTER SEVEN

# Music for Children with Special Needs

"It's not that easy being green, When green is all there is to be" sang our favorite Kermit the Frog as he appeared at the First International Very Special Arts Festival, From the Heart, at the Kennedy Center, Washington, D.C., Sunday, September 10, 1989, featured on NBC. Kermit echoed the theme for the vibrant and thrilling appearances of many celebrities—Kenny Rogers, Laureen Bacall, Jim Henson, Senator Edward Kennedy, Jean Kennedy Smith, and others—who introduced special children and their musical talents.

America responded to the music, which cut across all barriers. We responded

- to the blind pianist—"If you want to know me, know my music."
- to the artist and his painting—"It might not be art, but then again it might."
- to the visually impaired and blind dancers of the New Visions Dance Project of New York City
- to the guitarist from Nicaragua, a former thalidomide baby, playing the guitar with his toes
- to Jean Kennedy Smith's belief that "everyone is differently able"
- to the actress Ellen Burstyn, who expressed her belief "disabled people are not unable . . . all they need is a fair opportunity to develop their gifts"
- to the wheelchair-bound young girl "dancing with Zina Bethune"
- to the gifted performer of the Access Theatre who has dystonia, a muscular disease, yet shared his writing and insights.

There were many faces of creativity. All shared the same dream—that art (music) can take you anywhere, that it is the great enabler. The essence of the human spirit was displayed through music; the vibrancy and joy were electric.

It is with that same electric and enthusiastic spirit that those of us who work with all children ensure that music is a vital core of the activities that occupy each day. We recall Eisner's elegant comment (1979), "Each child, so to speak, is a custom job." We remember to think first of the child, separate from his or her fellows, then of differences and likenesses among all children. The key to working with any child is to know his or her areas of strength and build upon them, as a part of the total life pattern. Learning for children should be a holistic process—they are not compartmentalized.

## LEAST RESTRICTIVE ENVIRONMENT

Many authorities, writing of children with special needs, stress the importance of a least restrictive environment for providing the best opportunities for learning. Certainly, this should be the goal for all children. The authors take the position that anyone responsible for the well-being of children is presumed to have a solid and thorough knowledge of human growth and development and to build upon that knowledge.

A least restrictive environment is achieved first by realistically assessing one's own skills, attitudes, and abilities, as well as one's breadth of knowledge regarding children with special needs. If there are gaps in information, excellent textbooks and articles in popular and professional journals enrich understanding. Observation of children, talking to others whose daily work involves special children, or working on a one-to-one basis with a child who needs extra attention will quickly build one's confidence and capacity to recognize the special abilities or disabilities.

A least restrictive environment infers a variety of instructional styles. Some children will show a preference for a particular sensory modality; some learn at a slower pace than others; some are more easily distracted; some respond more readily to visual cues and some to action cues. We need to expand our repertoire, learn as much as possible about the nature of special needs, and then adapt our techniques to the individual child.

A least restrictive environment also provides a broad variety of materials and manipulatives, carefully selected for an advantageous ''fit'' between child and media. In this multimedia world of VCRs, cassette tapes, recorders, books, instruments, musical toys, puppets, satellites, and networking, the primary task is one of screening and selecting the best in music for children with special needs.

We must look with a critical eye at the work and play space of the child with special needs. What are the elements that facilitate and enhance learning? Which elements inhibit and frustrate? Is there a cacophony of sound, glaring color, distractions? Is the environment one in which participation and appreciation of music will flourish? Will music provide a socializing factor and develop individual skills regardless of limiting conditions? Perhaps the reader will define least restrictive environment in a new light.

As a music resource, this text cannot develop fully the range of exceptionality exhibited by the children one might encounter in a classroom, day care center, nursery school, or other child care environment. In most situations, the number of such children is small. Typically, a teacher/care giver might ask, ''What activities are appropriate for all the children who are my responsibility?'' or ''What modifications or adaptations are useful for special children?'' Usually the major modification needed is slower pacing in a more structured setting. Careful observation of special children and their behavior pattern is a given. How might an adult's creative abilities be used with this particular child to use music in the daily routine? There are aspects of music that can be enjoyed and learned by any child, regardless of handicapping condition. The current trend of placing the exceptional child with normal children in regular classrooms and social groups should ensure that these children will derive the benefits of music in a natural setting. Music offers the potential for growth that recognizes no handicap.

The basic areas of singing, rhythms, informal use of instruments, and music listening experiences are a part of the music education of all children. For the child with special needs, different techniques might be applied, but whatever the method, working on a one-to-one basis or in small groups is strongly recommended. Determine what works, then adapt and refine.

Children in a music setting show the following responses:

- sheer fun and enjoyment
- attentive listening
- increased attention span
- participation with others
- relaxed demeanor
- a cooperative spirit

- nonverbal exchanges such as smiling, foot tapping, finger snapping, clapping, keeping time, swaying, rocking
- more fluent language and speech clarity

The needs of the exceptional child are not unlike those of the normal child. They include a need for

- security
- self-respect and gratification
- love and affection
- movement
- positive interpersonal relationships
- a sense of belonging, worth, and acceptance
- a feeling of accomplishment and contribution

Music can play a major part in satisfying these needs. However, specific uses of music must be determined for individual children.

Particularly with special children, teachers must be patient, realistic about the rate of progress, and supportive, providing reliable feedback to reinforce self-concepts and successful efforts. Ego support is paramount. Recognize that there are more similarities than differences between handicapped and nonhandicapped children and that all conditions have a range of severity. Plan your musical activities accordingly. Let your daily encounters with the children reflect your understanding. Continue to build your professional knowledge background regarding special needs.

## GENERAL SUGGESTIONS FOR CHILDREN WITH SPECIAL NEEDS

Teachers who work with children with special needs should include the following musical activities in their programs:

- Songs of identification: names, families, pets
- Favorite songs: ''Happy Birthday,'' ''Good Morning,'' television jingles, rhymes, family favorites
- Action songs involving specific body parts and motions: clapping, hopping, and nodding
- Circle games
- Humorous songs or those with surprises
- Special day songs on holidays
- Songs that can incorporate rhythm instruments such as drums, bells
- Songs utilizing balls, puppets, scarves
- Songs with a definite rhythm
- Songs that require the following of directions
- Name exercises in songs

## GOOD TEACHING TECHNIQUES

Teachers should use the following good techniques:

- Use many different approaches with a variety of media; vary level and pace

- Use small segments
- Build familiarity, give experience
- Provide a choice of activities
- Offer levels of difficulty
- Recognize differences in attention span
- Avoid overstimulation, lengthy activity
- Remember balance of activities
- Inform, avoid surprises
- Build success

Remember, children will show the way!

## MUSIC FOR SPECIAL NEEDS

Most authorities consider the physically disabled, those with visual and hearing impairments, those with speech and language disorders, the mentally retarded, the learning disabled, the gifted, and those with behavior and emotional disorders to have special needs. Deiner (1983) adds the culturally distinct.

### Physically Disabled Children

Physical disabilities include cerebral palsy, spina bifida, multiple sclerosis, poliomyelitis, and other neurological impairments and convulsive disorders (Hallahan and Kauffman, 1986). Children with such limitations must cope with a restriction of mobility. In these cases the attitude of the adult is crucial in promoting achievement.

Singing offers relaxation and eases tension. Rhythms, too, can be enjoyed if the child can manage lightweight, simple instruments such as sticks, bells, sand blocks, tambourines, or drums. Sometimes body rhythms such as nodding, swaying, moving the upper body, and tapping fingers and hands are possible. Some physical therapists do mat exercises with music. Simple fingerplays set to music offer opportunities for musical appreciation and enrichment and the release of pent-up feelings. Coordination and control will often improve and muscles strengthen through use of rhythms.

It is productive for the adult working with a physically handicapped child to consult with other individuals involved: the therapist, the physician, and certainly the parent. Adaptations in programming in the music environment may be helpful. Keep in mind that children with multiple handicaps may withdraw into themselves and operate within a small radius. They may have problems with laterality and directionality; concepts such as *up, down, over, under,* and *around* may confuse them. Music can be used quite successfully to help the children master these concepts. Those with multiple handicaps may take part peripherally, and security soon builds because there is no right or wrong in music and no competition.

A relatively large group of children suffer from *cerebral palsy*. In cerebral palsy, damage to the central nervous sys-

tem affects one side of the body or the entire body. Speech and language are sometimes impaired. The adult care giver must respond to the needs of each child and adapt the music participation level correspondingly.

*Muscular dystrophy* may present other problems as muscles slowly deteriorate. Singing and movement through rhythmic activities should be encouraged.

*Spina bifida, arthritis,* and *epilepsy* may be slight or advanced in young children under adult care. Problems with gross motor activities, locomotion, and control may limit participation. A child with arthritis, in particular, may have difficulty using rhythm instruments or being involved in simple dances. Movement is beneficial, but check for signs of pain or discomfort in the child. It is important to provide ample time for rest and relaxation for children with these handicapping conditions. Remember the therapeutic quality of music and its power to soothe and relax.

For children with limited mobility or loss of mobility in limbs or extremities, some adaptations can be made in music activities and simple musical instruments to enable children to experience the joy of music and the well-being that results from participation.

*Neurologically handicapped children* are often described on the basis of their actions, and their disorder can be confused with many others. Behaviors are nearly always exaggerated, extreme, and persistent.

1. Rigidity (wanting everything to be as always, for example, the same song or the same key and tempo; disturbed and disoriented by change)
2. Hyperactivity (irritable attention; paying too much attention to everything; unable to distinguish between important and less important)
3. Emotional lability (exhibiting inappropriate and extreme expressions, laughter)

Those working with the neurologically handicapped report that such children often respond strongly to music. For many, music is the first medium that holds their attention.

### Children with Visual and Hearing Impairments

Children with *visual impairment*, those who read and write in Braille, or those who are able to read enlarged print can particularly profit from music activity because they may not be able to participate in other art forms. Through music these children may venture into new activity and explore a larger world. Young children with visual impairment require little in the way of special adaptation to music activities; auditory and primary learning styles can be employed. Auditory memory can be enhanced through music. Concrete experiences and tactile aids should be provided, especially exploration of the rhythm instrument and opportunities to touch and to play other instruments. Do not forget the tape recorder, the record player, and the many excellent records now available. Resources offered by the American

Printing House for the Blind in Louisville, Kentucky, and Recording for the Blind in New York City are valuable to the adult planning activities for these special children.

Many blind children are now enjoying keyboard instruments as well as rhythm instruments. Contemporary piano music is available in Braille. The popular music star Stevie Wonder is an excellent role model for children with vision handicaps.

*Hearing impaired children* need exposure to music activities that help promote flexibility, relaxation, and hearing activity. They profit from sitting close to the adult, to modification of sound volume, and to the use of visual stimuli. The social stimulation of music and the sense of belonging to the group can be invaluable.

Deaf children can participate in rhythmic activities, folk dances, and keyboard experiences. Ballet and simple folk dances are recommended as well as the use of piano, cymbals, records, accordion, guitar, and chord organ. The harp or Autoharp can offer an unusual experience; have the children touch the vibrating strings and put their ears against the instrument to "hear" the music. Headsets can be used to amplify the music to develop concepts of loud and soft, near and far, and high and low. Playing musical instruments also increases muscle strength and joint motion and develops coordination.

Singing may be enjoyed by both hearing and hearing impaired children. Encourage the hearing impaired to use their bodies wholeheartedly in many rhythmic experiences.

Deaf children can be helped to learn nursery rhymes by emphasizing the tactile sense—placing their fingers on the lid of the piano to feel vibrations or sitting on the floor near the piano or the drum. Remove the front of the piano to permit children to see the action.

Much repetition is necessary for deaf children to feel the rhythm. Strong rhythmic actions such as marches, hopping, and skipping can make music a personal experience for them. These actions also improve body coordination and speech rhythm. When we consider the magnitude of the handicap of deafness, we can see why music is not always emphasized. Clear speech is of paramount importance to deaf children; thus involvement in music can be extremely beneficial. Songs, chants, choral speaking, and poetry put into rousing folk songs and country music all offer avenues of expression and possibilities for speech and language development. Further investigation should encourage the expansion of musical opportunities for the deaf.

The music classroom can serve as an excellent vehicle for the integration of hearing impaired and hearing children; it offers enjoyment for all.

## Children with Speech and Language Disorders

A *speech-deficient* child needs singing—its phrasing, rhythm, and emphasis. Music sharpens the ear and aids the development of focused and listening skills.

Nearly two-thirds of the children who are speech impaired suffer from articulation defects. When they speak or sing, sounds are distorted, substituted, or omitted, the most common being the *d*, *l*, *r*, and *s*. Songs that incorporate these sounds in a kind of speech game are useful.

Sing, sing,
Say your name.
Sing, sing, sing,
All the same.

La, la, la,
Sing, sing, sing.
La, la, la,
Ring, ring, ring.

La, la, la,
Ding, dong, ding.
La, la, la,
Sing, sing, sing.

Sally, Sally, Sally,
Sing your name.
Sally, Sally, Sally,
Say your name.

Ring around the rosies,
Sing your name.
Ring around the rosies,
Play the game.

Select songs of reasonable length and difficulty. Teach a song in phrases. Have the children listen and then repeat each phrase. Because articulation and listening are most important, be a good model in speaking and singing.

Cleft-palate speech, delayed speech, and stuttering are other defects in which music may alleviate distress through relaxation of the muscles and vocal chords. Often severe stutterers can sing without stuttering and yet stutter when speaking. Mel Tillis of "Hee-Haw" is a good role model.

Many of the traditional, simple songs of early childhood offer excellent memory and speech training opportunities. The repetition, lively movement, and humor of such rhymes as "Three Blind Mice," "Row, Row, Row Your Boat," "Baa, Baa, Black Sheep," "This Old Man," "Pop Goes the Weasel," "Old MacDonald Had a Farm," "Ten Little Indians," "One, Two, Buckle My Shoe," and "Shoo, Fly" make these songs particularly good for nonverbal children. In fact, adults working with speech-deficient children might deliberately select songs that promote strong language and speech development. Even television commercials, jingles, and popular songs are appealing. Watch a group of young children enjoying and participating in "Sesame Street" or Saturday morning cartoons. Even the youngest quickly learns the sprightly tunes; these tunes encourage speech production. Use pictures to illustrate the songs, or experiment with choral verse in which children participate as one. Tape the child's voice as he or she speaks and sings and then play the tape back for him or her to encourage speech production.

*Autistic* children may also benefit from the qualities of music. Such children appear to be oblivious and unaware of surroundings; music may break through this barrier. Often such a child will rock to music, sing or hum, or follow along with the singer. Usually autistic children require a one-to-one learning situation and progress is slow. There is some evidence that autistic children tend to prefer just a few types of music, which are simple and repetitive in nature. Often one-syllable verbal instructions, one-gesture signs, moving and speaking in synchrony with the child, and adapting a rhythm to that of the child increase attention and learning. Much remains to be investigated in discovering the causes of autism. We believe music may add a dimension to the life of an autistic child.

*Aphasic* children, whose power to use or understand language is lost or impaired, seem to find new interest and strengthened morale through singing and rhythms. Simple, repetitive songs with strong emotional appeal should be selected for the autistic and aphasic child. From infancy on, participation in music builds good speech habits and patterns and provides the exceptional child with a comfortable and enjoyable means of learning to alleviate deficiencies. Aphasic children often reveal extreme physical rigidity, depression, and withdrawal. Movement and rhythmic activity tend to relax and give vitality to these children.

## Culturally Distinct Children

The *culturally different* or *culturally distinct* child is also considered a child with special needs. The opportunities presented to the teacher/care giver to use music to promote communication and participation among these children are many. Penny Deiner's *Resources for Teaching Young Children with Special Needs* (1983) offers excellent suggestions and activities for integrating music into the lives of children from different cultures. Celebration of special holidays of ethnic groups, using folk and popular songs of Americans, demonstration of musical styles of different cultures, exposure to a variety of traditional instruments—maracas, castanets, bagpipes, drums, flutes, dulcimers, lute, harpsichord, and mandolin, to name a few—will create excitement and develop appreciation for the richness of the many family groups in our midst. The UNICEF resource, ''Musical Instruments of the World'' is excellent.

Language differences and dialects also find a place in musical selections. It is important to remember that most of the behavior patterns children learn are related to the family and to the culture. Keep in mind that children labeled verbally deficient may simply be using language in their own way to fit the situation. The adult who is well informed about the backgrounds of children in the group will understand passivity on the part of some, nonverbal responses from others, fear of failure, bilingual exchanges, etc. Some will seldom volunteer and others will not look directly at adults. Children bring with them a wide range of family and cultural expectations. Learning to sing or play an instrument can have significant long-term value to a child with limitations in language or social functioning.

Music is everywhere, and therein lies its appeal. It can cross the boundaries that separate cultures and nationalities; it can transcend emotional differences. There is some form of musical expression attractive to each child. We need to develop awareness of both cultural differences and similarities. Often adults in the community can be used as resource persons to share the folk music, dances, musical instruments, and even some of the rhythms of a language ''strange'' to the ears.

Young children learn quickly and are eager for new experiences. If made to feel comfortable, they will often participate willingly in small groups. They strive to please. The culturally different child can thrive and blossom in the nonpunitive, nonthreatening atmosphere music provides.

Deiner (1983) offers the following insight:

> Just as there is no one white American culture, there is also no one Asian American, black American, Hispanic American, or native American culture (pp. 242–243).

The role of the teacher is to discover differences, appreciate them and incorporate such learnings into the daily lives of children. Music can be a valuable aid in achieving such goals. Music is particularly useful in enhancing adult/ child and peer/peer interaction (Nelson et al. (1984).

## INTELLECTUAL DIFFERENCES AND MUSIC

The slow learner, the gifted, the perceptually handicapped, and the severely retarded can all profit from musical activities. Early identification of these special differences can facilitate planning appropriate programs for each. Guidance and support from adults provide the contact, security, and encouragement necessary for these and all children. Music has a unique value; it develops self-confidence and opens up channels of communication.

Authorities agree that music experiences should begin at the earliest possible age; some say even before birth! Teachers and parents should seek every opportunity to provide stimulating musical experiences. The child then learns to value music by anticipating enthusiasm and excitement, thus growing musically as well as socially.

*Slow learners* and *mentally challenged* children need simple songs. Find songs appropriate to the age level and use illustrative and repetitive materials. Encourage the children to imitate and then to sing along. There are many so-called mentally retarded children who participate wholeheartedly in music, particularly if the songs are family favorites. These family tunes and even television jingles are useful in developing attentiveness, coordination, listening ability, and vocabulary growth.

Old favorites such as ''I'm a Little Teapot,'' ''Humpty Dumpty,'' ''Hickory, Dickory, Dock,'' ''Sing a Song of Sixpence,'' ''Little Miss Muffet,'' and ''Little Bo-Peep'' can be introduced with colorful illustrations and movements to facilitate learning. For the slow learner who is very young, music can strengthen memory and concentration, thus promoting achievement.

Drums, resonator bells, cymbals, zithers, and Autoharps can be used. Music with short phrases and repeated tones is suggested. Keep selections brief, varying the length with age and ability of the group. Wrist bells, sticks, wood blocks, and triangles can be used to develop eye–hand coordination. Strong melody appeals, mixing rhythm instruments and singing, however, are not advised for these children.

The rate of development in the retarded child is uneven. Background is acquired at a slower pace, and musical experiences need to be repeated more often and in many different ways. Never be discouraged while working with the retarded child. Responses may be hidden.

The retarded child's attention span will be short. Singing, playing instruments, and moving to music is enjoyed. Rote learning of songs, repetition, melody, and a sequential presentation are usually successful. Visual aids and devices for manipulation are useful and add to understanding and enjoyment. Try both instrumental and vocal media.

Rocking the body to music, clapping, and brisk marching can be demonstrated and then enjoyed. A song such as "Row, Row, Row Your Boat," is appealing. "Jack Be Nimble" can be chanted and acted out. Short phrases, familiar topics, a strong rhythm, and repetition are most successful. Many authorities suggest that singing be the focal point for these children. Give them ample opportunity to sing, and emphasize enjoyment. The record player, tape player, piano, and chord organ have all found a place in the lives of retarded children.

Creativity, ingenuity, understanding, and patience, coupled with a wide variety of musical activities, can enrich the lives of both adult care givers and the slow learner as they work together.

Another group of children with special needs has been identified—those with *learning disabilities* or *perceptually handicapped* children. A learning disability (LD) is a subtle problem not as easily discovered as a physical handicap. Usually found in a child with a normal or higher IQ, it is a malfunctioning or immaturity of the central nervous system that affects the child's ability to receive, organize, store, and transmit information. Such a child may show deficiencies in auditory or visual learning, may have difficulty with concentration, coordination, directionality, memory, and shutting out details, and may display inconsistent performance. Often children with learning disabilities do not develop language and communication skills as rapidly as their peers.

Many children labeled hyperactive, immature, or unstable may, in fact, have perceptual problems. Often the behavior of these children is misunderstood, and they may exhibit aggressiveness, withdrawal, or other social maladjustment.

The child with learning disabilities may well experience difficulty with music—performing with instruments, maintaining attention, or remembering melody lines. He or she may also have difficulty doing two things at once, for example, singing and playing, clapping and singing, or swaying and singing. Every music opportunity should include a variety of simple tasks such as movement, rhythm, or singing. However, emphasis on enjoyment of music provides a common ground and basis for success.

The same music may not soothe all individuals. Some children will respond favorably, others adversely. The reactions of each child are unique.

Make it possible for these children to experience music with their whole bodies whenever possible. Talk through all activities to be sure there is no misunderstanding. Demonstrate actions and new vocabulary when feasible. Carefully check the activity level and the total room environment for distractions. Frustration may be a problem, as these children are easily discouraged at their inability or slowness in mastering an activity. Enjoyment, humor, and simplicity are desired goals.

Because music is highly structured and noncompetitive, many children can thrive within the music environment. Be aware of and capitalize upon the fact that music activities can serve as a catharsis for anger, frustration, hyperactivity, and depression. All of us have experienced times when we have been upset, disorganized, or overburdened, and music has lifted our spirits or made things right.

*Gifted* children will usually want to extend music activities, to experiment with a variety of instruments, to develop record and tape collections, to enjoy hearing musicians, to learn about the lives of the performers, and to emulate the stars of the day. Often gifted children can be precocious with melody or composing. However, the musically talented child should enjoy the normal activities suited to any young child. Outside the school setting, children gifted musically may be deeply involved in performance and practice. We need to avoid exploiting or displaying such a child.

There are no special procedures for the gifted child and music—all approaches can be considered. Enrichment activities should be appropriately complex to challenge and stimulate. Quality should be stressed as well as individual initiative. Here is an instance in which the teacher/care giver might well learn from the child as they share music experience, appreciate new selections, and explore new modes. We are not all musicians, but we can all learn from one another.

Most important, parents and other adults need to be aware of resources and enrichment opportunities within the community that will expand the musical interests of the gifted child. Investigate area libraries, theater and dance groups for children, church groups, and civic groups. But remember to consider the child first, the talent second.

*Behavior disordered* and *severely emotionally disturbed* children are usually placed in special group situations. Here again, individual study and observation of particular children is encouraged. Seek out the appropriate resources available in the community; obtain expert opinion and build a personal professional library.

Most authorities agree that music has therapeutic qualities and can be of value in the daily schedule of children with behavior disordered conditions. Special considerations include early prevention with a curriculum similar to that of normal children. There may be wide differences in behavioral characteristics and achievement. The teacher/care giver might well follow the suggestions and activities given in earlier chapters of this text. Experimentation with various types of musical activity, with songs and simple instruments, may encourage this group of children to participate more fully and develop moderated behavior.

A slower rate of progress, a multifaceted approach in learning, a concentration on broad general skills such as listening, speaking, attending, and appreciating should be the rule. As music is inherently stimulating and reinforcing, it can be a powerful educational and therapeutic tool in a least restrictive environment.

Music has a critical role in programming for special children; it can build group spirit and cohesion; it can extend memory; it can offer a much needed place in the spotlight; it can rehabilitate the spirit; it can provide a beginning, an introduction into the world of all children, and a first opportunity to be like others.

## KEY IDEAS

1. Think about "everyone is differently able."
2. Special children differ from normal children only in degree of condition.
3. Like normal intelligent individuals, children with special needs possess varying ranges of musical talent and ability.
4. Music, because it is nonverbal, may be an entree to participation in everyday activity for special children.
5. Music develops self-confidence and opens up expanded language development and channels of communication.
6. Music provides a way for children with special needs to belong to a group and make a positive contribution to it.
7. Music can be a great enabler. It cuts across all barriers—time, age, race, and status.
8. Disabled people are not unable.

## SUMMARY

The goals of music for special children are much the same as those for all other children. Emotional and aesthetic benefits are paramount. Auditory, visual and kinesthetic skills are stressed, as is *quality* of musical experience. Because music is a nonthreatening and nonpunitive medium, its use can open avenues for communication, thus enabling the special child to feel a part of the "real" world. Each child responds in a unique way to music. Children grow in special ways and adapt to their individual need for the benefits and joys of music.

## QUESTIONS TO CONSIDER

1. Due to the increasing numbers of culturally diverse children in our schools, add to your collection at least ten songs appropriate to a typical group setting. Illustrate activities for each song.
2. Select three songs from Chapter Six. Describe how each could be adapted to meet the needs of special learners.

3. Explore the community in which you live. What resources are available for children with special needs? Cite instances where music is a unifying influence.
4. Cite examples of music as a great enabler.
5. How might you use Kermit's opening song with children in your care?
6. What examples can you give of individuals in public life who have overcome limiting physical conditions?
7. Participate in the activities of the Special Olympics in your area. How does this event contribute to community well-being?

## REFERENCES AND SUGGESTED READINGS

Anderson, William M., and Lawrence, Joy E. *Integrating music into classrooms.* Belmont, Calif.: Wadsworth, 1985.

Andress, Barbara, and Boardman, Eunice. *The music box.* New York: Holt, Rinehart and Winston, 1983.

Arnoff, Frances W. *Move with music: Songs and activities for young children.* New York: Turning Wheel Press, 1982.

Bailey, Donald B., Jr., and Wolery, Mark. *Teaching infants and preschoolers with handicaps.* Columbus, Ohio: Merrill, 1984.

Bissett, Donald J. "Poems and verses to begin on." In Book 1: *Poetry and verse for urban children.* San Francisco: Chandler Publishing, 1967.

Blair, John F. *Classroom success for learning disabled.* Winston-Salem, N.C.: John F. Blair, 1984.

Brand, Manny, and Feroric, David E. "Music in early childhood curriculum." *Childhood Education,* May/June 1983, 59(5), pp. 321–326.

Cardareli, Aldo F. *Twenty-one ways to use music in teaching the language arts.* Eric Document 176–268. Evansville Indiana State University, 1979.

Cazden, Courtney B. *Language in early childhood education.* Washington, D.C.: National Association for the Education of Young Children, 1981.

Chinn, Peggy L. "The mentally retarded child during infancy and early childhood." In Phillip C. Chinn, Clifford J. Drew, and D. R. Logan (eds.), *Mental Retardation: A life cycle approach,* pp. 115–135. St. Louis: C. V. Mosby, 1955.

Chukovsky, Kornei. *From two to five.* Translated by M. Morton. Berkeley: University of California Press, 1968.

Coates, Patricia S. "Make Mainstreaming Work." *Music Educators Journal,* Fall 1986, 89, pp. 53–57.

Cohen, Dorothy H., and Rudolph Marguerita. *Kindergarten and early schooling.* Englewood Cliffs, N.J.: Prentice-Hall, 1977.

Cowen, John E. (ed.). *Teaching reading through the arts.* Newark, N.J.: International Reading Association, 1983.

Curtis, Sandra. "Joy of movement." *Day Care and Early Education,* Fall 1984, 12(1), pp. 18–19.

Curtis, S. R.; *The joy of movement in early childhood.* Song Picture Books for Language Disabled Children. *Exceptional Children,* Winter 1984, 16(2), pp. 114–119.

Darrow, Alice Ann. "Music for the deaf." *Music Educators Journal,* Fall 1985, 71, pp. 33–35.

Davis, Gary A., and Rimm, Sylvia B. *Education of the gifted and talented.* Englewood Cliffs, N.J.: Prentice-Hall, 1985.

Davis, Hazel Grubbs. "Reading pressures in the kindergarten." *Childhood Education,* November /December, 1980, 37(2), pp. 76–79.

Day, David E. "The curriculum." *In early childhood education: A human ecological approach,* pp. 246–267. Glenview, Ill.: Scott, Foresman, 1983.

Deiner, Peggy Law. *Resources for teaching young children with special needs.* New York: Harcourt Brace Jovanovich, 1983.

Delisle, James R. *Gifted children speak out.* New York: Walker, 1984.

Dlink, Howard. "Words and music." *Language Arts,* April 1976, 53(4), pp. 401–403.

Duerkesen, George, et al. *Learning packages for the music education of handicapped students.* Lawrence: University of Kansas Department of Art, Music Education and Music Therapy, 1981.

Eastland, Joyce. "Working with the language deficient child." *Music Educators Journal,* November 1980, 67(3), pp. 60–63.

Eisner, Elliott W. *The educational imagination: On the design and evaluation of school programs.* New York: Macmillan, 1979.

Evans, David. *Sharing sounds.* London: Longman Ltd., 1978.

Feeney, Stephanie; Christensen, Doris; and Moravcik, Eva. *Who am I in the lives of children?* 3rd ed. Columbus, Ohio: Merrill, 1987.

Fithiani, Janet (ed.). *Understanding the child with a chronic illness in the classroom.* Phoenix: Oryx Press, 1984.

Flowers, Sister Evelyn. "Musical sound perception in normal children with Down's syndrome." *Journal of Music Therapy,* Fall 1984, 21(8), pp. 146–154.

Gearheart, Bill R. Learning disabilities. In *Educational strategies,* 4th ed. Columbus, Ohio: Merrill, 1985.

Gfeller, K. E. "Musical mnemonics for learning disabled children." *Teaching Exceptional Children,* Fall 1986, 19, pp. 28–30.

Graham, Richard M. "Barrier-free music education: methods to make mainstreaming work." *Music Educators Journal,* January 1988, 75, pp. 29–33.

Graham, Richard M., and Beer, Alice S. *Teaching music to the exceptional child.* Englewood Cliffs, N.J.: Prentice-Hall, 1980.

Hallahan, Daniel P., and Kauffman, James M. *Exceptional children: Introduction to special education,* 3rd ed. Englewood Cliffs, N.J.: Prentice-Hall, 1986.

Hardman, Michael L., Drew, Clifford J.; and Egan, W. Winston. *Human exceptionality: Society, school, and family.* Boston: Allyn and Bacon, 1884.

Hayden, Alice, et al. *Mainstreaming preschool children with learning disabilities.* Washington, D.C.: U.S. Government Printing Office, 1978.

Hildebrand, Verna. "Guiding children's literature, language and music activities." Chapter 14 in *Guiding young children,* 3rd ed. pp. 247–249. New York: Macmillan, 1985.

Jalongo, M. R., and Bromley, K. "Developing linguistic competence through song picture books." *The Reading Teacher,* May 1984, 37(9), pp. 840–845.

Lapp, Diane, and Flood, James. *Teaching reading to every child,* 2nd ed. New York: Macmillan, 1983.

Lasky, Lila, and Mukerjii, Rosa. *Art—Basic for young children.* Washington, D.C.: National Association for the Education of Young Children, 1980.

Lawrence, Marjory. *A beginning book of poems.* Menlo Park, Calif.: Addison-Wesley, 1967.

Lee, Dorris M., and Rubin, Joseph B. *Children and language: Reading and writing, talking and listening.* Belmont, Calif.: Wadsworth, 1979.

Leeper, Sarah Hammond; Witherspoon, Ralph L.; and Day, Barbara. "Creative expression and music and movement." In *Good schools for young children,* 5th ed., pp. 377–417. New York: Macmillan, 1984.

Lloyd, Mavis J. "Teach music to aid beginning readers." *The Reading Teacher,* December 1979, 32(3), pp. 323–327.

Logan, Lillian M., and Logan, Virgil G. "Through poetry to creative reading." *Childhood Education,* February/March 1980, 56(4), pp. 206–209.

Marley, Linda S. "The use of music with hospitalized infants and toddlers." *Journal of Music Therapy,* Fall 1988, 21, pp. 126–132.

Marsh, Mary Val, Rinehart, Carroll; and Savage, Edith. *The spectrum of music.* New York: Macmillan, 1980.

Mathias, Sandra L., and Fango, Mary E. Massa. "Blending reading instruction with music and art." *The Reading Teacher,* February 1977, 30(7), pp. 494–500.

Matter, Darryl E. "Musical development in young children." *Childhood Education,* May/June 1982, 58(5), pp. 305–307.

Maxim, George W. "Music." In *The very young: Guiding children from infancy through the early years.* Columbus, Ohio: Merrill, 1989.

McCarthy, Melodie A., and Houston, John P. *Fundamentals of early childhood education.* Cambridge, Mass.: Winthrop, 1980.

McDonald, Dorothy. "Music and reading readiness." *Language Arts,* September 1975, 52, p. 876.

McDonald, Dorothy, and Ramsey, Jonny H. "Awakening the artist: Music for young children." *Young Children,* January 1978, 33(2), pp. 26–32.

McGinnis, Ellen, and Goldstein, Arnold P. *Skillstreaming the elementary school child: A guide for teaching preschool skills.* Champaign, Ill.: Research Press, 1984.

McGuire, Gary N. "How arts instruction affects reading and language: Theory and research." *The Reading Teacher,* May 1984, 37(9), pp. 835–839.

Michael, Donald E. *Music therapy: An introduction, including music in special education,* 2nd ed. Springfield, Ill.: Charles C. Thomas, 1985.

Moomaw, Sally. *Discovering music in early childhood.* Boston: Allyn and Bacon, 1984.

Morsink, Catherine Voelker. *Teaching special needs students in regular classrooms.* Boston: Little, Brown, and Company, 1984.

*Mother Goose melodies.* New York: Dover, 1970.

Murray, Joseph N., and McLoughlin, Caven S. (eds.). *Childhood disorders: Preschool and early elementary years.* Springfield, Ill.: Charles C. Thomas, 1984.

Nelson, David J., et al. "Music activities as therapy and other pervasive developmental disorders." *Journal of Music Therapy,* Fall 1984, 21, pp. 100–116.

Nye, Vernice Trousdale. *Music for young children,* 3rd ed. Dubuque, Iowa: William C. Brown, 1983.

Ramsey, Marjorie E. (ed.). *It's music!* Wheaton, Md: Association for Childhood Education International, 1984.

Remmington, Lloyd. "Let's get physical in science." *Science and Children,* April 1982, 19(7), pp. 13–17.

Rinehart, Carroll A. "The state of the art. Music: A basic for the 80's." *Childhood Education,* January 1980, 26(3), pp. 140–145.

Roberts, John A. "Music is everyday." In *It's Music!* Marjorie E. Ramsey (Ed.). Wheaton, Md: Association for Childhood Education International, 1984.

Russell, Philippa. *The wheelchair child: How handicapped children can enjoy life to its fullest.* Englewood Cliffs, N.J.: Prentice-Hall, 1985.

Safford, Philip L. *Integrated teaching in early childhood.* White Plains, N.Y.: Longman Inc., 1989.

Saracho, Olivia N. "Mainstreaming: The role of the teacher." *Day Care and Early Education,* Winter 1984, 12(2), pp. 17–23.

Shapiro, Lawrence E. *The new short-term therapies for children.* Englewood Cliffs, N.J.: Prentice-Hall, 1984.

Silver, Larry B. *The misunderstood child: A guide for parents of learning disabled children.* New York: McGraw-Hill, 1984.

Smardo, Frances A. "Using children's literature as a prelude of finale to music experiences with young children." *The Reading Teacher,* April 1984, 37(8), pp. 700–705.

Staum, M. J. "Music rotation to improve the speech prosody of hearing impaired children." *Journal of Music Therapy,* Fall 1987, 24, pp. 146–159.

Tanner, Don R. "Music and the special learner." *Education,* Fall 1980, 101(1), pp. 46–49.

Taylor, Barbara J. *A child goes forth,* 5th ed. Provo, Utah: Brigham Young University Press, 1980.
_____. *When I do, I learn,* 5th ed. Provo, Utah: Brigham Young University Press, 1980.

Taylor, Gail Cohen. "Eric-RCS report: Music in language art instruction." *Language Arts,* March 1981, 58, pp. 363–368.

Tompkins, Gail E., and Tway, Eileen. "Adventuring with words: Keeping language curiosity alive in elementary school children." *Childhood Education,* May/June 1985, 61(5), pp. 363–365.

United Nations Children's Fund. "Musical Instruments of the World." New York: Facts on File Publications, 1976, pp. 264–300.

Westling, David L. *Introduction to mental retardation.* Englewood Cliffs, N.J.: Prentice-Hall, 1986.

Withers, Carl (collector). *Counting-out rhymes.* New York: Dover Publications, 1970.

Worstell, Emma Victor. *Jump the rope jingles.* New York: Collier Books, 1961.

Zinar, Ruth. "Reading, writing and music." *Education Summary,* January 1974, 26(13), p. 8.

# CHAPTER EIGHT

# Music: A Child's Heritage

As the popular American song says, "This land was made for you and me." Wherever children gather—playground, day care center, shopping mall, classroom, amusement park, or city streets, we are struck by their infinite diversity. For children of all shapes and sizes, all ethnic backgrounds, chubby or thin, effervescent or solemn-faced, music appears to create a bond and sense of belonging.

Music brings color, excitement, and joy to the child in a rapidly changing and shrinking world. Whether in city or country, San Jose, Wichita, San Antonio, Tokyo, or Taipei, children are chanting, humming, and improvising tunes, as well as tapping and clapping, shaking and moving to the rhythms of others or themselves. Because music is nonverbal, it constitutes a universal medium for establishing contact, communication, and interaction. Its inherent order and structure provide predictability and a feeling of security (Flowers, 1988).

## A CHANGING AMERICA

Beginning in the early 1900s, America experienced an unprecedented influx of refugees and immigrants attempting to build new lives. Today, increased pressure to relax quotas adds to this national wave of infants, young children, and adults—Vietnamese, Laotians, Hmongs, Cambodians, and large numbers of Amerasians. Our day care centers, kindergartens, and preschool centers reflect this joining of cultures. Hispanic, Greek, Indian, Chinese, Japanese, and Jamaican children contribute to what *Time* called the "changing face of America" (July 8, 1985). "The enormous migration is altering the racial makeup, the landscapes and skyscapes, the food and clothes and music" (pp.

26–27). California, Texas, Florida, Minnesota, and Tennessee, in fact most of the nation's large cities, are feeling the impact of diverse groups of people, many of whom come speaking little English and holding high expectations.

The *Music Educators Journal* (May 1983) describes statistically what it terms the American Ethnic Palette—the statistics that tell us who we are. Any care giver will find that the listing probably typifies the composition of many groups of children on our playgrounds or in our centers.

Jeptha Green (November 1988), speaking to a leadership group, expressed the view that the task of this generation is to strike the creative balance between celebrating the uniqueness of diverse cultures and continuing to create the common culture. She felt the energies of cultural diversity are centripetal; they create more layer cakes than melting pots.

Phillips (1988) reminds us that culture is more than a collection of artifacts and holidays. It is a set of rules for behavior by which we organize and give meaning to the world.

Music can create the bridge to natural understanding and appreciation for this "layer cake" of children with whom we work. Children *are* the carriers of tradition. They share the songs and the music that are part of their heritage. They preserve a vast storehouse of games, songs, chants, and rhymes, and they add, revise, edit, and interpret as the situation warrants.

For the parent, teacher, or care giver who is responsible to the young child, the blending of cultures presents perhaps an unparalleled opportunity to discuss the matrix of cultural values and to tap the richness of the music and customs of each group. Music as a social activity can help cement relationships within groups where children gather, can fos-

ter appreciation and enjoyment of likenesses and differences, and can deepen understanding of who and what we are. Music can become the common denominator that encourages communication among groups of children with diverse backgrounds.

As we encounter children from Africa, the Orient, the Caribbean, the inner city, and Appalachia, we tap the unique resource of their music, which can be shared with other children and lead to a growth in their self-esteem, status, and a sense of worthy contribution to the music of the world. If the music is supplemented with costuming, regalia of all kinds, dance, pictures, and oral history, the classroom can become a spirited and welcoming haven to children seeking to establish a place in a new environment. Fine periodicals such as *National Geographic*, *Smithsonian*, *Travel and Leisure*, *Ranger Rick*, and travel posters from airlines and governmental agencies can further extend learning and appreciation for cultural groups. An offshoot of musical activity to extend further the delight of working and playing with children of diverse groups could be a food festival, which offers cooking and eating, tasting parties, and demonstrations. Picture children sampling tortillas, cornbread, pita bread, leechee nuts, and sushi, then listening to and participating in music and dance representing the

culture from which each food comes. Adults and children alike will cherish the experience!

Garfias (1983) expands our thinking on the multiplicity of musical languages now developing. He feels that music exists in every human society and is fundamental to the nature of humankind. However, it functions in the context of the personal and worldview of each culture—of each society. O'Brien and O'Brien (1984) vividly describe the universality of music and how music is an integral part of the lives of children in several societies. Of singular interest are the examples of musical instruments and the objectives of music education found in each society.

If as care givers we believe that music is for all children, we must in present-day America seriously consider the cultural diversity represented everywhere. To the immigrant groups already described add our native Americans (Indian and Alaskan), the Asian and Pacific Islanders, African Americans, and Hispanic Americans and we have a richness of resources in music never before realized.

## THE CHILD'S MUSIC HERITAGE: FAMILY CUSTOMS

Many authors (Tait and Haack, 1984; Dodds, 1983; Anderson and Lawrence, 1985; May, 1980; Werner and Burton, 1979; Kendall, 1983; Miller and Brand, 1983; Shehan, 1984; and Wilson, 1985) have heightened awareness of the need to emphasize and capitalize upon the music of the many ethnic groups represented in the community. All agree that music adds luster to the lives of young children and that a broad variety of music—ballads, jazz, country, folk, classical, pop, and rock—should be available to children. Interrelationships of music and other aspects of a culture are stressed. A two-pronged approach is needed to nourish an interest in music: developing the talents of those young children showing musical promise, and making every effort to elicit participation from those who either have had limited exposure to music or who appear uninterested in it. Fortunately, most young children, whatever their background, quickly become active in a music environment when adults lead the way. Both the sensitivity of the care giver to the unique qualities of ethnic groups and the willingness to experiment and share the delights of music provide the proper combination for musical leadership.

## BALLADS, FOLK SONGS, OPERA

Many of the ballads and folk songs of ethnic groups provide the opportunity for total participation of lead singer and audience. The singing of songs from Haiti, Jamaica, other West Indian islands, and West Africa, as well as old Louisiana Creole songs, spirituals, anthems, railroad ballads and work songs, melodic calls, and children's ring games, all evoke deep-rooted response patterns. It is as though each singer lives the experience of the other and echoes or affirms mutual feelings; a sense of community is established and shared.

Brown (1983) speaks of preserving Appalachian traditions through hand puppet productions with accompanying ballads. He deplores the loss of the oral tradition and the fact that many contemporary mountain children are virtually unaware of the scope and richness of mountain music. How rewarding it would be for children to share this richness by acting as carriers of traditions!

Folk song traditions in cultures as diverse as France, India, China, and Ghana are easily identified and enjoyed by children as a result of characteristic sound.

Folk music and dance in the United States are a composite of European, African, and Hispanic elements. Folk music combines folk calls, hollers, work songs, rhythmic chants, spirituals, and blues. It includes Mexican mariachi bands, Caribbean salsa music, steel-drum bands from Trinidad, and music of Japanese, Chinese, and Asian origins—a host of musical dialects.

## MUSICAL INSTRUMENTS

An exciting avenue for increasing enjoyment in music and possible participation is through the sharing of musical instruments.

Envision within the schools or the children's center the anticipation engendered from "trying out" the many musical instruments: castanets, recorder, guitar, banjo, ukulele, maracas, reed pipes, bongo drums, Japanese lute,

gamelan, violin, Chinese Er-Hu, steel drum, piano, balalaika, dulcimer, and harp. Guest artists such as fiddlers, limbo dancers, or flutists might well be drawn from the community. Children should be encouraged to interview performers.

The history of musical instruments (UNICEF, 1976) can enrich understanding and appreciation of our diverse heritage. African musicians, notably drummers, are usually trained from a young age. Rattles, xylophones, flutes, trumpets, drums of every type, bows, harps, fiddles, and zithers make the music that permeates almost every aspect of African life.

In the Americas, drums, rattles, flutes, wind instruments, guitars, and the harp were early instruments. The Pueblo Indians played gourd rattles and drums in the Cornhusk dance. The Incas of early times enjoyed the panpipes.

The folk music culture of Europe was rich with the hurdy-gurdy, bagpipes, zither, flute, and accordion. Different countries reflected characteristic musical styles.

Cultural traditions of Islam dominated the music of the Middle East, Northern Africa, and U.S.S.R. Classical musicians commonly used the lute, flute, and drums. India has long cherished the guitar, fiddles, and reed pipes.

Chinese music was a major influence in the Far East. Spike fiddles, gongs, mouth organs, or bamboo pipes accompanied theatrical performances and still do in modern Chinese acrobatic exhibitions. Solo music for lutes, zither, or samisen is also featured.

Indonesian children are familiar with the music of the gamelan, gongs, gong chimes, drums, flutes, and fiddles. Oceania has its stamping sticks, scrapers, drums, trumpets, and folk harps.

We know that the history of musical instruments began many thousands of years ago when early humans first used natural objects as sound makers. In Europe, over twenty-five thousand years ago, the earliest "instruments" were the clapping hands and stamping feet of family groups. Bone, stone, wood, clay, and, later, metal were used for instruments.

Before the arrival of the Europeans, Indian civilizations of Central and South America developed a rich musical culture using flutes, whistles, panpipes, drums, and rattles, but no stringed instruments.

From such early beginnings have come the string groups, cello, trombone, oboe, harpsichord, and modern electric guitar, electric organ, and synthesizers well known to today's children. The military and marching bands with their horns, trumpets, cymbals, and drums add to our heritage. Children and adults alike respond to the stirring musical sounds of bands at sporting events.

If you are near a campus school, plan a field trip to watch band practice or attend a football game. Invite band members to demonstrate instruments or invite a nearby city symphony to participate in an arts festival.

Children gain a sense of belonging and pride when they share a family heritage of music.

## OUR WEALTH OF MUSIC

All over the world people enjoy making music in groups. Consider the wealth of music accessible today. Tait and Haack (1984) state, "At the mere flick of a switch we can hear vast libraries of music from rock to pop, opera to symphony, music from Africa or Asia, and music that is sacred or secular or anything in between. We have musical environments of staggering proportions." How bewildering the music must be to the young child. On a typical Saturday morning, music provides background for cartoons and sells toothpaste and soft drinks. Even on the streets and play-grounds of China, one author was startled to hear the humming of commercial jingles popular in the United States, as well as American jazz.

In the United States, the child is heard humming and chanting nursery rhymes, nonsense verses, jump-rope jingles, and popular music. Often, children will sing songs without knowing the meaning of the lyrics, singing merely what they think they heard. For example, the growth of country music appeals even to the young, who might not understand the words, but nevertheless hear the messages of loneliness, sadness, disappointment, love, and ambition—the age-old themes that reflect every society and cultural group.

From childhood recollection we have savored:

- "Yankee Doodle"
- "Casey Jones"
- "Church in the Wildwood"
- "Swing Low Sweet Chariot"
- "Home on the Range"
- "Blue-Tailed Fly"
- "O, Christmas Tree"
- "America"
- "Battle Hymn of the Republic"

Each of us draws upon a different heritage of song. Once learned, who can forget "Waltzing Matilda" or "Down in the Valley"? We bring ourselves to music, and it becomes a part of us. We recall events through music. Perhaps we need more singing bees or sing-a-longs!

Children today have daily exposure to popular music, theme songs from commercials, cartoons, films, and videos. They may speak of jazz, rock, and heavy metal because others have mentioned them. Parents will often ask for recommendations in purchasing tapes and records and express concern about the lyrics of television programming.

## DANCE

Dance is also an effective medium for cultural appreciation. Werner and Burton (1979) suggest as examples the folk dances indigenous to the United States, the play-party games, round dances, line dances, and square dances. Folk dances such as "Mulberry Bush," "Paw Paw Patch," "Shoo Fly," "Polly Wolly Doodle," and "Pop Goes the Weasel" are relished by children. Action and delight come from mastering the Mexican hat dance, the Highland fling, German folk dances, the dances of native Americans, and ballet. And across the mountains and in the South, clogging is a favorite of children as well as adults, producing keen competition at country fairs and festivals. The phenomenon of break dancing from the inner city, moreover, has received plaudits throughout the world and has been enjoyed at both the Lincoln Center and the Kennedy Center. Music is truly a powerful force in bringing children and their heritage together.

## MUSIC AS THERAPY

Discussions of music as therapy are relatively new in the literature, as we begin to explore the relationship between music and good health. Wilson (1985) believes that music has been an essential ingredient of human personal and social life for as long as thirty thousand years. He believes music may be capable of providing one of the most powerful experimental tools we have ever had for studying the workings of the human brain. The July 1985 issue of *Health* treats briefly the subject of musical healing, based upon increasing evidence that music can help the body as well as the mind. Research appears to indicate that, as one listens to music, more alpha rhythms, associated with relaxation, are produced, as are more endorphins, the body's natural defenses.

Preliminary results from Amsterdam's University Hospital (September 1989) indicate infants with respiratory problems need less oxygen in their incubators if soft disco music is played. Because oxygen can damage babies' corneas, a method had been sought to lower the oxygen content of the incubators used for premature babies. Results indicate that for twenty-four premature infants, 90 minutes of disco music daily reduced oxygen need by 1 to 20 percent.

For these children the music of Perry Como did not suffice! When music was changed to disco rhythm, the breathing rhythm improved as the "beat seemed to pull them along."

For children entering a strange and new community, music may provide a familiarity and sense of recognition. In music there is no time or place, no right or wrong. The child can be comfortable and natural; he or she can enjoy, participate in, or choose not to participate in the music, depending on the motivational power of the selection.

We appear to be on the verge of a major breakthrough in the use of music as therapy. The concept of relating music to wellness bears further exploration, with implications spreading to home and classroom.

## EXTENDING OUR KNOWLEDGE

Each ethnic group displays unique patterns of child rearing; children absorb those patterns and emulate the adults most valued within their immediate environment. Kendall (1983) reminds us that, "Ideally the teacher does not view any child as a cultural or ethnic representative but responds to each one as an individual for whom culture or ethnicity is merely one aspect of her or his personality" (p. 123). Additionally, Kendall feels that in a monocultural setting, regardless of the culture represented, it is especially important that the teacher provide a hypothetical multicultural environment through thoughtful selection of curriculum materials and learning activities that reflect a multicultural society (p. 63). Reinforcement is thus offered for the thesis of this chapter that, given the increasing ethnic diversity of our children and the fact that we still have many centers filled with children of the same cultural background, care givers should exploit every avenue to obtain a broad range of instructional materials. Resources for extending cultural understanding as well as musical experiences are listed at the end of this chapter.

Become acquainted with the patriotic music of the parade, circus music, and songs related to the holidays of represented ethnic groups. Attend folk festivals, set a goal to visit sites of historic interest in the community, develop a resource file of individuals (including parents) who may speak of their cultural roots, and recommend relevant public television productions to children. One kindergarten teacher began the study of heritage by developing a family tree for the classroom guinea pigs. She then went on to a full-scale project tracing the family trees of the students. Entire families caught the enthusiasm, and everyone enjoyed the music, art, costumes, photographs, and keepsakes contributed.

A child's song shows features of melody, rhythm, form, and text topic that transcend culture. "Ten in a Bed" (Anglo-American), "James Brown" (African-American), "Riverboat Song" (Chinese-Lao), and "Step Back Sally" (Jamaican) reflect a culture's uniqueness.

Become a field investigator. With a battery-operated tape recorder, cassette tapes, extra batteries, notepad, and pencil (to record words and movements), capture the richness of each child's music heritage. Explore near and far, in the most unlikely places. As people learn to trust you, you will be shown the variety and luster of the many songs and rhythms of this new America.

Begin a collection of excellent folk songs, records, and poetry to be shared with children. Begin singing with children each day, and realize the potential contributions of the ethnic groups of the community to children's cultural and musical learning. What better way to promote communication and participation than through the heritage of music!

Remember, even Benjamin Franklin experimented with music. His development of the glass harmonica—twenty-four glass bowls filled with varying amounts of water and played with moistened fingers—is part of each child's heritage. We want each child—whatever his or her ethnic origin—to acknowledge proudly commonalities and differences and be able to shine.

**FAVORITE SONGS AND RHYTHMS**

# THIS LITTLE LIGHT OF MINE

Spiritual

This lit - tle light of mine, I'm gon - na let it shine.

This lit - tle light of mine, I'm gon - na let it shine.

This lit - tle light of mine, I'm gon - na let it shine, let it

shine, let it shine, let it shine.

This little light of mine, I'm gonna let it shine,
This little light of mine, I'm gonna let it shine,
This little light of mine, I'm gonna let it shine,
Let it shine, let it shine, let it shine.

This big world of ours, I'm gonna help it shine,
This big world of ours, I'm gonna help it shine,
This big world of ours, I'm gonna help it shine,
Help it shine, help it shine, help it shine.

# HI-YO-WITZI (Morning Song)

Melody and Words by Chief White Eagle
(North American Indian) Abridged

*Drum*

Hi - yo    hi - yo - wit - zi    nai - yo,

Hi - yo    hi - yo - wit - zi    nai - yo.

Hi - yo    nai - yo    hi!

If a drum is used, a steady beat should continue throughout the song. A tone bell (middle C) could be used on the last three measures.

# THE LITTLE STICK

Folk Song from South America
English Version by Verne Muñoz
Arranged by Pablo Garcia Todoña

*Playfully*

Jump a-cross the lit-tle stick the way I do;
*Brin - ca la ta - bli - ta yo ya la brin - que,*
*Breen - kah lah tah - blee - tah yoh yah lah breen - keh,*

Back and forth a-cross the stick, it's fun to do.
*Brin - ca la de vuel - ta yo ya me can - se.*
*Breen - kah lah deh vwehl - tah yoh yah meh kahn - seh.*

Jump a-cross the lit-tle stick the way I do;
*Brin - ca la ta - bli - ta yo ya la brin - que,*
*Breen - kah lah tah - blee - tah yoh yah lah breen - keh,*

Back and forth a - cross the stick —I'm tired! Aren't you?
*Brin - ca la de vuel - ta yo ya me can - se.*
*Breen - kah lah deh vwehl - tah yoh yah meh kahn - seh.*

From *Cancioncitas Para Chiquitines* by Emma H. Jimenez and Cinchita M. Puncel. © 1969 Bowmar/Noble Publishers, Inc., and the Economy Company, Oklahoma City, Okla. Used by permission.

Have children pretend there is a little stick lying across their lap. As the song is sung, lead them in keeping the steady beat by making their hands jump back and forth over the "stick." Then have a child jump across a flat stick (a yardstick is a good choice as it will not roll or trip the child) to the rhythm of the song. Have that child invite another classmate to carry on this delightful folk song.

# CHIAPANECAS

Mexican folk tune

Arranged and adapted by K. BAYLESS

2. Come, let us stamp feet like this, (stamp, stamp)

For variation children may count 1–2 as they clap hands.

# LOOBY LOO

Old English folk game

Arranged by K. BAYLESS

Here we dance Loo - by Loo, Here we dance Loo - by light,
(go)

Here we dance Loo - by Loo, All on a Sat - ur - day night. I

put my right hand in, I put my right hand out, I

give my right hand a shake, shake, shake, And turn my - self a - bout.

2. left hand    3. right foot    4. left foot    5. head right in    6. whole self

# SANDY MALONEY

English singing game

1. Can you dance, San - dy Ma - lon - ey? Can you dance, San - dy Ma - lon - ey?

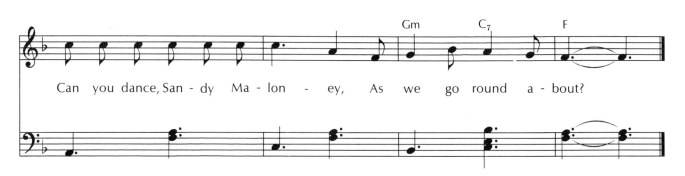

Can you dance, San - dy Ma - lon - ey, As we go round a - bout?

2
Put both your hands on your shoulders,
Put both your hands on your shoulders,
Put both your hands on your shoulders,
And turn you round about.

*Chorus*
Here we dance, Sandy Maloney,
Here we dance, Sandy Maloney,
Here we dance, Sandy Maloney,
As we go round about.

3
Put your hands behind you,
Put your hands behind you,
Put your hands behind you,
As we go round about.

*Chorus*

Continue to have children create additional verses.

# LONDON BRIDGE

Mother Goose

English singing game
Arranged by K. BAYLESS

1. Lon - don Bridge is fall - ing down, fall - ing down, fall - ing down,

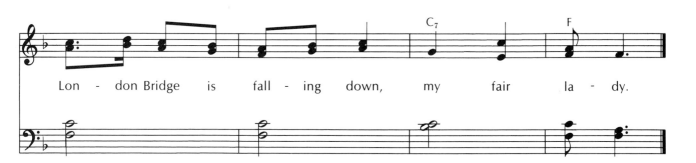

Lon - don Bridge is fall - ing down, my fair la - dy.

2. Build it up with iron bars,
3. Iron bars will bend and break,
4. Build it up with gold and silver,
5. Gold and silver I've not got,
6. Here's a prisoner I have got,

7. What'll you take to set him free,
8. One hundred pounds will set him free,
9. One hundred pounds we have not got,
10. Then off to prison he must go,

Two children are chosen to make an arch by raising their arms above their heads to make a bridge for the other children to pass under. These children secretly decide which one represents silver and which one gold. The other children then pass under the bridge as the song is sung. At the words "My fair lady," the bridge falls. The child who is caught is asked which he prefers, gold or silver. This child then stands behind the one who represents his choice. The game continues until all the children have been chosen.

## FIVE LITTLE BUNS

Traditional English song

Arranged by K. BAYLESS

1. Five lit-tle buns in a bak-er's shop, Nice and round with sug-ar on the top, A-

long came a (boy) with a pen-ny one day, And bought a sug-ar bun and took it right a-way.
        (girl)

# HOW D'YOU DO, MY PARTNER?

Swedish singing game

Arranged by K. BAYLESS

How d'you do, my part - ner, How d'you do to - day_____?

Will you dance in a cir - cle? I will show you the way.

Children stand in a circle facing the center. One child stands in the center and skips to a child in the circle. They shake hands, then join hands and skip around the inside of the circle. Other children clap hands. The song is repeated with the two children choosing new partners, etc.

## ST. PATRICK'S DAY

Traditional

1. We're wear - ing green for the I - rish, We're wear - ing green for the

I - rish. We're wear - ing green for the I - rish On this St. Pat - rick's Day.

2. We'll dance a jig for the Irish,
We'll dance a jig for the Irish.
We'll dance a jig for the Irish,
On this St. Patrick's Day.

3. Me fither and mither were Irish,
Me fither and mither were Irish,
Me fither and mither were Irish,
And I am Irish, too.

4. We kept a pig in the parlor,
We kept a pig in the parlor,
We kept a pig in the parlor,
And he is Irish, too.

## AIKEN DRUM

Traditional
Scottish

1. There was a man lived in the moon, lived in the moon, lived in the moon, There

was a man lived in the moon, and his name was Ai - ken Drum.

Chorus: And he played upon a ladle, a ladle, a ladle,
And he played upon a ladle, and his name was Aiken Drum.

2. And his hat was made of cream cheese, etc.
3. And his shirt was made of good roast beef, etc.

# THERE'S A LITTLE WHEEL

Spiritual

Arranged by K. BAYLESS

Other verses that may be added to "There's a Little Wheel a-Turning":

2. Oh, I feel so very happy in my heart,
3. There's a little drum a-beating in my heart,
4. There's a little harp a-strumming in my heart,

5. There's a little bell a-ringing in my heart,
6. There's a little bit of kindness in my heart,
7. There's a little song a-singing in my heart,

---

*If the A is too low, sing middle C instead.

# ALL NIGHT, ALL DAY

Spiritual

Arranged by K. BAYLESS

All night, all day, An - gels watch-ing o - ver me, my Lord.

All night, all day, An - gels watch-ing o - ver me.

# ALOUETTE

French Canadian

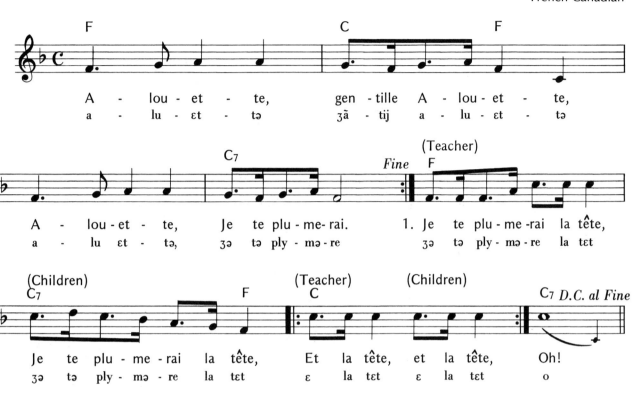

A - lou - et - te,     gen - tille A - lou - et - te,
a - lu - ɛt - tə     ʒã - tij a - lu - ɛt - tə

A - lou - et - te,     Je te plu - me - rai.     1. Je te plu - me - rai la tête,
a - lu ɛt - tə,     ʒə tə ply - mə - re     ʒə tə ply - mə - re la tɛt

Je te plu - me - rai la tête,     Et la tête, et la tête,     Oh!
ʒə tə ply - mə - re la tɛt     ɛ la tɛt ɛ la tɛt     o

2. Le bec (lə bek)—the beak     4. Le dos (lə do)—the back     6. Le cou (lə ku)—the neck
3. Le nez (lə ne)—the nose     5. Les pattes (le pat)—the feet     *Note:* la tête (la tet)—the head

---

Each of the three French songs in this chapter contains a verse in French in addition to its English verses. The French is printed in phonetic symbols to help parents and teachers with the pronunciation.

# FRÈRE JACQUES

French

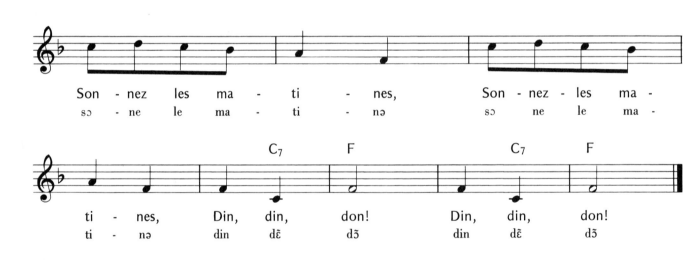

Translation of verse:
Are you sleeping, Are you sleeping, Brother John, Brother John?
Morning bells are ringing, Morning bells are ringing,
Ding, Ding, Dong, Ding, Ding, Dong.

# LES PETITES MARIONNETTES
## (Little Puppets)

French folk song

English version by JUDITH GREEN
Arranged by K. BAYLESS

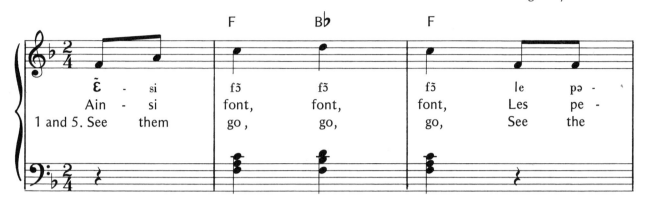

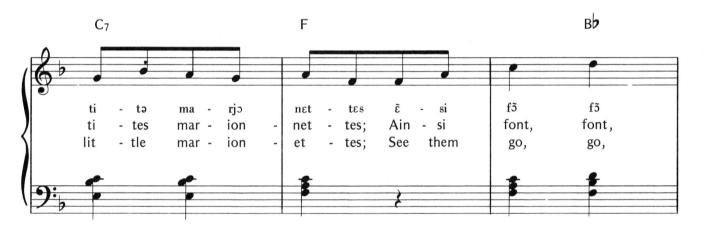

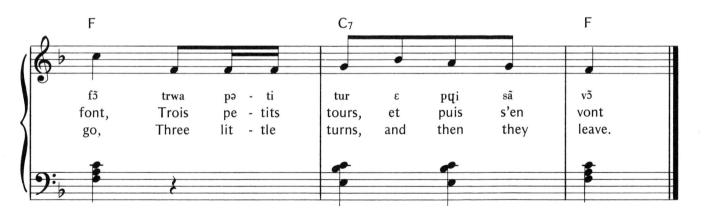

2
See them move their heads,
See the little marionettes;
See them move their heads,
Three little nods, and then they
  leave.

3
See them move their arms,
See the little marionettes,
See them move their arms,
Three little claps, and then they
  leave.

4
See them move their legs,
See the little marionettes;
See them move their legs,
Three little jumps, and then they
  leave.

217

# GO AWAY PARTNER

Source unknown

German singing game
Adapted by K. BAYLESS

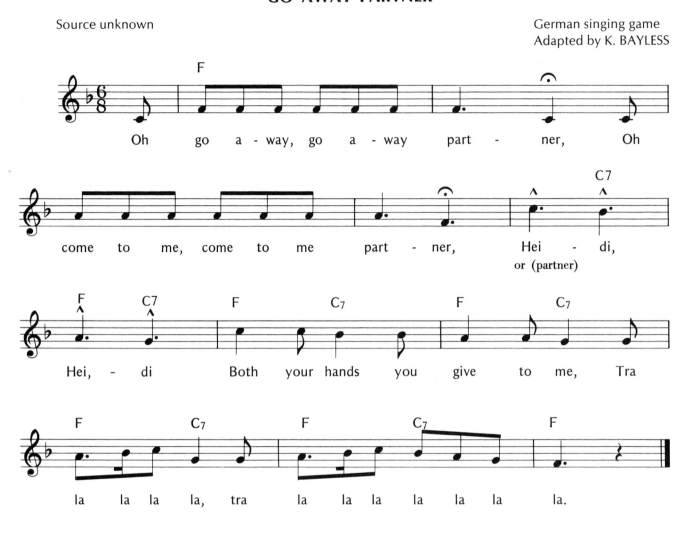

Oh   go a - way, go a - way part - ner,   Oh

come to me, come to me part - ner,   Hei - di,
or (partner)

Hei, - di   Both your hands you give to me,   Tra

la   la la la, tra   la la la la la la   la.

*Formation:*

```
            O Boy
            X Girl
    XO          XO
            O
            X
```

Four boys and four girls stand in formation, facing partners. Raise arms and hands with palms out toward the partner. On the words "Oh go away, go away partner," the arms and palms are moved forward and back in rhythmic movement, keeping the palms toward the partner. On the words "Oh come to me, come to me partner," the palms are turned toward the player, and the rhythmic movements are repeated. On the words "Both your hands you give to me," partners join hands and dance in a circle until the end of the song. At this point, the inside group of four children remain in position. The group of children on the outside move clockwise to the next partner, and the song is then repeated. (*Note:* It is easier to use this kind of formation when only the outside group change partners.)

## DANCE FROM HANSEL AND GRETEL

Germany

This song and dance from *Hansel and Gretel* is one of the most popular selections for young children. The singing range is really too wide for young children since it goes from middle C to high F, but because the song is so beloved by children, it is included in our collection.

# DINOSAUR DIET

Slovak folk tune
Adapted words

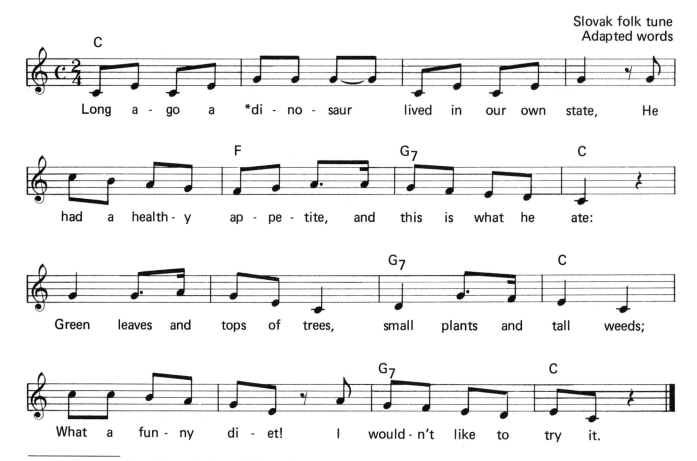

Long a-go a *di-no-saur lived in our own state, He had a health-y ap-pe-tite, and this is what he ate: Green leaves and tops of trees, small plants and tall weeds; What a fun-ny di-et! I would-n't like to try it.

*bron-to-saur-us, pter-o-dac-tyl (may substitute particular type)

From ABC Music Series, Book copyright 3, © 1959. Used by permission of D.C. Heath and Company.

## SEE THE LITTLE DUCKLINGS

German folk tune

See the lit - tle duck - lings, swim - ming here and there,

Heads are in the wa - ter, tails are in the air.

## LADYO, LADYO

Old Swiss melody

Down the moun-tain side we go, La - dy - o, La - dy - o.
We feel hap - py all day long, La - dy - o, La - dy - o.

Gai - ly through the drift - ing snow, La - dy, La - dy - o.
Come and lis - ten to our song, La - dy, La - dy - o.

___

***Musical Concept:*** *Children can learn how to control the voice by ''yodeling'' on the word ''Ladyo''*

(If possible, bring in a resource visitor who can play the accordion and yodel.)

# STODOLA PUMPA

Czech folk tune

Sto-do-la, sto-do-la, Sto-do-la pump-a, sto-do-la pum-pa. Sto-do-la pum-pa,

Sto-do-la, sto-do-la, sto-do-la pum-pa, sto-do-la pum-pa, pum, pum, pum.

**Suggestions**

Slap each knee once for each ''stodola.'' Clap twice for each ''pumpa.'' Clap for each ''pum'' at the end of the song.

# KOLYADA (Yuletide)

Ukrainian folk tune

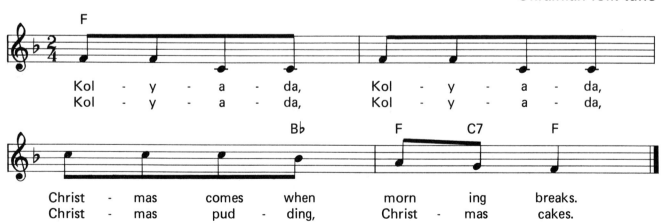

Kol - y - a - da,    Kol - y - a - da,
Kol - y - a - da,    Kol - y - a - da,

Christ - mas    comes    when    morn    ing    breaks.
Christ - mas    pud - ding,    Christ - mas    cakes.

## OJO MA R Q

Nigerian folk song

Written and sung by OMOTE AWANI

Pronunciation key: ojo, as in old Joe: ã, as in apple; I, as in eat; u, as in soothe; a, as in apple; ọ, as in up; ẹ, as in set; o, as in old.

This is a song about rain. It means "Rain please fall. You are refreshing."

# MY DREYDL*
## My Top

S. S. Grossman

S.E. Goldfarb

1. I have a lit - tle drey - dl, I made it out of clay; And When it's dry and read - y Then drey - dl I shall play. O drey - dl, drey - dl, drey - dl, I made it out of clay; O drey - dl, drey - dl, drey - dl, Now drey - dl I shall play.

*A dreydl is a four-sided top with a Hebrew character on each side.

## LIGHT A LITTLE CANDLE

Adapted from a folk melody

ROSE ENGEL
JUDITH BERMAN

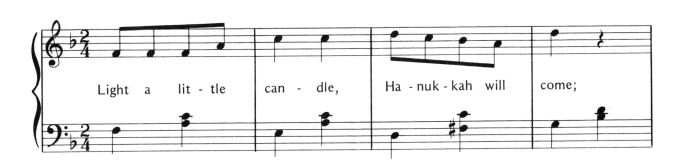

Light a lit-tle can-dle, Ha-nuk-kah will come;

Eat a lit-tle lat - ke,* Yum, yum, yum, yum, yum! I'm

count-ing on my fin-gers and I'm count-ing on my thumb,

Just how man-y days till Ha-nuk-kah will come!

*Potato pancake customarily eaten during Hanukkah.

# HANUKKAH LATKES

Not too fast

FREDA BRECK

Take a po - ta - to, pat, pat, pat,

Roll it and make it flat, flat, flat,

Fry in a pan with fat, fat, fat,

Ha - nuk - kah lat - kes, clap, clap, clap.

# KOOKABURRA

Australia

Written by M. SINCLAIR

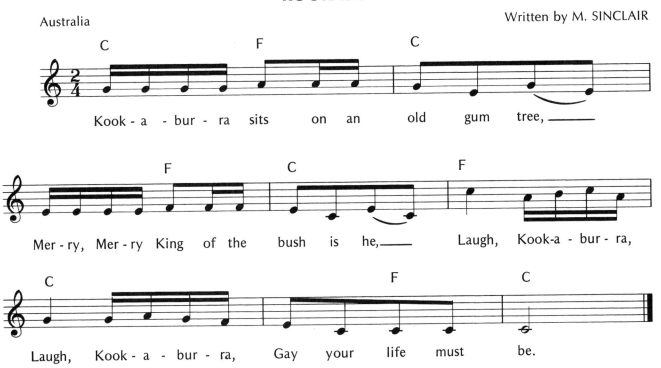

Kook - a - bur - ra sits on an old gum tree, _____

Mer - ry, Mer - ry King of the bush is he, _____ Laugh, Kook - a - bur - ra,

Laugh, Kook - a - bur - ra, Gay your life must be.

# TANGALAYO

Source unknown

West Indian song

Tan - ga - lay - o! Come lit - tle don - key come; Tan - ga - lay - o! Come lit - tle don - key come My don - key walk, my don - key balk, my don - key has a fun - ny talk! My don - key go, my don - key stop, my don - key look and then he drop!

## TRES PAJARILLOS

L. W.                                                                L. W.

U - no, dos, tres,   u - no, dos, tres,   Tres pa - ja - ri - llos,
One,   two,   three,   one,   two,   three,   Three lit - tle birds,

tres pa - ja - ri - llos,   Can - tan a - sí,   can - tan a - sí,
three lit - tle birds   Sing like this,   sing like this,

Pip - a - ri - a - ri - a,   Pip - a - ri - a - ri - a,   Can - tan a - sí, can - tan a - sí.
Peep - a - ree - a - ree - a,   Peep - a - ree - a - ree - a,   Sing like this, sing like this.

From SING A SONG OF PEOPLE by Roberta McLaughlin and Lucille Wood. By permission of the publisher, Phoenix Learning Resources Inc. Copyright 1973.

Select E, D, and C from the resonator bells. Help the children find the melody patterns using these pitches. Play the patterns on the bells and determine which move up and which move down.

# AFTER SCHOOL

Grace Boynton

Chinese Folk Melody

School is out as the sun goes down;

Books in my bag I go through the town,

Home are my par - ents who smile at me

I make a nice low bow like this you see.

This song should be sung with light, soft voices and at a rather slow tempo. Children can use instruments that suggest the sound of rain to accompany the song. This selection is a good example of a pentatonic song using the pitches of C, D, E, G, and A. Children can create their own *ostinatos* (repeated melodic or rhythmic patterns) by playing C, D, E, G, and A in various melodic patterns.

## JAPANESE RAIN SONG

Lightly

Japanese folk song contributed by
ELIZABETH CLURE and HELEN RAMSEY
English words by ROBERTA McLAUGHLIN
Arranged by ALBERT DeVITO

1. Pit - ter -pat - ter, fall - ing, fall - ing, rain is fall - ing down.

Moth - er comes to bring um - brel - la, Rain is fall - ing down.

*Refrain:*

Pi chi, pi chi, cha pu, cha pu, ran, ran, ran.

2. Underneath the dropping willow stands a little child.
   No umbrella, child is weeping, rain is falling down.

## KEY IDEAS

1. Children from many ethnic groups are changing the faces of classrooms, day care centers, and society.
2. Music provides a bridge of communication between cultures in which all can participate, appreciate, and learn.
3. By using culturally diverse music, children begin to appreciate other life-styles.
4. Much potential for learning exists in the music of cultural groups.
5. Become a field explorer and collect a variety of songs to enrich your work with all children.

## SUMMARY

We never outgrow the vitality, humor, nonsense, and fun of the music about us. Music surrounds us, offers relaxation and enjoyment, and encourages spirited participation. Old and young can travel the world through music, reveling in song and dance. Through music we learn geography, history, language, and cultural patterns. Through music children can come to understand and accept other children. Together, teacher/care giver and child can reconstruct a musical heritage and begin to construct a heritage for the present and future.

## QUESTIONS TO CONSIDER

1. Recall family customs shared in your childhood. How could music reinforce these customs? Give illustrations for the classroom.
2. Music as therapy is relatively new in the literature. Select four songs that would be suitable for such a use and describe their presentation in a particular setting.
3. Select a family representative of a culture different from your own. Interview the primary care giver as to musical influences in the family background. Record your findings.
4. Select four folk songs from different ethnic groups. Outline ways in which each might be used to extend cultural understanding.
5. Develop a bulletin board featuring cultural diversity in America. Ask children to contribute pictures as illustration.

## REFERENCES AND SUGGESTED READINGS

Anderson, William M., and Lawrence, Joy E. "Integrating music with the study of people and places." In *Integrating music into the classroom*, pp. 251-292. Belmont, Calif.: Wadsworth, 1985.

"Babies dig soft beat of disco," *The Commercial Appeal*, Memphis, Tennessee, September 9, 1989.

Barkan, Emmanuel. *Children's songs*. New York: Board of Jewish Education of Greater New York, undated. (A collection of 21 simple Hebrew melodies about nature, the classroom, and the home. Each song appears in Hebrew, transliterated Hebrew, and English.)

Blacking, John. *Venda children's song: A study in ethnomusicological analysis*. Johannesburg, South Africa: Witwatersrand University Press, 1967.

Brown, Tom. "Sugar in the gourd: Preserving Appalachian tradition." *Music Educators Journal*, November 1983, 70(3), pp. 52–55.

Chubb, Deborah M. "More refugees coming." *The Commercial Appeal*, Memphis, Tennessee, September 9, 1989, B1, 3.

Coopersmith, Harry. "Music for the Jewish school." In Richard Neumann, *A song curriculum and teaching guide*, 2d rev. ed. New York: Board of Jewish Education, 1975.

Courlander, Harold. *Negro Folk Music, U.S.A.* New York: Columbia University Press, 1963.

Deiner, Penny Low. "Needs: Culturally distinct." In *Resources for teaching young children with special needs*, pp. 461–470. New York: Harcourt Brace Jovanovich, 1983.

Dodds, Jack, P. B. "Music as multicultural education." *Music Educators Journal*, May 1983, 69(9), pp. 33–34.

Eistein, Judith, and Prensky, Freida. *Songs of childhood*. New York: The United Synagogue Commission of Jewish Education, 1955.

Feeney, Stephanie; Christensen, Doris; and Moravcik, Eva. *Who am I in the lives of children?* 3rd ed. Columbus, Ohio: Merrill, 1987.

Friedrich, Otto. "Changing face of America." *Time*. July 8, 1985, 126(1), pp. 26–27.

Garfias, Roberta. "Music in the United States: Community of cultures." *Music Educators Journal*, May 1983, 69(9), pp. 30–31.

Greer, Jeptha V. "Commentary: Cultural, diversity and the test of leadership." *Exceptional Children*, November 1988, 55(3), pp. 199–201.

Griffin, Louis. *Multi-ethnic books for young children*. Washington, D.C.: National Association for the Education of Young Children, undated.

Hale, Janice. "Black children: Their roots, culture and learning styles." *Young Children*, January 1981, 36(2), pp. 37–50.

Hansman, Jerome J. *Arts and schools*, New York: McGraw-Hill, 1980.

Hoffer, Charles R., and Hoffer, Marjorie L. *Teaching music in the elementary school classroom*. New York: Harcourt Brace, 1982.

"The immigrants: The changing face of America." *Time*, July 8, 1985, 126(1), pp. 24–101.

Jalongo, Mary Renck, and Collins, Mitzi. "Singing with young children. Folk songs for non-musicians." *Young Children*, January 1985, 40(2), pp. 17–22.

Kebede, Ashenafi. *Roots of black music*. Englewood Cliffs, N.J.: Prentice-Hall, 1962.

Kendall, Frances E. Diversity in the classroom: *A multicultural approach in the education of young children*. New York: Teachers College, Columbia University, 1983.

Larkin, Marilynn. "Musical healing." *Health*, July 1985, 17(7), p. 12.

May, Elizabeth (ed.). *Music of many cultures*. Berkeley and Los Angeles: University of California Press, 1980.

Miller, Samuel D., and Brand, Manny. "Music of other cultures in the classroom." *Social Studies*, March/April 1983, 74(2), pp. 62–64.

"Multicultural Education." *Theory into Practice*. Spring 1984, 33(2).

O'Brien, James, and O'Brien, Shirley. "Music is universal." In *It's music!* Marjorie E. Ramsey, ed. Wheaton, Md.: Association for Childhood Education International, 1984.

Palmer, Hap. *Movin'*. Freeport, N.Y.: Educational Activities. (album)

Peters, David G., and Miller, Robert P. *Music teaching and learning*. New York: Longmans, 1983.

Phillips, Carol Brunson, "Nurturing diversity for today's children and tomorrow's leaders." *Young Children*. January 1988, 43(1), pp. 43–47.

Ramsey, Majorie E. (ed.) *It's Music!* Wheaton, Md.: Association for Childhood Education International, 1984.

Schmidt, V. E., and McNeil, E. *Cultural awareness: A resource bibliography*. Washington, D.C.: The National Association for the Education of Young Children, 1978.

Schreibaer, J. E. (ed.). *Using children's books in social studies: Early childhood through primary grades*. Washington, D.C.: Council for the Social Studies, 1984.

Scott, C. R. "Preschool music education and research on the development of preschool children, 1900–1980." *The Bulletin of the Council for Research in Music Education*, Spring, 1986, 87, pp. 57–61.

Shehan, Patricia K. "Finding a national music style: Listen to the children." *Music Educators Journal*, May 1987, 73(3), pp. 38–43.

Shehan, Patricia K. "Teaching music through Balkan folk dance." *Music Educators Journal*, November 1984, 71(3), pp. 47–51.

Smith, John A. "Four music activities to sharpen language skills." *Music Educators Journal*, November 1984, 71(3), pp. 52–54.

Soldier, Lee Little. "To soar with the eagles: Enculturation and acculturation of Indian children." *Childhood Education*, Jan./Feb. 1985, 61(3), pp. 185–191.

Sutton–Smith, Brian. *The folk stories of children.* Philadelphia: University of Pennsylvania Press, 1981.

Tait, Malcolm, and Haack, Paul. *Principles and processes of music education: New perspectives.* New York: Teachers College Press, Columbia University, 1984.

"The multicultural imperative." *Music Educators Journal.* May 1982, 69(9), pp. 26–66.

United Nations Children's Fund. "Musical Instruments of the World." New York; Facts on File Publications, 1976, pp. 264–300.

Vulliamy, George. *Pop, rock and ethnic music in school.* Cambridge: Cambridge University Press, 1982.

Werner, Peter H., and Burton, Elsie C. *Learning through movement: Teaching cognitive content through physical activities.* St. Louis: C. V. Mosby, 1979.

White, Rene Boyer. "Reflecting cultural diversity in the music classroom." *Music Educators Journal,* December 1968, 75, pp. 50–54.

Wignall, Harry James. "Marionettes, children and the magic of opera." *Music Educators Journal,* December 1988, 75, pp. 55–58.

Wilson, Frank R. "Music as basic schooling for the brain." *Music Educators Journal,* May 1985, 71(9), pp. 39–42.

# APPENDIX A

# Musical Approaches for Young Children

## DALCROZE EURHYTHMICS

The Dalcroze approach was developed by Emile Jaques-Dalcroze, a Swiss composer and educator (1865–1950). "Dalcroze believed that rhythm is the fundamental, motivating force in all the arts, especially in music" (Landis and Carder, 1972, p. 12). Dalcroze's theories were stated in two principal books: *Rhythm, Music and Education* (1921) and *Eurhythmics, Art and Education* (1930). When Dalcroze died in 1950, his legacy to the musical world, along with his books on music theory and movement, included a large number of songs for children. A majority of his ideas are taught by means of personal instruction rather than written materials.

Dalcroze's approach has enjoyed much success and is used all over the world. The Dalcroze School in New York City offers not only a wide variety of courses of instruction for adults and youngsters but also a comprehensive course in the Dalcroze System for teachers who wish to learn to use it firsthand. Several universities and institutions in the country offer courses in Dalcroze Eurhythmics, including Kent State University, Kent, Ohio, and the Cleveland Institute of Music.

Today many people refer to Dalcroze's entire approach as *Eurhythmics* (rhythmic movement). The concept of Eurhythmics, however, is much more extensive than simply rhythmic movement. If one undertakes complete Dalcroze training, the comprehensive studies that comprise a music major's program will be emphasized (Landis and Carder, 1972, p. 7).

Dalcroze's Eurhythmic approach begins with the belief that children should develop an awareness of music through body movement. The child's body is used as a musical instrument to interpret what is heard. Rhythmic sense, voice, and body coordination are all learned simultaneously through the synchronization of body movement and music. Sensory and intellectual experiences are fused together. The Dalcroze approach helps children become aware of the total possibilities of their bodies.

According to Dalcroze, it is very important to sequence a student's musical experience. Dalcroze was determined that instrumental study should not begin before ear training and rhythmic movement. His approach starts with the simplest of rhythmic responses from children and proceeds step by step to the most difficult and complicated.

The Dalcroze approach consists of three parts: (1) Eurhythmics (rhythmic movement), (2) solfege (vocal exercises using the *sol-fa* syllables that help develop a good ear for sound), and (3) piano improvisation by the teacher. With rhythmic movement as the basic mode of instruction, Dalcroze taught rhythm, melody, harmony, dynamics, form, and phrasing. He felt that as music is heard, a person should experience an immediate physical response in order to fully comprehend a musical idea (Landis and Carder, 1972, p. 12).

In a Dalcroze Eurhythmics class the children dramatize freely with their bodies and respond to the improvised music played by the teacher. Listening to musical changes is important. For example, children listen to the music played on the piano and move their bodies along with what they hear. Children do exercises such as tiptoeing to music, freezing to silence, and stepping more heavily to louder sounds and more lightly to softer sounds. This is only a

All readers are urged to read *The Eclectic Curriculum in American Music Education: Contributions of Dalcroze, Kodaly, and Orff* (1972) by Beth Landis and Polly Carder, Music Educator's National Conference, 1902 Association Drive, Reston, VA 22091.

235

small list of concepts and skills that can be explored using this approach.

Readers are encouraged to obtain Elsa Findlay's book *Rhythm and Movement, Applications of Dalcroze Eurhythmics* (1971). This is an excellent resource that provides information on the application of this approach. A wealth of ideas and activities for the teacher are also presented. The material is comprehensive and easily understood. Early childhood teachers are especially urged to obtain this book. In addition, teachers would find it most helpful to take a course in Dalcroze Eurhythmics. Eurhythmics should be included as an important part of every early childhood education program.

## THE KODÁLY METHOD

Another popular music approach used for the young child is the Kodály method, developed by Hungarian composer and educator Zoltán Kodály, 1882–1967 (Nye, 1983, pp. 80–81). Kodály is responsible for this educational philosophy, which proposes that a child's education in music begins when he starts to "make" his own music. Thus the child's voice is his first and most important instrument. Kodály did not believe in the continued use of the piano to accompany children's singing. In fact, he thought it was a distraction and that if a song were always accompanied, the beauty of the pure melodic line could be destroyed. Instead of using piano accompaniment, Kodály suggests that childlike percussion and barred instruments (such as the xylophone) be used to accompany children's songs. The child should learn to appreciate music as a pure, unadulterated melody emanating from himself, this appreciation being achieved through the use of ear-training exercises. To this end, Kodály developed play songs, chants, and games to assist in the teaching of rhythm, meter, and accent. He created hand signals for each scale tone, in which the hand moves up or down according to the ascending or descending tones. This system serves to reinforce what the child hears.

Kodály was a great supporter of play and believed that song and play belonged together. According to Kodály, a simple song, well written, makes play more interesting. Kodály used authentic children's games, nursery songs, and authentic folk music extensively in his teachings. He used melodies with simple meters (2/4, for example) and songs employing the pentatonic scale. He felt that ear training of children developed faster if songs were learned first through their melody line before the text was introduced. Kodály was most critical of the many teachers who used songs with large interval leaps, thereby endangering the vocal development of young children.

Wheeler, in *Orff and Kodály Adapted for the Elementary School* (1977), states that one of Kodály's prime objectives was to teach children to read and write music through singing. This teaching is done in gradual, sequential steps. In the Kodály approach, the feeling for the basic beat is reached through clapping and stepping with the beat, gradually progressing to a greater grasp on word rhythms and their respective musical symbols.

Kodály strongly believed that it is possible to bring music to the general public with his approach. His followers contend that this approach could be part of the general school curriculum for the "average" child. With occasional help and advice, the classroom teacher could handle this technique. The workbooks that include the structured songs and games are the only equipment required.

A study conducted by Harper et al. (1973, pp. 628–629) of the Kodály approach used in kindergarten indicated very positive results. A comparison was made between children in the program and control children on the following criteria: auditory discrimination, visual-motor integration, and first-grade level academic skills. The children in the Kodály program displayed higher levels of skills in all areas, a better self-image, and a readiness for first grade. Many teachers have found Zoltán Kodály's musical approach very helpful in their work with young children.

## THE ORFF APPROACH

The Orff, or Orff-Schulwerfe approach, was introduced by Carl Orff (1895–1982), the well-known contemporary German composer. This musical approach emphasizes the use of specially designed percussion and keyboard instruments for young children.

Orff was influenced by Dalcroze's thinking, by the surge of interest in physical education and gymnastics, and by the advent of a new kind of dancing that has since become known as modern dance. Orff, like Dalcroze, had a great interest in the theater. He opened a school for gymnastics and dance in 1924 and combined the study of music with gymnastics. This fusion became the key to his concept of music education. Orff began to create music for the young dance students in his school. By 1948, he had developed an educational system specifically for music.

The contrast and variation of rhythm are the primary elements in Orff's style of musical composition, and percussion instruments that produce this rhythm naturally play a primary role in these works. Thus Orff invented new percussion instruments to meet his demand for novel effects. These unique instruments distinguish Orff's approach from others. The instruments are easy to play and are of excellent quality. Since rhythmic responses are so natural to the young child, Orff was convinced that these melodic percussion devices would allow children the opportunity for creative improvisation and ensemble experience. The child memorizes pitch and rhythmic patterns with facility and lack of inhibition.

Orff felt that children should play instruments from memory and that the study of piano should come only after the development of other musical skills. Drill is to be avoided. Orff believed that a gradual progression from speech patterns to rhythmic activities to song was the best and most natural for the child. The playing of instruments follows. Children try out and play various rhythm patterns and melodic and ostinato figures on instruments. Orff felt the instruments provide a comprehensive and sound musical foundation for the child.

Originally, Orff based his approach on the folklore and music of childhood that originated in Germany. (Orff's music for children is now available in the English language adaptations.) It might be appropriate for teachers to use American folk music and children's songs in the pentatonic mode in utilizing the Orff approach. These songs can be accompanied by the Orff instruments. The prized Orff instruments are manufactured in Germany but can be readily obtained in the United States. Despite the fact that the teacher must be fairly well trained and that the instruments are fairly expensive, this approach is used throughout the United States with success and popularity.

The authors have been very impressed with the range of possibilities in using the Orff instruments. Teachers are encouraged to pursue the Orff approach in more depth. Today, the Orff Institute, established in 1963 in Salzburg, offers training in the Orff approach for teachers from many parts of the world. Music schools throughout America can provide information on the Orff approach. (Also, read *The Eclectic Curriculum in Music Education: Contributions of Dalcroze, Kodály and Orff* by Landis and Carder, 1972, and Vernice Nye's description of Orff's method in *Music for Young Children*, Third Edition, 1983.)

## THE SUZUKI METHOD, OR TALENT EDUCATION

The Suzuki method, or Talent Education, was developed by Dr. Shinichi Suzuki, a violinist and Japanese language teacher. The approach received worldwide recognition and acclaim when three-, four-, and five-year old children demonstrated their ability to play demanding sonatas and concertos on their miniature-sized violins. Suzuki's method of instruction employs a psycholinguistic approach. The child learns to respond to and repeat music in the same manner that he learns to speak his native tongue, playing first by ear rather than by reading notes. Suzuki regards two elements as being very important in his method: ''(1) The child must be helped to develop an ear for music. (2) From the very beginning, every step must by all means be thoroughly mastered'' (Suzuki et al., 1973, p. 12).

The method not only involves the student, but requires close supervision by the parent and the teacher. The student must listen, practice, and perform. The parent is asked to attend each weekly lesson and to supervise daily practice sessions. Parental involvement not only ensures that the student follows the teacher's instructions, but gives encouragement and praise for the child's efforts. The children have the opportunity to play for each other in informal recitals. Frequent opportunities to play before an audience build a child's self-confidence.

The Suzuki method now encompasses the instruction of piano, cello, flute, and viola as well as violin. Although each particular instrument has its own music repertoire, Suzuki's basic techniques, principles, and philosophy still apply.

Having enjoyed the success of his students, Suzuki believes that his instructional procedure can be used in all forms of teaching. Now many schools are employing the Suzuki method and the instrumental technique that relies primarily on the human ear.

Obviously, each approach discussed here offers a unique musical experience to the young child. Whatever approach feels most comfortable to the teacher will be the most successful one for the students.

## EDUCATION THROUGH MUSIC (ETM)

Education Through Music (ETM) is the experience of learning through music, movement, singing, sharing, and exploring. Mary Helen Richards, a well-known authority on music education, is the director of the Richards Institute, 149 Corte Madera Road, Portola Valley, CA 94025. The Richards Institute sponsors ETM courses and workshops around the United States and in Canada.

Initially, the ETM program began with the approach called Threshold to Music. After researching and refining the Threshold to Music approach, Richards developed the ETM program. Teachers who have attended these courses and workshops have been most complimentary about the benefits received from this unique approach. Information regarding future workshops and courses may be obtained from the Richards Institute.

## INTRODUCING THE CONCEPT OF BEAT COMPETENCY*

The following article explains the concept of beat competency presented by Bonnie Draeger and Linda White. These two young women make up the PARADIDDLES® Music Team, which was created in 1977 to fill the need for quality musical experiences for young children and quality in-

---

*By Bonnie Wendt Draeger. © 1984 by Bonnie Wendt Draeger and Linda Boyte White. PARADIDDLES Music/Arts Newsletter, Columbus, Indiana. Used by permission.

service musical training for current early childhood teachers and care givers. Since that date, PARADIDDLES has become known throughout the midwest through lectures, inservice workshops, and parent-child participatory workshop-performances called PARADIDDLES PRESCHOOL MUSICAL EXPERIENCES. Both teachers hold music degrees and taught elementary music prior to devoting full time to early childhood music. They can be contacted at P.O. Box 1348, Columbus, IN 47202, (812) 342-9325.

Children are born with an innate sense of timing. They repetitively bounce, tap, rock and sway. Once through the infant stage, tots begin walking "to the beat of a different drummer," both philosophically and physically. Their steps, at first hesitant and unsteady, soon become confident and encompass the elements of a "steady beat."

Researchers are finding that each has his/her own sense of 'personal timing' and that many aspects of our lives and learning are connected to this inner sense of 'beat.'

When a very young child pats along to a musical selection, the pats may be steady and even; however, the synchronization with the actual beat and tempo of the musical selection will often not occur. This is an experimental stage and is quite acceptable and, in fact, may be necessary for musical development. (It is interesting to note that in keeping with the faster pace of the child's life in general, the tempo of the young child's beat is often considereably faster than that of adults.)

It can often take months or years to progress beyond this stage of experimentation. It is important then to provide preschool and kindergarten children with many opportunities to experience and express their own beat—tapping and bouncing and moving along at their own pace without criticism. It is *imperative* then, also, to refrain from introducing activities

requiring rhythmic responses, and to work solely with beat, until beat competency is attained. (For more information, please refer to: *Teaching Movement & Dance* by Phyllis S. Weikart, High/Scope Press.)

As children grow, they will finally be ready to move beyond their own sense of personal timing. They must develop the ability to relate to the timing of others, be it keeping pace in the reading class or keeping an accurate beat to a musical composition. This may occur as early as one year of age or as late as six to eight years old. This developmental stage is not solely related to musical talent but is strongly linked to the amount of beat-related activities the child has experienced to date.

At the same time, it is essential that children progress through the various stages of physical development and coordination required to be able to move, play and physically express themselves comfortably. Activities to foster this development are often included in the preschool and kindergarten curriculum and should continue to be encouraged.

Uniting these elements of developing physical coordination and developing beat awareness results in attaining beat competency. Beat competency can most easily be measured by the child's ability to walk, move, and imitate a steady beat on his/her own initiative without outside direction. As many as 75 percent of American first graders cannot accomplish this task, according to initial findings of Phyllis Weikart, University of Michigan professor.

Following successful pilot projects, Professor Weikart is directing an in-depth research project on the educational implications of beat competency in the classrooom. Professor Weikart asserts that attaining beat competency prior to formal schooling will strongly enhance the child's opportunities for success in the classroom including increased self-confidence, improved spatial awareness, better coordinative and attending skills, and improved reading readiness.

## REFERENCES AND SUGGESTED READINGS

Becknell, Arthur F. "A history of the development of Dalcroze eurhythmics in the United States and its influence in the public school music program." Ph.D. diss., University of Michigan, 1970.

Chosky, Lois. *The Kodály method.* Englewood Cliffs, N.J.: Prentice-Hall, 1974.

Findlay, Elsa. *Rhythm and movement: Application of Dalcroze eurhythmics.* Evanston, Ill.: Summy-Birchard Music, 1971.

Garson, Alfred. "Learning with Suzuki: Seven questions answered." *Music Educators Journal,* February 1970, 56, pp. 64–65.

Garson, Alfred. "Suzuki and physical movement." *Music Educators Journal,* December 1970, 60, pp. 34–37.

Harper, Andrew; Flick, Marty; Taylor, Karen; and Waldo, Renee. "Education through music." *Phi Delta Kappan,* May 1973, 54, pp. 628–629.

Hermann, Evelyn. *Shinichi Suzuki: The man and his philosophy.* Athens, Ohio: Ability Development Associates, 1981.

Landis, Beth, and Carder, Polly. *The eclectic curriculum in American education: Contributions of Dalcroze, Kodály, and Orff.* Reston, Va: Music Educators National Conference, 1972.

Markel, Roberta. *Guide to music education.* New York: Macmillan, 1972.

Nye, Vernice. *Music for young children.* 3rd ed. Dubuque, Iowa: William C. Brown, 1983.

Richards, Mary Helen. *Hand singing and other techniques.* Belmont, Calif.: Fearon Pitman, 1966.

Richards, Mary Helen. *Language arts through music.* Portoria Valley, Calif.: Richards Institute of Music Education and Research, 1971.

Rubin-Rabson, Grace. "A Kodály symposium." *The American Music Teacher,* April 1974, 23, pp. 14–16.

Spector, Irwin. "Bring back Dalcroze." *American Music Teacher,* July 1972, 21, pp. 19–21.

Suzuki, Shinichi; Miller, Elizabeth; Ferro, Mae; Schreiber, Marian; Behrend, Louise; Jempelis, Anastasia; Kendall, John; Mills, Harlow; Rowell, Margaret; Tillson, Diana; and the American Institute-West. *Suzuki concept.* Berkeley, Calif.: Diablo Press, 1973.

Weikart, Phyllis S. *Teaching movement & dance.* Ypsilanti, Mich.: The High/Scope Press, 1982.

Wheeler, Lawrence. *Orff and Kodály adapted for the elementary school.* Dubuque, Iowa: William C. Brown, 1977.

Willour, Judith. "Beginning with delight, leading to wisdom: Dalcroze." *Music Educators Journal,* September 1969, 56, pp. 42–43.

Zahtilla, Paul. *Suzuki in the string class.* Evanston, Ill.: Summy-Birchard, 1972.

# APPENDIX B

# Music Terminology

## MUSICAL CONCEPTS

The following list of musical concepts will help parents and teachers as they expand on and enrich the music experiences of the preschool or kindergarten-age child. For most children, this will be just a beginning to their understanding of music. Children's awareness of musical concepts should grow out of their natural experiences with music. Parents and teachers can plan for and guide these discoveries. Most of the musical selections throughout this book include one or more of the following concepts.

I. *Melody*
   A. Direction—discover whether the melody of a song moves up or down.
   B. Pitch differences (high-low)—respond to high or low sounds.

II. *Rhythm*
   A. Steady beat—respond to a steady beat of music by tapping, clapping, or playing percussion instruments.
   B. Tempo (fast-slow)—experience songs, both fast and slow. Move in response to music that gets faster or slower.
   C. Rhythm patterns—echo simple rhythm patterns and repeat them by clapping or playing a percussion instrument. Recognize repeated patterns in a song.
   D. Rhythmic activities—walk, run, gallop, skip, hop (locomotive movements) and bend, push, pull, reach, sway (nonlocomotive movements) to music.

III. *Form*
   A. Beginning and ending—learn to respond to beginnings and endings of music. Start when the music begins; stop when it comes to an end. Draw a "map" of the song in the air, from beginning to end.
   B. Two-part song (AB or ABA)—respond in one way to one section or part of the music and in a different way to the other.
   C. Individual or group (call and response)—imitate musical tone calls or phrases.
   D. Verse and refrain—recognize the difference between a verse and a refrain.

IV. *Tone color*
   A. Instruments—begin to identify instruments by sight and sound. Begin with strings, winds, and percussion. Be exposed to different methods of playing instruments such as blowing, striking, and bowing.
   B. Natural and environmental sounds—experience clapping, snapping, whistling, tongue-clicking, etc. Identify different environmental sounds such as trains, sirens, machines, and owls.
   C. Voices—recognize the difference in men's, women's, and children's speaking and singing voices.
   D. Dynamics (soft-loud)—recognize the difference between loud and soft in music. Also, recognize when music gets louder and softer.

V. *Texture-harmony*
   A. Have the experience of adding harmony to a song by playing simple bell parts, strumming on an Autoharp, etc.
   B. Have opportunities to hear songs with and without accompaniment.

## GLOSSARY

**accent**    A stress or emphasis given to certain notes.

**beat**    The audible or visual markings of the metrical divisions of music. Pulse that can be heard or felt in music.

**direction**    The upward or downward movement of a melody.

**duration**    The length of time that sound persists (short or long).

**\*dynamics**    The loudness or softness of sounds in music.

**fermata**  ⌢    The sustaining of a note, chord, or rest for a duration longer than the indicated time value, with the length of the extension at the performer's discretion.

**form**    Scheme of organization that determines the basic structure of a composition. Often designated by letters—AB form, ABA form, etc.

**forte (f)**    A direction to play a composition loud or strong.

**harmony**    The simultaneous combination of tones (sounding at one time).

**interval**    The difference in pitch between two tones.

**measure**    Music contained between two vertical bars.

**melody**    The succession of single tones (moving upward or downward) in a musical composition.

**ostinato**    A short rhythmic or melodic pattern that is repeated.

**pentatonic scale**    A five-tone scale (do, re, mi, sol, la). It can originate on any tone.

**phrase**    A division of a composition—a "musical sentence." Commonly a passage of four or eight measures.

**piano (p)**    A direction to play a composition softly.

**pitch**    The highness or lowness of a tone.

**rest**    A sign (symbol) in music indicating an interval of silence.

**scale**    A succession of ascending or descending tones arranged according to fixed intervals.

**staccato**    Short, detached sound.

**steady beat**    Regular, even pulsation.

**\*tempo**    The speed or rate of beats in music.

**timbre**    The quality of a sound (voice or instrument).

**tonal music**    Music that has a "home base"; that is, it is written in a particular key.

**tone color**    Sound that makes an instrument or voice different from another.

## GRAND STAFF AND PIANO KEYBOARD

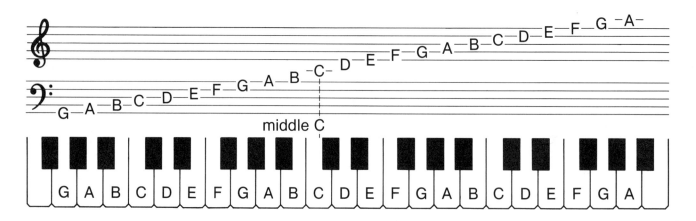

**\*Dynamics (Terms):**
**crescendo**    Gradually growing louder.
**diminuendo**    Gradually growing softer.
**mezzo forte (mf)**    Moderately loud.
**forte (f)**    Loud.
**fortissimo (ff)**    Very loud.
**mezzo piano (mp)**    Moderately soft.
**piano (p)**    Soft.
**pianissimo (pp)**    Very soft.
**sforzando (sf)**    Forcefully.

**\*Tempo (Terms):**
**accelerando**    Gradually getting faster.
**allegretto**    Moderately fast.
**allegro**    Fast.
**presto**    Very fast.
**andantino**    Slightly faster than andante.
**andante**    Moderately slow.
**lento**    Slow.
**largo**    Very slow.

## MUSIC FUNDAMENTALS

### Staff

Music is written on a staff that consists of five lines and four spaces. Notes are placed upon the staff to indicate *pitch,* which is the highness or lowness of tone.

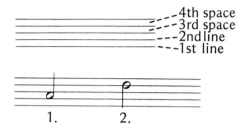

To indicate where a note is located, the lines and spaces are always counted from the bottom of the staff up to the top, as shown above:

1. This note is in the second space.
2. This note is on the fourth line.

When a note is below the third line, the *stem* goes up on the right side of the *head*. When the note is on the third line, the stem can go in either direction, but if the note is above the third line, the stem extends down on the left side, as follows:

### Letter Names

The first seven letters of the alphabet are used to name the lines and spaces. These are used consecutively and repeatedly to correspond with all the white keys on the piano.

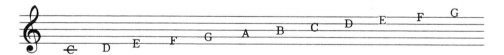

### Great Staff

The combined bass and treble staffs are called the Great Staff. The letter names of the lines and spaces of the Great Staff are as follows:

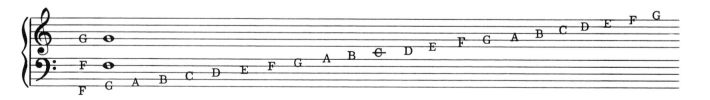

### Clefs

For vocal and piano music the treble and base clefs are used almost exclusively. Middle C has the same pitch in each of these clefs.

Treble or G Clef locates the
pitch G above Middle C.

Bass or F Clef locates the
pitch F below Middle C.

In making the treble clef sign, be sure the two lines of the sign cross on the fourth line of the staff and the G line or second line is crossed three times.

### Other Terms

1. *Bars.* Lines drawn vertically through the staff are called bars.
2. *Double bars.* These are used at the end of a composition to indicate the completion of a composition.
3. *Measure.* The music contained between two bar lines is one measure. The rhythm of the music is measured.
4. *Accent marks.* These are used for accent or emphasis.
5. *Tie.* The curve line connecting two or more notes of the same pitch (in the same place on the staff) is called a tie. The note is sounded or played once and held for the duration or value of all the notes.

6. *Slur.* The curve line connecting two or more notes of different pitch is called a slur. One word or syllable of a word is sung on the two or more tones.
7. *Repeat signs.* Two dots before a bar indicate that the music of the preceding section is to be repeated. Go back to the preceding double bar or, in case there is no double bar, go back to the beginning and continue to the end or the sign ''Fine.''
8. *Fermata* or *Hold.* The note under this sign is to be held longer than usual, the length of time dependent on the interpretation being given the music.
9. *Sharp.* This sign in front of a note indicates a tone one-half step (next adjacent key on the piano or bells) higher than the normal pitch of that tone.
10. *Flat.* This sign indicates a tone one-half step lower than the normal pitch.
11. *Natural.* This sign removes the effect of a sharp or flat or takes away the sharp or flat.

a. Placed before a flatted note, the natural has the same effect as a sharp and raises that tone one-half step higher than the pitch represented by the flatted note.

b. Placed before a sharped note, the natural has the same effect as a flat and lowers that tone one-half step below the pitch represented by the sharped note.

12. *Half step.* A step is a unit for measuring distance in music. The tone nearest to any given tone, either above or below, is a half step from the given tone. The half steps that occur normally on the staff are between B and C (*12a*) and E and F (*12b*). As another example, on the keyboard the half steps are from white key G to black key G# (*12c*) and from white key A to black key A♭ (*12d*).

13. *Whole step.* A whole step consists of two half steps. On the keyboard the whole steps are from a white key to the next white key or from a black key to the next black key (except from B to C and from E to F).

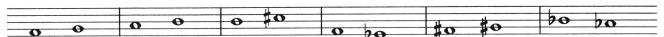

14. *Chromatic.* Sharps, flats, or naturals (other than those in the signature) placed before notes in a composition are called chromatics or accidentals. When sharps, flats, or naturals are used in a measure of music, they affect only the same note when repeated in the same measure. The measure bar automatically cancels these accidentals.

**Notes and Their Corresponding Rests**

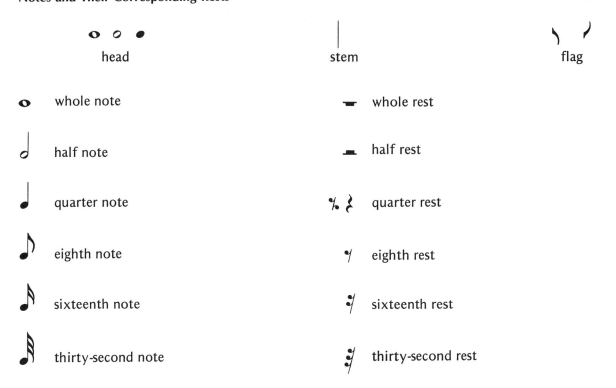

head                       stem                      flag

| note | | rest |
| --- | --- | --- |
| whole note | | whole rest |
| half note | | half rest |
| quarter note | | quarter rest |
| eighth note | | eighth rest |
| sixteenth note | | sixteenth rest |
| thirty-second note | | thirty-second rest |

**Placement of Rests on the Treble Staff**

|  | 1. | 2. | 3. | 4. | 5. |
|---|---|---|---|---|---|
|  | Whole | Half | Quarter | Eighth | Sixteenth |

1. Whole rest is placed down from the fourth line of the staff.
2. Half rest is made up from the third line.
3. Quarter rest is started in the third space and goes down into the second space.
4. The flag of the eighth rest is made in the third space and on the left side of the stem.
5. The flags of the sixteenth rest are made on the third and fourth lines and on the left side of the stem.

**Dotted Notes**

A dot following a note adds one half of the value of the note. The most commonly found dotted notes are:

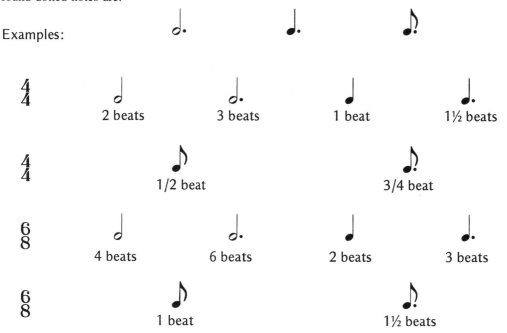

**Signature**

The term *signature* includes clef sign, sharps or flats, and numbers. The sharps or flats indicate the *key signature*. The numbers indicate the *time* or *meter signature*.

1.   Treble clef key of D
     6/8 meter

2.   Bass clef key of E♭
     4/4 meter

**Rules for Meter (Time) Signatures**

Meter signatures are numerical indications of the regular recurrence of a beat or pulse. They are composed of two numbers placed one above the other. The upper figure tells the number of beats in a measure. The lower figure tells the kind of note that receives one beat.

## Examples of Meter Signatures

$\frac{4}{4}$  $\frac{3}{4}$  $\frac{2}{4}$    The 4 on the bottom means that the <u>quarter</u> note gets one count or beat.

**C** means common time, the same as $\frac{4}{4}$ time.

| 4 beats | 2 | 1 beat | 1/2 | 1/4 | 3 | 1½ | 3/4 |

$\frac{3}{8}$  $\frac{6}{8}$    The 8 means that the <u>eighth</u> note gets one count or beat.

| 4 beats | 2 | 1 beat | 1/2 | 6 | 3 | 1½ |

Typical complete measures of these meter signatures are:

## Finding the Key of a Song

Songs are written in various keys. The key of a song is determined by the scale tones used. Thus a song in the key of C uses the tones in the scale of C:

In this scale, the pitch of C is considered to be the key center or the pitch that begins and ends the scale series, and in this scale it is given the number 1. In the C scale the pitch of D is number 2, E is number 3, F is number 4, G is number 5, A is number 6, B is number 7, and C again is number 8, or the octave of 1. In the scale of C none of the pitches is either sharped (#) or flatted ( ♭ ), so in a song in the key of C no sharps or flats are shown at the beginning of the song. Songs in other keys show key signatures that use sharps or flats because they are based on scales that have to use pitches either sharped or flatted. Thus a song in the key of G, the tones of which are derived from the scale of G, has to use a sharp (F#) in its signature because in the scale of G this pitch (F) has to be sharped:

Key of G

This sharp is placed on the staff after the clef sign. In each case the key signature denotes the pitch considered to be the key center for the song. The pitch so considered is always given the number 1.

In order to play or sing a song in its proper key setting, it is important to be able to tell from the key signature in what key the song is to be played or sung. The technique of determining the key from a given key signature is not difficult.

In songs having flats in their signatures, call the line or space of the staff on which the last flat (the one to the far right of any others shown) is placed ''four'' (4) and count downward each consecutive line or space of the staff until the line or space number one (1) is reached. The pitch for that line or space of the staff is then the key center (*x*) or key tone (keys of B♭, E♭, A♭, and D♭):

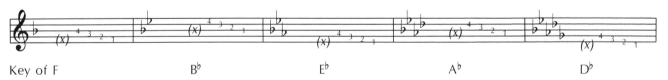

Key of F                    B♭                    E♭                    A♭                    D♭

In songs having only one flat in their signature, call the line of the staff on which it is placed ''4,'' and count down to 1 (key of F above).

In order to find the key of songs with sharps, move up one line or space of the staff from the last sharp, which is the one to the far right of any others shown in the key signature. If the last sharp is located on a line, the key center will be located on the next space. If the last sharp is located in a space, the key center will be located on the next line:

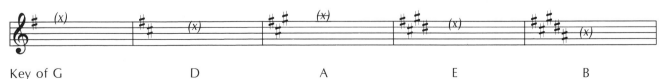

Key of G                    D                    A                    E                    B

# APPENDIX C

# Resource Materials

## PROFESSIONAL ORGANIZATIONS, NEWSLETTERS, AND JOURNALS

### Organizations

**A.C.E.I.**
Association for Childhood Education International
11141 Georgia Ave.
Suite 200
Wheaton, Md. 20902

**D.C.C.D.C.A.**
Day Care and Child Development Council of America, Inc.
1401 K St., N.W.
Washington, D.C. 20005

**ERIC/ECE**
Educational Resources Information Center/Early Childhood Education
805 West Pennsylvania Ave.
Urbana, Ill. 61801

**MENC**
Music Educators National Conference
1902 Association Dr.
Reston, Va. 22091

**N.A.E.Y.C.**
National Association for the Education of Young Children
1834 Connecticut Ave., N.W.
Washington, D.C. 20009

**U.S. DHEW**
U.S. Department of Health, Education, and Welfare
Office of Child Development
Children's Bureau
Washington, D.C. 20201

### Newsletters

*ERIC/ECE Newsletter*
805 West Pennsylvania Ave.
Urbana, Ill. 61801

*Report on Preschool Programs*
Capitol Publications, Inc.
1300 North 17th St.
Arlington, Va. 22209

*Today's Child* News Magazine
Edwards Publications, Inc.
Roosevelt, N.J. 08555

### Journals

*Childhood Education*
Association for Childhood Education International
11141 Georgia Ave.
Suite 200
Wheaton, Md. 20902

*Children Today*
U.S. Department of Health, Education, and Welfare
Office of Child Development
Children's Bureau
Superintendent of Documents
U.S. Government Printing Office
Washington, D.C. 20402

*Child Development*
Society for Research in Child Development
University of Chicago Press
5801 Ellis Ave.
Chicago, Ill. 60637

249

*Music Educators Journal*
Music Educators National Conference
1902 Association Dr.
Reston, Va. 22091

*Merrill-Palmer Quarterly of Behavior and Development*
Merrill-Palmer Institute
71 East Ferry Ave.
Detroit, Mich. 48202

*Young Children*
National Association for the Education of Young Children
1834 Connecticut Ave., N.W.
Washington, D.C. 20009

## MUSIC TEXTS FOR TEACHING MUSIC TO YOUNG CHILDREN

Andress, Barbara. *Music experiences in early childhood.* New York: Holt, Rinehart & Winston, 1980.

Aronoff, Frances Webber. *Music and young children.* New York: Holt, Rinehart and Winston, 1969.

Haines, B. Joan E., and Gerber, Linda L. *Leading young children to music.* 2d ed. Columbus, Ohio: Merrill, 1984.

Moomaw, Sally. *Discovering music in early childhood.* Boston: Allyn and Bacon, 1984.

Nye, Vernice. *Music for young children.* Dubuque, Iowa: William C. Brown, 1983.

Pugmire, M.C. *Experiences in music for young children.* Albany, N.Y.: Delmar, 1977.

Wilt, Michele. *Music experiences for young children.* New York: The Center for Applied Research in Education, 1982.

## MUSIC SERIES BOOKS

*Music for Early Childhood* (1980)
Choate, Kjelson, Berg, Troth, Peterson
New Dimensions in Music
American Book Co.
New York, N.Y.
*Resource collection for teachers and parents of children two through five years old. All the songs and related activities are based on a part of the curriculum for this age.*

*Silver Burdette Music Kindergarten Centennial Edition* (1985)
Teacher's Edition K
Aubin, Crook, Hayden, Walker
Silver Burdette Company
Morristown, N.J.
*Familiar, singable songs. Informal experiences with specific qualities of music.*

*The Music Book—Teacher's Resource Book for Kindergarten* (1984)
Boardman and Andress
Holt, Rinehart & Winston
New York, N.Y.

*The Spectrum of Music* (1980)
Music Teacher's Resource Book
Marsh, Rinehart, Savage
New York, N.Y.
*Hearing, singing, and playing songs and selections ranging from traditional to contemporary. Optional activities for Orff and Kodály methods, plus many other outstanding features.*

## SONGBOOKS

*A Fiesta of Folk Songs from Spain and Latin America* (1967)
Edited by Henrietta Yurchenco
G.P. Putnam's Sons
New York, N.Y.
*Collection of songs about animals and nature and singing games and dances with pronunciation guide.*

*All Day Long Songs* (1979)
Minnie O'Leary
Shawnee Press, Inc.
Delaware Water Gap, Pa.
*Good collection.*

*American Folk Songs for Children* (1948)
Ruth Crawford Seeger
Doubleday & Co., Inc.
Garden City, N.Y.
*An excellent collection of American folk songs for children.*

*A Song Is a Rainbow* (1982)
Patty Zeitlin
Scott, Foresman and Company
Glenville, Ill.
*Music, movement, and rhythm. Instruments in the nursery school and kindergarten. Excellent.*

*Do Your Ears Hang Low?* (1980)
Tom Glazer
Doubleday & Co., Inc.
Garden City, N.Y.
*Fifty fingerplays set to music. Tom Glazer's second set of musical fingerplays.*

*Elephant Jam* (1980)
Sharon, Lois, & Bram
McGraw-Hill Ryerson Limited
Toronto, Ontario, Canada
*A trunkful of musical fun for youngsters, friends, and families. Games, favorite camp songs, and other excellent activities.*

*Eye Winker, Tom Tinker, Chin Chopper* (1973)
Tom Glazer
Doubleday & Co., Inc.
Garden City, N.Y.
*Contains 50 fingerplays. There are familiar fingerplays set to music, as well as some beautiful new songs and famous folk songs with brand new fingerplays.*

*Holiday Singing & Dancing Games* (1980)
Esther L. Nelson

Sterling Publishing Co., Inc.
New York, N.Y.
*Songs and dances passed down from generation to generation. Some dances are authentic; others are new. Folk and traditional songs included.*

*Jim Along Josie* (1970)
Nancy and John Langstaff
Harcourt Brace Jovanovich, Inc.
New York, N.Y.
*Collection of folk songs and singing games for young children. This book contains traditional singing games that involve the child in singing, dancing, and acting out words. There are many action songs especially suited to the youngest child. Included are piano accompaniments, guitar chords, and some optional percussion accompaniments for use with simple instruments.*

*Juba This and Juba That* (1969)
Selected by Virginia A. Tashjian
Little, Brown and Company
Boston, Mass.
*Book contains chants, poetry, stories, fingerplays, riddles, songs, tongue twisters, and jokes that are fun to sing, tell, and play.*

*Mockingbird Flight* (1975)
Patricia Hoglund Nielsen, Floyd Sucher, and Charlotte D. Garmon
The Economy Company
Oklahoma City, Okla.
*Good collection.*

*Music Activities for Retarded Children* (1965)
David R. Ginglend and Winifred E. Stiles
Abingdon Press, Tenn.
*This book was planned to assist the special music teacher, classroom teacher, and recreation or volunteer leader to initiate a developmental beginning music program for special children or young "normal" children.*

*Musical Games, Fingerplays and Rhythmic Activities for Early Childhood* (1983)
Marian Wirth et al.
Parker Publishing Company, Inc.
West Nyack, N.Y.
*Over 200 musical games, camp and folk songs, chants, and other activities. Excellent and comprehensive collection.*

*Music for Fun, Music for Learning* (1977)
Lois Birkenshaw
Holt, Rinehart & Winston of Canada, Ltd.
Toronto
*Music for regular and special classrooms.*

*Reaching the Special Learner Through Music* (1979)
Sona D. Nocera
Silver Burdette Company
Glenville, Ill.
*An excellent source of songs and activities for developing music skills and learning.*

*Singing Bee* (1982)
Compiled by Jane Hart

Lothrop, Lee & Shepard Books
New York, N.Y.
*125 songs, beautifully illustrated, that should be a part of every child's musical heritage. Excellent.*

*Sing Through the Day* (1968)
Compiled and edited by the Society of Brothers
The Plough Publishing House
Firton, N.Y.
*Ninety songs for young children. Beautifully illustrated.*

*The Animal Song Book*
Edward Fisher
St. Martin's Press, Inc.
New York, N.Y.
*Includes songs about lions, porcupines, and other creatures; songs are excellent for creative movement.*

*The Fireside Song Book of Birds and Beasts* (1972)
Edited by Jane Yolen
Simon and Schuster
New York, N.Y.

*The Fireside Song Book of Children's Songs* (1966)
Collected & Edited by Marie Winn
Simon and Schuster
New York, N.Y.

*The Fireside Book of Folk Songs* (1963)
Songs selected by Margaret Boni
Simon and Schuster
New York, N.Y.

*The Great Song Book* (1978)
Edited by Timothy John
Doubleday & Co., Inc.
Garden City, N.Y.
*A collection of the best-loved songs in the English language, based on traditional versions. Excellent.*

*The Illustrated Disney Song Book* (1979)
Introduction by David E. Tietyen
Hal Leonard Publishing Corporation/Random House
New York, N.Y.
*Disney songs have become an important part of our American heritage. The book is a collection in sheet-music format of more than 80 of Disney's most popular songs.*

*The Raffi Singable Songbook*
Chappell
14 Birch Avenue
Toronto, Ontario, Canada
*A collection of 51 songs from Raffi's first three records for young children.*

## MUSIC BOOKS BY "MISS JACKIE"* AND OTHERS

*Hello Sound* (1979)
*Hello Rhythm* (1977)

---

*"Miss Jackie," 10001 El Monte, Overland Park, Kansas 66207.

*The Great Big Book of Rhythm* (1986)
*Sniggles, Squirrels and Chicken Pox* (1984)
*Songs to Sing with Babies* (1983)
*Excellent collection.*

*Piggyback Songs* (1983)
*More Piggyback Songs* (1984)
Compiled by Jearn Warren
Totline Press
Warren Publishing House
P.O. Box 2255
Everett, Wash. 98203
*New songs sung to the tune of childhood favorites.*

*Wee Sing—Children's Songs and Fingerplays* (1984)
*Wee Sing Silly Songs—Collection of ''Silly Songs''* (1982)
*Wee Sing and Play—Musical Games and Rhymes for Children* (1981)
Pamela Conn Beall and Susan Hagen Nipp
Price/Stern/Sloan Publishers
Los Angeles, Calif.

## SOURCES FOR ORDERING INSTRUMENTS

Children's Book & Music Center
2500 Santa Monica Blvd.
Santa Monica, Calif. 90404

Lyons Band
P.O. Box 1003
Elkhart, Ind. 46515

Oscar Schmidt/Music Education Group
230 Lexington Dr.
Buffalo Grove, Ill. 60090

Peripole, Inc.
Brown's Mills, N.J. 08015-0146

Rhythm Band, Inc.
P.O. Box 126
Fort Worth, Tex. 76101

## BOOKS ON MAKING INSTRUMENTS

*Make Your Own Musical Instruments*
Muriel Mandell and Robert E. Wood
Sterling Publishing Co., Inc.
419 Park Avenue South
New York, N.Y. 10016

*Music and Instruments for Children to Make (Book One)*
*Rhythms, Music and Instruments to Make (Book Two)*
John Hawkinson and Martha Faulhaber
Albert Whitman & Co.
560 West Lake St.
Chicago, Ill. 60606

*Simple Folk Instruments To Make and Play*
Ilene Hunter and Marilyn Judson
Children's Book & Music Center
2500 Santa Monica Blvd.
Santa Monica, Calif. 90404

*Making Musical Instruments*
Rebecca Anders
Lerner Publications Company
Minneapolis, Minn. 55401

*American Indian Music and Musical Instruments*
George S. Fichter
McKay Publishers
New York, N.Y. 10016

## SOURCES FOR ORDERING RECORDINGS*

A & M Records of Canada Limited
939 Warden Ave.
Scarborough, Ontario MIL 4C5

Bowmar/Noble
P.O. Box 251308
1901 N. Walnut St.
Oklahoma City, Okla. 73125

Capital Records, Inc.
1290 Avenue of the Americas
New York, N.Y. 10019

Childcraft
Education Corp.
20 Kilmer Rd.
Edison, N.J. 08817

Children's Book & Music Center
2500 Santa Monica Blvd.
Santa Monica, Calif. 90404

Columbia Records
51 West 52nd St.
New York, N.Y. 10019

Decca Records
445 Park Ave.
New York, N.Y. 10022

Disneyland Records
800 Sonora Ave.
Glendale, Calif. 91201

Educational Activities, Inc.
P.O. Box 391
Freeport, N.Y. 11520

*Readers are encouraged to send for up-to-date catalogs. Full descriptions of the recordings are usually given. Every effort was made by the authors to obtain the latest names and addresses of the companies listed.

Education Records Sales
157 Chambers St.
New York, N.Y. 10007

Educational Recordings of America
P.O. Box 210
Ansonia, Conn. 06401

Educo
P.O. Box 3005
Ventura, Calif. 93003

Folkways Records & Service Corp.
632 Broadway—Ninth Floor
New York, N.Y. 10012

Honor Your Partner Records
P.O. Box 391
Freeport, N.Y. 11520

Kimbo Educational
P.O. Box 477
86 South 5th Ave.
Long Branch, N.J. 17740

Ladyslipper, Inc.
P.O. Box 3124
Durham, N.C. 27705

Lyons Band
P.O. Box 1003
Elkhart, Ind. 46515

MCA Records, Inc.
70 Universal City Plaza
Universal City, Calif. 91608

Melody House, Inc.
819 N.W. 92nd St.
Oklahoma City, Okla. 73114

Michael Brent Publications, Inc.
Golden Records
Winding Wood Rd.
Port Chester, N.Y. 10573

Miss Jackie Music Co.
10001 El Monte
Overland Park, Kans. 66207

MMB Music, Inc.
10370 Page Industrial Blvd.
St. Louis, Mo. 63132

Oscar Schmidt/Music Education Group
230 Lexington Dr.
Buffalo Grove, Ill. 60089

R & D Records
254 Cambridge
Ashland, Ore. 97520

Tom Thumb Productions
Rhythm Productions

Whitney Bldg.
Box 34485
Los Angeles, Calif. 90034

## EXAMPLES OF FAVORITE RECORDINGS*

### Alfred Publishing Co., Inc.
*It's Time for Music* by Mary Louise Reilly & Lynn Freeman Olson—A complete teaching package. Excellent! Every teacher of young children should have these materials. Songbook, recordings, and teacher handbook. Contains guidelines for planning appropriate singing, playing, and moving experiences for the young child age three to seven. One of the best and most complete music education programs available.

### Children's Book & Music Center
### Lyons Band
*The Small Singer,* Records 1 and 2—Good collection of songs for the young.
*The Small Dancer*—Short orchestral pieces for interpretive movement.
*The Small Listener*—Short classics for young listeners.
*The Small Player*—Short classics for rhythm instruments.
*Folk Songs For Little Singers*
(The Bowmar Musician Series has long been a favorite.)

### Children's Book & Music Center
*Our Dinosaur Friends*—Perfect for the early years.
*Peter, Paul and Mary*—Good. "Puff The Magic Dragon," "Going to the Zoo."
*Dance-A-Story/Sing-A-Song*—"The Wooden Doll Story." Side 2 contains nine multicultural songs.
*Sounds Like Fun*—Folk songs, games, and poems for children accompanied by folk and Orff instruments.
*Birds, Beasts, Bugs and Little Fishes*
*Adventures in Sound*—Contains many different types of sounds with narration.
*American Folk Songs for Children*—Collection of 94 familiar folk songs.
*Burl Ives: The Best of Burl's for Boys and Girls*—"Aunt Rhody," "Hush Little Baby."

### Educational Activities, Inc.
*Won't You Be My Friend?* by Patty Zeitlin and Marcia Berman.
*Circle Games, Activity Songs, and Lullabies* by Patty Zeitlin and Marcia Berman.
*I'm Not Small*—Simple circle games and activity songs. Lullabies, songs for listening and resting.
*Be a Frog, a Bird, or a Tree* by Rachel Carr—Creative yoga exercises for children.

---

*For the convenience of the reader, we are listing some of the companies from which the following records can be obtained. Many of these records may also be obtained from other companies listed in this appendix. Records are grouped by composer or company. This sampling is taken from preschool teachers.

*I Know the Colors of the Rainbow* by Ella Jenkins—Rhythmic, musically compelling. Listening and appreciation album. Songs about other cultures.

*You'll Sing a Song and I'll Sing a Song* by Ella Jenkins—Excellent! A favorite.

*Play Your Instruments and Make a Pretty Sound* by Ella Jenkins—Instrument identification, conducting, creative movement, use of instruments.

*Learning Basic Skills Through Music* by Hap Palmer, vol. 1—Contains the popular song "This Is the Song About Colors."

*Patriotic and Morning Time Songs* by Hap Palmer.

*Folk Song Carnival* by Hap Palmer—Excellent! A must for the classroom and home.

*Witches Brew* by Hap Palmer—Excellent for oral language development.

*Sea Gulls* by Hap Palmer—Good for listening and relaxation.

*Getting to Know Myself* by Hap Palmer—One of his finest recordings.

*Easy Does It* by Hap Palmer—Motor skill development.

*Pretend* by Hap Palmer—Stimulates creativity, imagination.

*Ideas, Thoughts and Feelings* by Hap Palmer—Experience discovery and independent thinking.

*Homemade Band* by Hap Palmer—Enjoyable and easy-to-follow directions. Use with instruments.

*Finger and Foot Plays*

**Kimbo**

*Get a Good Start*—Aerobic activities designed for young children. Short, simple, fun, easy-to-follow directions. Excellent.

*Bean Bag Activities*—Excellent. Good for developing coordination.

*Walk Like the Animals*—Imitative animal walks.

*Toes Up, Toes Down*—Enjoyable activities to help develop body identification, spatial awareness.

*Sing a Song of Action*—23 progressive songs to act out rhythmically through fingerplays and games.

*Simplified Lummi Stick Activities*—Excellent! A favorite.

*One Elephant, Deux Elephants* by Sharon, Lois, & Bram—Excellent collection of children's songs.

*Smorgasbord* by Sharon, Lois, & Bram—Songs like "Peanut Butter," "Michael Finnigan."

*Mainly Mother Goose* by Sharon, Lois, & Bram—Parents' Choice Award.

*Music for 2'S & 3'S* by Tom Glazer—A fun collection of activity and game songs like *Music for 1'S & 2'S.*

*Children's Greatest Hits* by Tom Glazer, vols. 1 and 2.

*Let's Sing Fingerplays* by Tom Glazer.

*Singable Songs for the Very Young* by Raffi.

*More Singable Songs* by Raffi.

*Raffi's Christmas Album*

*Rise and Shine* by Raffi.

*We All Live Together Series* by Youngheart, vols. 1–4—Refreshing and enjoyable. Use of pop-rock tunes to develop readiness and motor skills.

*Share It* by Rosenshontz.

*Tickles You* by Rosenshontz.

*Once Upon a Dinosaur*

**Lyons**

*Chicken Fat*—Good. Orchestrated with vocal instructions.

*Fingerplay Fun* by Rosemary Hallum—Traditional fingerplays from the folk heritage as well as new ones.

*It's a Happy Feeling* (Tom Thumb Library)—Excellent! Auditory awareness, classification, left-right, self-concept.

*Favorite Folk Dances & Song Games,* Singing Games Albums 1 and 2.

**Melody House, Inc.**

*The Hokey Pokey and Other Favorites*—Very good. Music is slow for the very young and exceptional child, faster for the advanced.

**R & D Records**

*Sing a Song of Sunshine,* vol. II, by Randy Hitz and Diane Bruengo—Songs for creative movement, call-and-response, action and game songs. Original songs and games for young children. A fresh approach. Very enjoyable.

**Phyllis S. Weikart**

*Movement Plus Music: Activities for Children Ages 3 to 7.*
High/Scope Press
600 North River St.
Ypsilanti, Mich. 48198

## RECORDINGS AND BOOKS ABOUT INSTRUMENTS

*Big Bird Discovers the Orchestra* (Sesame Street)

*Big Bird Leads the Band* (Sesame Street)

*Homemade Band* (Hap Palmer)
Children's Book & Music Center, Educational Activities, Inc., Kimbo

*Modern Tunes for Rhythms and Instruments* (Hap Palmer)
Children's Book & Music Center, Educational Activities, Inc., Kimbo

*Play Your Instruments and Make a Pretty Sound* (Ella Jenkins)
Folkways, Children's Book & Music Center, Educational Activities, Inc.

*Rhythm Band Time* (Music to use with instruments)
Children's Book & Music Center

*The Great Big Book of Rhythm* ("Miss Jackie" Weissman)
10001 El Monte
Overland Park, Kans. 66207

*The Instruments of the Orchestra* (Ages 4 to 10—Cassette)
Children's Book and Music Center

*The Rhythm Makers* (Learning rhythm through activities and beginning rhythm instruments)
Children's Book & Music Center, Rhythms Productions

*The Orchestra* (Introduction to the instruments)
Children's Book & Music Center

*The Small Player* (Bowmar Series)
Kimbo, Children's Book & Music Center
  *Excellent*

*Tubby the Tuba*
Children's Book & Music Center

*Young Person's Guide to the Orchestra* (Benjamin Britten)
Children's Book & Music Center
  *Excellent*

*A Rainbow of Sound* (The instruments of the orchestra and their
    music)
Herbert Kupferberg
Charles Scribner's Sons
New York, N.Y.
*Resource book for teachers. Tells how different instruments con-
    tribute to the orchestra.*

*Tooters, Tweeters, Strings and Beaters*
Allen L. Richardson
Grosset & Dunlap
New York, N.Y.
*An excellent book showing 24 different instruments. Pictures and
    descriptions of instruments suitable for young children.*

## LISTENING AND APPRECIATION

It has often been said that the tastes of young children can
be shaped by the music we play for them. In order for
children to appreciate music of quality, they need to hear the
music played repeatedly. A list of recordings that develop
listening skills and music appreciation follows.

"Air on the G String" (Bach)
"Aragonaise" (Massenet)
"Ballet of the Unhatched Chicks" (Moussorgsky)
"Barcarolle" from *Tales of Hoffman* (Offenbach)
"Berceuse" (Chopin)
"Bridal Chorus" from *Lohengrin* (Wagner)
*Carnival of the Animals* (Saint-Saëns)
*Children's Corner Suite* (Debussy)
"Clown" from *Marionettes* (MacDowell)
"Country Gardens" (Granger)
"Danse Macabre" (Saint-Saëns)
"Dance of the Ballerina" from *Petrouchka* (Stravinsky)
"Entrance of the Little Fauns" (Pierné)
"Golliwog's Cakewalk" (Debussy)
*Grand Canyon Suite* (Grofé)
*Hansel and Gretel* (Humperdinck)
"Hornpipe" from *Water Music* (Handel)
"Knight of the Hobby Horse" (Schumann)
"Leap Frog" (Bizet)
"March Militaire" (Schubert)
"March of the Little Lead Soldiers" (Pierné)
"March of the Toys" (Herbert)

*Mother Goose Suite* (Ravel)
*Nutcracker Suite* (Tchaikovsky)
"Of a Tailor and a Bear" (MacDowell)
*Peter and the Wolf* (Prokofiev)
*Peer Gynt Suite No. 1* (Grieg)
"Pizzicato" (Delibes)
"Polka" (Shostakovich)
*Scenes from Childhood* (Schumann)
"Sleighride" (Anderson)
"Sweet Dreams" (Tchaikovsky)
*Symphony No. 94 in G Major* ("Surprise") (Haydn)
"The Dancing Doll" (Poldini)
"The Flight of the Bumblebee" (Rimsky-Korsakov)
"The Happy Farmer" (Schumann)
"The Skater's Waltz" (Waldteufel)
*The Sorcerer's Apprentice* (Dukas)
"The Swan" (Saint-Saëns)
"To a Water Lily" (MacDowell)
"Toy Symphony" (Haydn)
"Waltzing Doll" (Poldini)
*The Small Listener* (Bowmar Series)—Short classics for
    young listeners. Excellent. Can be ordered from the Chil-
    dren's Book & Music Center.
*A Child's Introduction to the Classics*, Children's Book &
    Music Center

## RECORDINGS

The following selected list identifies recordings that highlight certain instruments.

*Carnival of the Animals* (Saint-Saëns)
  *Piano, double bass, strings, flutes, clarinet, xylophone*

"The Swan" (Saint-Saëns)
  *Cello, piano*

"Waltz of the Flowers" (Tchaikovsky)
  *Harp*

"Stars and Stripes Forever" (Sousa)
  *Piccolo*

*Peter and the Wolf* (Prokofiev)
  *Oboe, bassoon*

"The White Peacock" (Griffes)
  *Flute*

*New World Symphony*, second movement (Dvořák)
  *English horn*

"Trumpet Voluntary in D" (Purcell-Clark)
  *Trumpet*

"Nocturne" from *A Midsummer Night's Dream* (Mendelssohn)
  *French horn, cello, bassoon*

"Dance of the Sugar Plum Fairy" (Tchaikovsky)
*Celesta*

"Prelude and Fugue in G Major" (Bach)
*Organ*

*11 Trovatore*, "Anvil Chorus" (Verdi)
*Tambourine, triangle*

Following are examples of selected classical recordings to use with movement.

### Creative Dancing
*Nutcracker Suite* (Tchaikovsky)
"Danse Macabre" (Saint-Saëns)

### Hopping
"Ballet of the Unhatched Chicks" (Moussorgsky)

### Jumping/Leaping
"Leap Frog" from *Children's Games* (Bizet)
"Aragonaise" from *Le Cid* (Massenet)

### Marching
"American Salute" (Gould)
"Entrance of the Little Fauns" (Pierné)
"March of the Little Lead Soldiers" (Pierné)
"Children's March" (Goldman)
"March Militaire" (Schubert)
"March" from *The Nutcracker Suite* (Tchaikovsky)

### Running
"Tag" (Prokofiev)
"Catch Me" from *Scenes from Childhood* (Schumann)
"The Ball" from *Children's Games* (Bizet)

### Skipping/Galloping
"Gallop" from *The Comedians* (Kabalevsky)
"Knight of the Hobby Horse" from *Scenes from Childhood* (Schumann)
"The Wild Horseman" from *Album for the Young* (Schumann)

### Sliding/Gliding
"The Swan" from *Carnival of the Animals* (Saint-Saëns)
"The Skaters Waltz" (Waldteufel)
"Waltz on Ice" from *Winter Holiday* (Prokofiev)

### Swaying/Rocking
"Waltz of the Dolls" (Delibes)
"To a Water Lily" (MacDowell)
"Barcarolle" (Offenbach)
"Waltz" from *Six Piano Pieces for Children* (Shostakovich)

### Tiptoe
"Dance of the Little Swans" from *Swan Lake* (Tchaikovsky)

### Walking
"Gavotte" (Handel)
"Bourree" (Telemann)
"Walking Song" from *Acadian Songs and Dances* (Thomson)

### Whirling
"Impromptu—The Top" from *Children's Games* (Bizet)
"Clowns" (Kabalevsky)
"Tarantella" from *The Fantastic Toy Shop* (Rossini-Respighi)

## STORIES FOR CHILDREN INVOLVING MUSIC

*The Fox Went Out on a Chilly Night* (1961)
Peter Spier
Doubleday & Co., Inc.
Garden City, N.Y.
*An old folk song beautifully illustrated.*

*Frog Went A-Courtin'* (1955)
John Langstaff
Harcourt, Brace & World, Inc.
New York, N.Y.
*Langstaff made one story out of the different versions of the ballad
that are sung in various parts of America.*

*Over in the Meadow* (1957)
John Langstaff
Harcourt, Brace & World, Inc.
New York, N.Y.
*The text is Mr. Langstaff's version of an old rhyme for children.
Not a traditional folk song.*

*One Wide River To Cross* (1966)
Adapted by Barbara Emberley
Prentice-Hall, Inc.
Englewood Cliffs, N.J.
*Includes the song "One Wide River To Cross."*

*The Cat Came Back* (1971)
Dahlov Ipcar
Alfred A. Knopf
New York, N.Y.
*Story plus the song "The Cat Came Back."*

*Hush, Little Baby* (1976)
Margot Zemoch
E.P. Dutton & Co., Inc.
New York, N.Y.
*Beautifully illustrated book of the popular folk song.*

*Six Little Ducks* (1976)
Chris Conover
Thomas Y. Crowell Company
New York, N.Y.
*One little duck leads his friends into mischief. Adaptation of an old
camp song.*

*We Wish You A Merry Christmas* (1983)
Dial Books for Young Readers
A Division of E. P. Dutton, Inc.
New York, N.Y.
*An illustrated version of the traditional English carol.*

*Twelve Days of Christmas* (1973)
Jack Kent
Parents' Magazine Press
New York, N.Y.
*An English folk song.*

*The Little Drummer Boy* (1968)
Ezra Jack Keats, Katherine Davis, Henry Onorati, and Harry Simeone
Macmillan Company
New York, N.Y.
*A classic for young children. Beautifully illustrated.*

*Over the River and Through the Wood* (1974)
Lydia Maria Child
Coward, McCann & Geoghegan, Inc.
New York, N.Y.
*An illustrated version of the favorite Thanksgiving song.*

*There Was an Old Woman* (1974)
Retold & drawn by Steven Kellogg
Four Winds Press, a division of Scholastic Magazines, Inc.
New York, N.Y.
*A cumulative song about the old lady who swallows a fly.*

*London Bridge Is Falling Down* (1967)
Ed Emberley
Little, Brown and Company
Boston, Mass.
*An illustrated version of the singing game.*

*London Bridge Is Falling Down* (1967)
Illustrated by Peter Spier
From The Mother Goose Library
Doubleday & Co., Inc.
Garden City, N.Y.

*Fiddle-I-Fee* (1979)
Traditional American chant
Illustrated by Diane Stanley
*A young girl invites farm animals to a special dinner party in her tree house. The animals fill the house with different sounds. Children can participate in making the animal sounds.*

*What Sadie Sang* (1976)
Story and pictures by Eve Rice
Greenwillow Books
New York, N.Y.
*Sadie sings a song to the tree on the corner, to the red fire hydrant, etc., as mother pushes her in a cart. Good for two- and three-year-olds.*

*Really Rosie* (1975)
Lyrics by Maurice Sendak
Music by Carole King
Colgems Music Corp.
*Contains "Chicken Soup With Rice" plus other songs.*

*The Boy Who Loved Music* (1979)
David Lasker
The Viking Press
New York, N.Y.
*The story is based on an actual incident about a boy who played horn in the orchestra of Prince Nicolaus Esterhazy. The book is beautifully illustrated and filled with humor.*

*Frère Jacques* (1973)
Barbara Schook Hazen
J.B. Lippincott Company
New York, N.Y.
*This is a story of a monk who has a terrible problem of oversleeping, especially when it is his turn to ring the morning bells. The problem is finally solved by a young choir boy. Includes words and music to the song.*

*Yankee Doodle* (1965)
Dr. Richard Schackburg
Prentice-Hall, Inc.
Englewood Cliffs, N.J.
*The story of how Yankee Doodle was written. Song is included.*

*The Old Banjo* (1983)
Dennis Hoseley
Macmillan Company
New York, N.Y.
*A story about old instruments (banjo, trumpet, violin) that are found by a farmer and his son in an attic and barn.*

*The Traveling Men of Ballycoo* (1983)
Eve Bunting
Harcourt Brace Jovanovich
New York, N.Y.
*The traveling men are minstrel brothers who take their songs and music throughout Ireland. After they become tired of traveling, the people come to them to hear their music.*

*Something Special For Me* (1983)
Vera B. Williams
Greenwillow Books
New York, N.Y.
*The story of Rosa, who takes money from a jar and can't decide what she wants to buy. She finally decides on a small used accordion and loves it.*

*The Willow Flute (A North Country Tale)* (1975)
D. William Johnson
Little, Brown and Company
Boston, Mass.
*Lewis Shrew goes out into the white woods to gather twigs for his stove. He finds a musty old room in a house. As he searches throughout the house, he finds a willow flute amid the wreckage on the floor. As he begins to play, winter disappears and spring returns.*

*Lentil* (1940)
Robert McCloskey
The Viking Press, Inc.
New York, N.Y.
*Lentil cannot sing but wants to be able to do so. When he opens his mouth, only strange sounds come out. He also cannot whistle. Lentil saves up enough money to buy a harmonica and saves the day when all the band members' lips pucker up and they can't play their instruments for Colonel Carter. The people give Lentil a warm welcome.*

*Ty's One-Man Band* (1980)
Mildred Pitts Walter
Four Winds Press
New York, N.Y.
*An American folktale about Andro, a peg-legged man who calls himself a one-man band. This lyrical story encompasses many emotions and all of the interesting sounds and rhythms of a hot summer day.*

*Peter and the Wolf* (1971)
Sergei S. Prokofiev
Gokkin Co., Ltd.
Tokyo, Japan
Distributed in the U.S. by Silver Burdette Co.
Morristown, N.J.
*One of the classics in music literature. Each character is represented by an instrument.*

*Carnival of the Animals* (1971)
Saint-Saëns
Gokkin Co., Ltd.
Tokyo, Japan
*Various instruments impersonate animals—for example, the double-bass impersonates an elephant, and the cello, a swan.*

# APPENDIX D

# Listening Activities

The following listening activities were contributed by Sally Roman, kindergarten teacher. The activities* are organized according to Wilt's successive levels of listening as discussed by Lerner.† Some of the wording in the levels was slightly modified.

I. *Auditory perception of nonlanguage sounds*
At this level the children will become aware of the contrast in sounds. They will associate sounds with objects and will listen for patterns.
A. *Contrasting sounds*
   1. Rhythm instruments such as a xylophone, bells, or piano can be used to play high and low sounds. The children can indicate whether the sound is high or low by pointing to parts of their bodies. For example, if the sound is very low, they point to their feet. They can also draw lines up or down as the sound varies. At first sounds should be grossly different. As the children improve their skill, the sounds can be made closer together.
   2. The piano and recorded music can be used to indicate whether sounds are soft or loud. At first the contrast should be great. Children can be asked to stand when the music is loud and to sit when it is soft.
   3. A variety of instruments can be used to demonstrate volume. The children determine when the instrument is playing loud tones and when it is playing soft tones. The drum is a good instrument to use for this purpose.
   4. Use recordings of animal sounds to demonstrate the difference between deep, growly sounds and high, squeaky sounds. The song "Old MacDon-

ald" can be used to help the children reproduce various animal sounds.
   5. Instruments can be used to depict the sounds of animals moving. For example, coconut shells split in half and clapped together make an excellent sound for galloping horses. (See pp. 279–280 for directions for making coconut shell clappers.)
   6. Hang a variety of metal objects from a rod. Allow the children to tap the objects and compare the sounds that they make.
   7. Play "Hunting for an Object." An object is hidden in the room, and several children look for it. While they are looking, music is played, and as the children get closer to the object, the music becomes louder. As they go away, the music is played more softly. A variation would be to have some of the children clap loudly or softly while the other children are looking for the object.
B. *Associating sound to object*
   1. Play a tape of people eating different kinds of food. Children have to guess what is being eaten.
   2. Make a tape of household sounds and have children identify them. The tape could be organized by rooms: kitchen sounds, bathroom sounds, etc.
   3. Use the record *American in Paris.* Have the children listen for automobile horns.
   4. Unseen by the children, place a small, familiar object in an opaque container. Shake the container. Have the children guess what the object might be.
   5. Make different sounds with paper behind a screen and have children identify what you are doing; for example, tearing, cutting, etc.
   6. Begin to introduce different orchestral instruments and have the children listen for their sounds. Young children can usually recognize the violin, clarinet, flute, French horn, and trum-

*Many of these activities can be modified to use with the different levels of listening.

†From Lerner, Janet W. *Children with learning disabilities.* Boston: Houghton Mifflin, 1971, pp. 162–165.

pet. Use music where the instrument is very prominent, such as Bowmar's record *The Young Listener*.

C. *Recognizing pattern*

1. Patterns of long and short duration can be introduced by clapping and having the children repeat the pattern. The teacher can also draw patterns on the board and then have the children guess what she is clapping; for example, _____ _____ \_\_ \_\_. The long marks stand for two long claps. The two short marks stand for two short claps. Patterns can be varied. At first, make the patterns easy to hear and reproduce. Then increase the difficulty as the children become more adept at doing them. For example, here is an easy pattern: _____ _____ _____. A more difficult pattern would be _____ _____ _____ \_\_ \_\_ \_\_.

2. Play the game "Pass It On." Children sit in a circle. One child claps a short pattern and gives it to the next child. That child then passes the pattern on to the next child. That child then passes the pattern on by clapping it for the next child. It is passed all the way around the circle. Another variation of this game is for the leader to play the pattern on a drum and have a child play the pattern back on sticks. The sticks are then passed on to the next child, and the leader sends him a pattern.

3. Meanings can be assigned to certain patterns. For example, let \_\_ \_\_ mean *stop* and _____ _____ _____ _____ mean *go*. Children can then walk, run, or skip in time to music and then listen for the signal to stop.

II. *Auditory perception and discrimination of language sounds*

The children will listen for words and letter sounds. They will respond to their similarities and differences. They will do likewise for rhyming words.

A. *Word sounds*

1. Make a tape on which you sing short phrases from songs. Sing the phrase twice—sometimes singing it the same, sometimes changing a word. Children listen and then indicate if the song was the same or different.

2. Have the children sing songs that have animal sounds in them. For example, the cow goes "moo, moo," the duck goes "quack, quack."

B. *Rhyming words*

1. Sing nursery rhymes often. They are excellent for helping children to hear rhyming words. For example, in "Jack and Jill" the teacher can help the children to understand that the words *down* and *crown* rhyme. One could also leave out a rhyming word and have the children supply it.

2. Use songs that have much rhyming in them, such as "This Old Man." Children then pick out the words that rhyme.

III. *Auditory perception of words and their meanings*

The children will develop a listening vocabulary and will understand action words, naming words, and concepts.

A. *Action words*

1. Use songs that require the children to act out motions, such as Hap Palmer's "Sammy," "Follow, Follow, Follow Me," and "This Is the Way We Wash Our Clothes."

B. *Words that name objects*

1. Show pictures of farm animals. Sing "Old MacDonald" and have the children choose a picture that represents that animal. Try and come up with some unusual animals. Another variation would be to sing the song, describing the animal but not naming it. The children then guess its name.

C. *Concepts*

1. Use songs that can help children to understand concepts. Examples of such songs might be "Ten Little Frogs" and "Pairs Are Things That Go Together."

IV. *Understanding sentences and linguistic units*

The children will begin to understand the structure of the sentence and the entire thought. They will begin to differentiate between a sentence and a question.

A. *Sentence understanding*

1. Use records and songs that require the children to follow directions; for example, the song "Turn Around" which asks, "Can you turn around with me?" This question is followed by the words "It's as easy as can be. Round and round about just so. Then *ker-flop* we're bound to go."

B. *Riddles*

1. Place several rhythm instruments in a box that has a hole just large enough for a child's hand to go through. The child reaches in and holds one instrument. He describes its sound and how it is played to the others who must then guess which instrument it is. *Note:* At first, place only two instruments in the box at a time.

2. Teach songs that ask questions; for example, "The Brownie Smile Song." Sing the song almost all the way through: "I've something in my pocket. It belongs across my face. And I keep it very close at hand in a most convenient place. I'm sure you couldn't guess it if you guessed a long, long while. So I'll take it out and put it on—it's a great big happy" (what?).

V. *Auditory memory*

The children will store auditory experiences, retrieve them, and relate them to other experiences.

A. *Songs related to curriculum areas or units being studied*

1. Teach songs such as "The North Wind" and other songs related to other seasons of the year. Discuss facts the children have learned from the lyrics of the songs. Ask children what kind of a sound the North Wind makes.

B. *Games with rules—remembering and associating directions*

1. *Tortoise and the Hare.* The children move in a circle or in scattered positions. The teacher assigns a drum beat to the hare, and the children move quickly. When the teacher says "tortoise" and changes the beat, the children move slowly like tortoises.

2. *Mother May I?* Use claps to indicate the number of steps to be taken. For example, two giant steps would be _____ _____, and two small steps would be ___ ___. Differences would have to be indicated by loudness and softness of claps or by longer and shorter claps.

VI. *Auditory or listening comprehension and critical thinking*

The children will combine listening and thinking skills and will be able to make judgments and evaluations.

A. *Following directions*
1. The teacher sings a song giving directions but does not follow those directions. For example, in the song "Put Your Finger in the Air" one of the directions is sung, "put your finger on your nose." The teacher sings, "put your finger on your nose," and while doing this she puts her finger on her chin. The children are encouraged to point out mistakes.
2. Use the record *Perceptual Motor Rhythm Games* by Capon and Hallum, which directs children to do movements by listening for musical cues.

B. *Sequencing events*
1. Use songs that have an order to them; for example, "Bingo" and "I Know an Old Woman."
2. Use songs that have several verses in which things happen in a sequence; for example, "Mary Had a Little Lamb."
3. Use pictures of verses of songs. Have the children arrange the pictures in order.

C. *Thinking critically*
1. Tape familiar, *appropriate* TV commercials that do not name the product. Permit the children to sing them. Then have the children name the product.
2. Invite to the room several adults that the children see each day and have each sing a song or songs for the children. This team might be composed of the classroom teacher, the cook, and the principal. Make a tape at the same time. At a later time, play the tape and have the children try to identify the person singing each song by relating the song to the person who sang it or by listening to the sound of the person's voice.
3. Play a variety of music. Discuss with the children the feelings that the music gives them and the actions it suggests.
4. Make a listening book. Play a piece of music with no words. The children then draw pictures and dictate a story to go with the music. Make a tape of the music. While listening on the earphones to the music, the children can follow along with the book.
5. Read a story. Have the children discuss the characters and the feelings conveyed. Then have them decide on appropriate musical instruments to accompany the storytelling, and make a tape of the story with the sound effects.

# A Practical Approach to Learning to Play the Autoharp

The Autoharp® is a relatively easy instrument to learn to play. The best way to become proficient in playing it is to learn the location of the bars and chords and then spend a great deal of time just playing and singing.

## CARE AND TUNING

The Autoharp should receive the same kind of treatment that one would give a fine piano or other instrument. Dampness and sudden changes of temperature will affect its playing qualities. When it is not in use, it is advisable to keep it in a box or case and to store it in a dry place of even temperature.

The instrument should be tuned frequently to keep it in perfect tune. This is not difficult to do if one has a good sense of pitch. It should either be tuned to a well-tuned piano, to some other instrument with a fixed pitch (such as an accordion), or to a pitch pipe. If one person plays the corresponding key on the piano while the other person tunes the Autoharp, the tuning can be done in approximately ten minutes.

Middle C should be tuned first, and the lower and higher octaves tuned in unison with it. In the same manner continue to tune the other strings. The tuning tool should be placed on each peg and turned *slowly* with either the right or left hand, either clockwise or counterclockwise until the tone produced by the string matches the tone of the corresponding key of the piano or other instrument. With the other hand, pluck the string with the thumbnail while turning the tuning tool. By turning the tool clockwise, the pitch of the string will be raised. Turning the tool counterclockwise lowers the pitch. When one is first learning to tune the Autoharp, it is most helpful to have one person playing the note on the piano while another person does the tuning. Continued practice in tuning the Autoharp should make one's ear more sensitive to changes in pitch.

When checking to see if the Autoharp is out of tune, press down the bars, one at a time, and slowly draw the pick across the strings to locate the string or strings out of tune with the chord. Usually, only a few strings will be out of tune at one time.

For optimum results it is extremely important to keep the instrument in tune. If one does not have a good ear for pitch, ask a music teacher or some other musical person for help.

## AUTOHARP CHORDING

This chart indicates the primary chords as they appear in the various Autoharp keys:

| Key* | Tonic I | Subdominant IV | Dominant V₇ | Tonic I |
|---|---|---|---|---|
| C major | C | F | $G_7$ | C |
| F major | F | B♭ | $C_7$ | F |
| G major | G | C | $D_7$ | G |
| D minor | $D_m$ | $G_m$ | $A_7$ | $D_m$ |
| A minor | $A_m$ | $D_m$ | $E_7$ | $A_m$ |

*Play the chord progressions in each key until you feel familiar with their individual qualities.

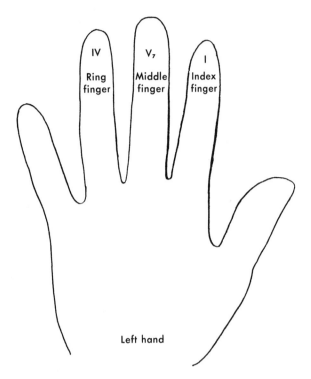

Left hand

The primary chords on the Autoharp, the I, the IV, and the V₇ in any of the keys, are played in the following manner. When the index finger is placed on the I chord of a given key, the middle finger falls on the V₇ chord and the ring finger on the IV chord of that key. For example, place the index finger on the F major bar. This would be the I chord in the key of F. The middle finger would fall on the C₇ bar (the V₇), and the ring finger would fall on the B♭ major bar (the IV chord).

The chart below indicates the chord markings for the twelve-bar Autoharp, the system used in this appendix:

| Bar label* | Chord produced | See note† |
|---|---|---|
| G Min. | G minor | $G_m$ |
| B♭ Maj. | B♭ major | B♭ |
| A Sev. | A seventh | $A_7$ |
| C Sev. | C seventh | $C_7$ |
| D Min. | D minor | $D_m$ |
| F Maj. | F major | F |
| E Sev. | E seventh | $E_7$ |
| G Sev. | G seventh | $G_7$ |
| A Min. | A minor | $A_m$ |
| C Maj. | C major | C |
| D Sev. | D seventh | $D_7$ |
| G Maj. | G major | G |

*On the Autoharp, ''Maj'' stands for the word *major,* and ''Min'' stands for the word *minor.* In a song a chord marking followed by a small *m* indicates that the chord is a minor one. A chord is considered major if it is not followed by a small letter.
†The letters and signs shown in this column are the same ones that are generally found in guitar chords on sheet music.

## VARIATIONS IN STRUMMING TECHNIQUE

Variations in rhythm or accent can be accomplished by strumming in different ways.

In order to strum rhythmically one must be acquainted with the time or meter signature found at the beginning of every song. Some of the more commonly used meter signatures are 2/4, 3/4, 4/4, and 6/8. The top number always indicates the number of beats or counts in each measure; the lower number indicates what kind of note or rest receives one beat or one count. For example, in 2/4 time the top number 2 shows there are two beats in each measure, and the lower number 4 shows that a quarter note (♩) receives one count. In 6/8 time, the top number 6 shows there are six beats in each measure; the lower number 8 shows that an eighth note (♪) receives one count.

Following are several suggested variations in strumming patterns*†:

- 2/4 time—One or two strokes per measure, depending on the tempo and style of the song. For one stroke per measure, strum on beat 1 and count silently on beat 2. For two strokes per measure, strum on both beats, 1 and 2.
- 3/4 time—One long, accented stroke or one long, accented and two short strokes, depending on tempo and style of the song. Strum one long, accented, full stroke, and count silently on beats 2 and 3, or strum one long, accented, full stroke from the bass strings up and two short, unaccented strokes on the higher-pitched strings.
- 4/4 time—One, two, or four strokes to the measure, depending on the tempo and style of the song. For one full stroke to a measure, strum on beat 1 and count silently on beats 2, 3, and 4. For two full strokes to a measure, strum on beats 1 and 3 and count silently on beats 2 and 4. For four strokes to a measure, use short strokes on all 4 beats.
- Banjo quality—Sharp, short strokes from the bass strings up or the higher-pitched strings down or stroking in both directions. The player can best decide on the desired length of stroke. A plastic pick is sometimes desirable to obtain the banjo effect.
- Harp quality—Full, long strokes from the bass strings up using most or all of the strings. One may also achieve the harp quality by strumming in both directions on the strings for certain desired effects. By strumming on the left side of the bars, one can obtain a realistic harplike effect. Play

*Press down one of the bar buttons with the index finger of the left hand and strum with the right, using the suggested variations.
†Chord markings for the songs in this book, placed above the music staff, are changed when the melodic line requires it. Additional chords are to be strummed between chord changes according to the rhythm of the song and the strumming patterns desired by the player.

smoothly without accent and only fast enough to keep the rhythmic pattern flowing.

- Broken rhythms—A combination of short and long strokes in either direction. If one can "feel" certain rhythmic patterns, it is usually not difficult with experimentation and practice to strum these patterns on the Autoharp.

When practicing the strumming patterns, press down firmly one bar button at a time with the fingers of the left hand. Strum with the right hand, using an easy, flowing action. Remember that the left-handed person may find it easier to reverse these positions. It is possible to obtain an endless variety of rhythm patterns by experimentation.

When playing the Autoharp, always try to strum and play it in such a way that it will help to create a mood that is appropriate to the song being played or sung.

### PLAYING

A good approach in learning to play the Autoharp according to chord markings is to select a familiar song that can be accompanied using only one chord. An example of this kind would be the round "Are You Sleeping?" Place the index finger of the left hand on the D major bar and stroke with the right hand on the first and third beats of each measure. Notice the song is written in 4/4 time. This means that there are four beats to a measure and a quarter note receives one beat. Hold the bar button down firmly while strumming. Strum each time the letter appears above the staff and note.

*Important:* When using the Autoharp to accompany singing, always strum the beginning chord several times in order to establish the key feeling for a song. If desired, one may pluck the beginning note of a song on the correct string indicated by the letter name shown beneath it.

## ARE YOU SLEEPING?

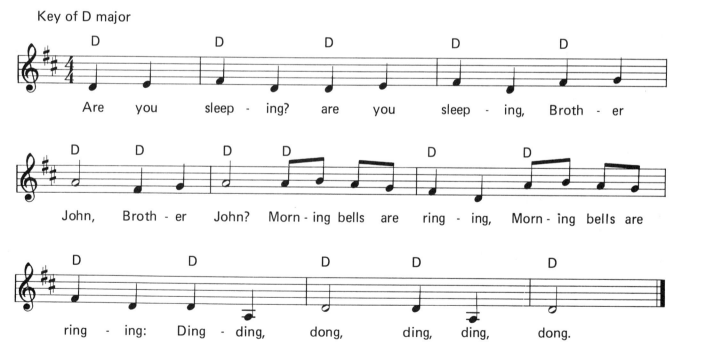

Key of D major

"Row, Row, Row Your Boat" is another example of a song that can be played using only one chord. Strum on the first beat of each measure or on both beats 1 and 2 if desired. Notice that this song has only two beats to a measure. Place the index finger on the C major bar.

# ROW, ROW, ROW YOUR BOAT

Key of C major

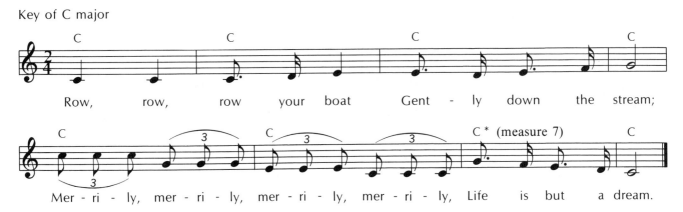

*After the song has been played once, play it a second time. At the beginning of measure 7 use the $G_7$ chord instead of the C chord. This should produce a more pleasing sound to the ear. In the last measure return to the C chord.

If the key of C is too low, try playing the song in the key of F. Place the index finger on the F major bar. In measure 7 use the $C_7$ chord. Return to the F major chord in the last measure.

Other songs that may be played with the use of only one chord are "Little Tom Tinker" and "Roll Over."

Continued early experiences in playing should be limited to songs with two chords, and the player should listen for the individual qualities of each of the chords used. Most songs having only two chords use a chord with the same letter name as the key in which the song is written, indicated by a I and called the *tonic chord*, and another chord that has the same letter name as the fifth tone of the scale in which the song is written, indicated by a $V_7$ and called the *dominant seventh chord*. The I chord gives the feeling of "completion" or "being at rest," whereas the $V_7$ chord has the quality of "unrest" and the need for resolution or completion, as was pointed out in the example of "Row, Row, Row Your Boat" (measure 7).

An example of a two-chord song would be "Mary Had a Little Lamb." Place the index finger of the left hand on the F major bar. The $C_7$ chord should be played with the middle finger of the left hand. Strum on the first beat of each measure.

The F major chord is the I chord, and the $C_7$ chord is the $V_7$ chord in this song.

## MARY HAD A LITTLE LAMB

Key of F major

Mar - y had a lit - tle lamb, lit - tle lamb, lit - tle lamb,

Mar - y had a lit - tle lamb, its fleece was white as snow.

Other songs that may be played using two chords are "Polly Wolly Doodle," "Down in the Valley," and "Skip to My Lou."

After mastering two-chord songs, three-chord songs should be explored for the distinctive quality of the third chord used. This third chord has the same letter name as the fourth tone of the scale in which the song is written and is indicated by a *IV* and called the *subdominant chord*. The chord progression from IV to I sounds much like the "Amen" that appears at the end of many hymns.

An example of a three-chord song is "Twinkle, Twinkle, Little Star." Notice the song is written in 2/4 time. Strum on the first beat of each measure or on beats 1 and 2 if desired. Place the index finger of the left hand on the C major bar button. The middle finger should play the $G_7$ chord and the ring finger the F major chord.

In this key, the C chord is the I chord, the $G_7$ chord is the $V_7$ chord, and the F chord is the IV chord.

Other songs that may be played using three chords are "Jingle Bells," "Home on the Range," "Brahms' Lullaby," "I've Been Working on the Railroad," and "Five Little Chickadees."

## TWINKLE, TWINKLE, LITTLE STAR

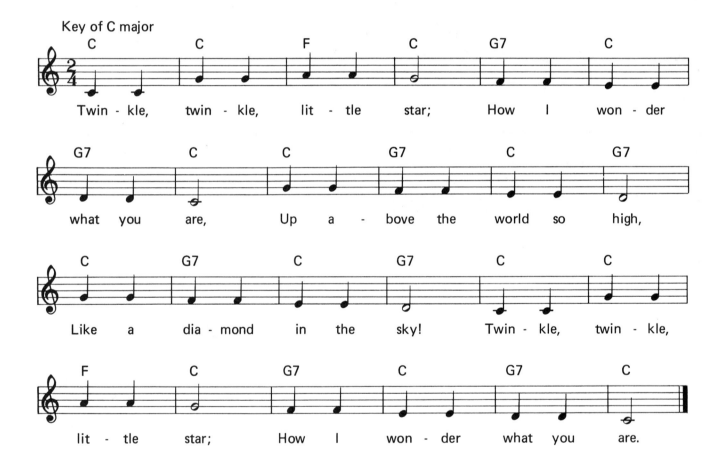

# APPENDIX F

# Fingering Charts for the Guitar and Soprano Recorder

**THE GUITAR AND ITS PARTS**

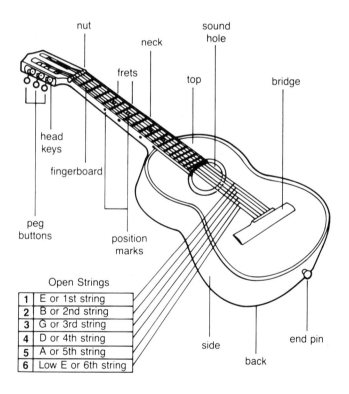

| Open Strings | |
|---|---|
| 1 | E or 1st string |
| 2 | B or 2nd string |
| 3 | G or 3rd string |
| 4 | D or 4th string |
| 5 | A or 5th string |
| 6 | Low E or 6th string |

## GUITAR FINGERING CHORDS COMMON TO THE MUSIC IN THIS BOOK

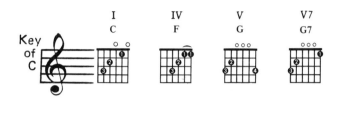

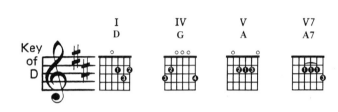

1    means first finger (forefinger)
2    means second finger
3    means third finger
4    means fourth finger
T    means thumb

The small circle (o) used on the diagrams indicates that those strings are to be played "open;" that isk they are not fingered.

A string that has no marking is not played. A slur "⌒" connecting two or more numbers on the diagrams means that those strings are to be pressed by one finger.

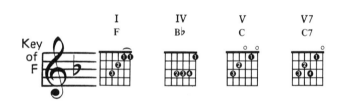

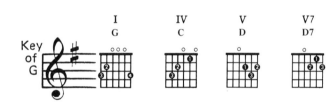

Dm(minor)    Gm(minor)

## PLAYING THE RECORDER

In the following recorder chart it should be pointed out that, unlike the traditional diagrams usually drawn for recorder, the fingering chart is shown from the player's view (rather than the observer's). Thus when the recorder is held in the position shown, all holes on the lower section of the chart should be played with the left hand, while those in the upper section should be played with the right hand. The numbers refer to fingers:

1 index finger
2 middle finger
3 ring finger
4 little finger

When playing the recorder, take care to blow gently and cover all holes completely except where indicated that the hole is left half open.

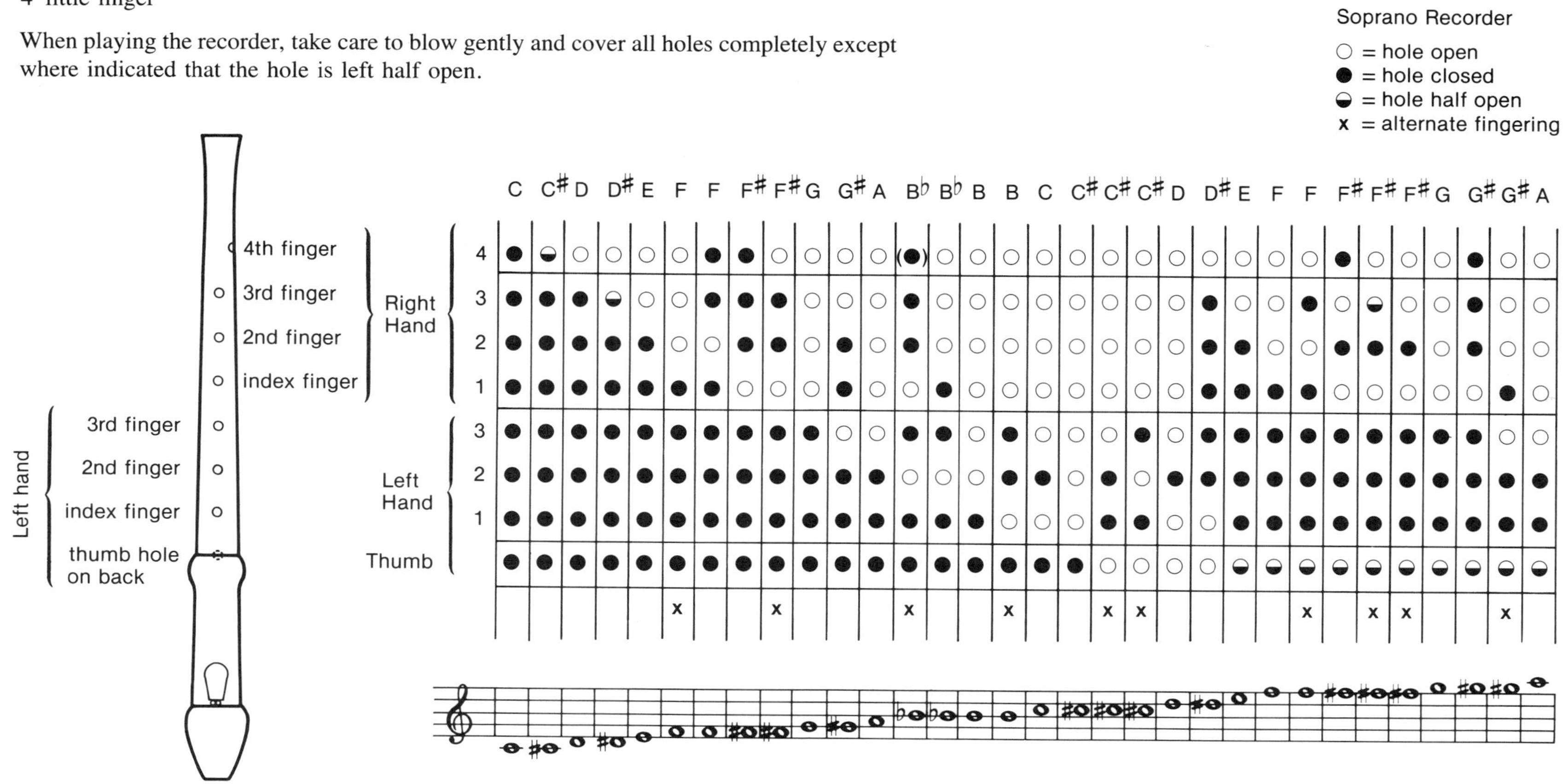

Soprano Recorder

○ = hole open
● = hole closed
◑ = hole half open
x = alternate fingering

From SONGS IN ACTION, Second Edition, by Phyllis Gelineau. © 1988. Reprinted by permission of the publisher, Parker Publishing Company, West Nyack, NY.

# APPENDIX G

# Instruments

## PERCUSSION, MELODY, AND CHORDING INSTRUMENTS

The following percussion, melody, and chording instruments are suitable for use with young children:

*Percussion instruments*

| | |
|---|---|
| rhythm sticks | gong |
| tone blocks | drums, small and large |
| wood blocks | bongo drums |
| temple blocks | tom-tom drums |
| tambourines | maracas |
| triangles | claves |
| finger cymbals | coconut shells |
| cymbals | |

*Melody instruments*

| | |
|---|---|
| piano | step bells |
| melody bells | xylophone |
| resonator bells | |

*Chording instruments*
Autoharp®
guitar
ukulele

## Drums

A drum is a versatile instrument to have in the home and classroom. A good drum is basic to any rhythm program for young children. One can make it do ever so many things. It can be played to tell when it is time to clean up the room or to call the children in from play. The syllables of a name can also be tapped out on a drum. One can play loud or soft, fast or slow, on this ''friendly'' instrument.

Drums can be purchased or made, and it is recommended that a variety of sizes and kinds be made accessible. Each drum should differ in pitch so that children have opportunities to hear and distinguish different levels of pitch. if possible, at times try to arrange several different drums close together, in a semicircle for example, so that children can discover the different sounds the drums produce as they tap one, then another. Children will soon discover that the drum produces different sounds depending on how, where, and with what they strike it. In good weather, the drums can be collected and taken outside where they can be experimented with. When this kind of opportunity is provided, children can accompany their rope-skipping games and create rhythms of their own. Parents and teachers are beginning to use some of the interesting drums from different parts of the world such as the Orient, Africa, and some of the Latin American countries.

## Rhythm Sticks

Rhythm sticks, two slender pieces of hardwood approximately 12 inches long, are good basic instruments for keeping time when marching, singing, or accompanying another instrument or a record. One stick from the pair is usually notched. A scraping sound can then be produced when the smooth stick is scraped across the stick that is notched. Sticks can be made from doweling. When making rhythm sticks, be sure the type of wood used produces a good tone quality.

## Wood Blocks

Two pieces of square- or rectangular-shaped wood with handles are used for this instrument. The size of the wood and the weight of the wood will depend on the age level of the children using the instrument. Some wood blocks are too heavy and large for use with the younger child. The instrument can be played by tapping or sliding one wood block against the other.

## Sand Blocks

Sand blocks are sandpaper attached by staples or thumbtacks to the sides of 2 wooden blocks, approximately 2½ × 4 inches each. Choose size and weight according to age level of children using them. Sand blocks are much easier to use if they are equipped with handles or holders. They are played by rubbing one sandpaper block against the other.

## Tone Blocks

A small block of wood, hollowed out with a cut on each side, and a wooden mallet make up the tone block. It is played by striking the mallet above the cut opening. This produces a hollow, resounding tone. When played correctly, the instrument provides a good underlying beat for musical selections.

## Wrist Bells

Sleigh bells, which should be of good quality, are mounted on a strap. The instrument is worn on the wrist or ankle and produces an effective sleigh bell sound to accompany songs and dances.

## Jingle Bells on Handles

Generally a single bell is mounted on the end of a handle. The instrument is held in one hand and shaken by the child in time to music.

## Tambourines

Six or more pairs of jingles are usually mounted in the instrument's shell. The plastic shell head comes in different sizes. The instrument may be shaken or struck with the hand, knee, or elbow, producing an interesting jingling effect.

## Triangles

The triangle consists of a steel rod bent into triangular shape, open at one corner, and struck with a small, straight, steel rod. We suggest that this instrument be purchased, since most homemade triangles have rather poor tone quality. The instrument is held by a holder and struck with a

metal rod. It may also be played by placing the rod inside the triangle and striking it back and forth against the sides.

## Maracas

Maracas are gourd or gourd-shaped rattles filled with seeds or pebbles. The instruments are shaken to produce rhythmic effects and can be played singly or by holding one maraca in each hand.

## Castanets

Castanets are a pair of concave pieces of wood, which may be held in the palm of the hand and clicked together or attached to a handle for easier use by small children. The sound makes an interesting accompaniment for dancing.

## Finger Cymbals

Two small cymbals with finger holders are held with each hand and struck together. The instrument also may be played by placing the loop holder of one cymbal over the thumb and the loop of the other cymbal on the middle finger. The two finger cymbals are then struck together.

## Hand Cymbals

Concave plates of nickel, silver, bronze, or brass produce a sharp, ringing sound when struck. Cymbals may be played in pairs by striking one against the other or singly by striking one cymbal with a drumstick.

## Autoharp®

This string instrument has buttons or bars that, when depressed by the finger, dampen all the strings necessary to the chord desired. It can be played by strumming or plucking. The number of bars on Autoharps® varies; the most common types have twelve or fifteen. Persons with little or no musical training can learn to play the Autoharp® in a relatively short time.

## Melody Bells

Melody bells are arranged like notes on the piano keyboard and are mounted on a frame. The bells are played with mallets. Sets come in various ranges.

## Step Bells

These bells are mounted on an elevated frame, include chromatic tones, and come in various ranges. Some frames are collapsible, allowing easy storage. Children can easily see whether the melody moves up or down.

## Resonator Bells

Mounted individually on a block of wood or plastic, these bells are arranged in a luggage case. Mallets are used to play the bells. The keyboard is similar to the piano keyboard. Each bell may be removed from its case and played individually. These are excellent for use by both child and teacher.

## HOMEMADE MUSICAL INSTRUMENTS

Making and using simple instruments can be a real source of pleasure and satisfaction for individuals of all ages, and it offers delightful hours of wholesome, cooperative activity for children in schools and for family groups. The possibilities for experimenting with materials are endless. Creating new instruments is fascinating and challenging, and much learning through problem solving takes place. It is not uncommon for the entire family to get involved in the process of creating new sound-making instruments. Some of the instruments described on the following pages are just as good as, and in some instances better, than those that are commercially made.

### Tom-toms, Drums

Played with the hands, tips of fingers, or sticks.

#### *Nail Kegs with Muslin Tops*—Materials

1. Nail keg—may be obtained from hardware store, lumberyard, factory, drugstore, antique shop, farm sale (kegs are becoming more difficult to obtain)
2. Airplane glue—hobby shop
3. Unbleached muslin
4. Large thumbtacks

*Directions.* Cut muslin about 3 inches larger than open top. Soak and stretch absolutely taut, fastening with thumbtacks or bright upholstery tacks. Do not remove rim of keg. When dry, paint top with airplane glue, giving it at least four coats. (*Caution:* Glue should be applied in a well-ventilated place, since it is highly flammable.) Do not paint kegs because this can affect the tone quality of the drum. A binding on the outside over the rim may be made from large rubber bands, inner tubing, or plastic tape. The sides of the keg may be decorated with cut-out figures. (See p. 276 for variations.)

#### *Cylindrical Containers of Cardboard*—Materials

1. Large ice cream cartons, large cottage cheese cartons, oatmeal boxes
2. Airplane glue
3. Unbleached muslin
4. Large thumbtacks

*Directions.* Tops for the cardboard containers are constructed like the nail keg tops.

#### *Large Tin Cans*—Materials

1. Potato chip cans, No. 10 food cans, oil cans from filling stations
2. Inner tubing
3. Sturdy lacing if needed

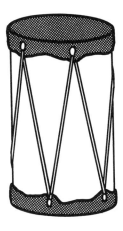

*Directions.* Use the best part of the inner tube for the drum head. Start by cutting the tube completely around the inner edge. Find the best part of the tube as you open it, and draw it over the end of the can. Cut out the round piece for the drum end, making it large enough to have a 3-inch overlap around the can. Repeat the same procedure for the second end. Cut eight holes in each piece of the rubber that was just prepared above, each hole about ¾ inch from the edge of the can. Place one of these rubber pieces on each end, and you are now ready to lace them onto the can. Prepare the lacing material by following along the inner edge of the tube and cutting strips ½ inch wide (or just wide enough to prevent tearing when stretching), or use another type of sturdy lacing. Thread loosely from one rubber end-piece back to the other, all around at first. Fasten, then keep on tightening and retying until the strips are taut and will snap back when pulled. These should be very tight. This type of drum will give a softer, more mellow tone than the other drums.

### Small Tin Cans—Materials

1. Empty, round tin cans—any size will do; the larger the can, the greater the volume and the deeper the tone
2. Discarded inner tube from an automobile tire; the thinner rubber gives a more pleasing tone
3. Flat paint; colored quick-drying enamel, turpentine
4. Small, round sticks, 10 to 12 inches long for drumsticks

*Directions.*    Select a sturdy can, free from dents, and remove one or both ends with a can opener that rolls the ends underneath so there are no sharp points. Remove the paper label with hot water, dry thoroughly, and give the can a coat of flat white paint. While this is drying, the design may be planned. Two coats of quick-drying enamel are recommended for finishing the drum.

When the finish is thoroughly dry, cut a circular piece from the inner tube to get a large rubber band ½ inch wide. Next, split the tube and cut a round piece for the drum head following the procedure used for the large tin can. One or two people are needed to help in putting the head on the drum, since the circular piece of rubber must be held tightly across the open end of the can while the ½-inch band is stretched around the can twice in a figure-eight fashion to hold the head in place. A little patience and practice will develop the necessary skill in this process. Tighten the head by placing the hands on opposite sides of the can and pulling the circular head down by means of the part that projects below the band. Trim off uneven parts, leaving sufficient rubber to prevent slipping and to provide for later tightening.

### Miscellaneous Drums

1. Drums may be made also by tacking a circular piece of inner tubing over the top of a wooden bowl. The large,

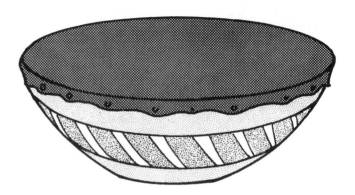

rather shallow type found in most homes is quite satisfactory. These offer fine opportunities for interesting decorations, and they give a nice tone.

2. More temporary, but very satisfactory and inexpensive drums can be made from round cardboard cereal boxes. Instead of using the muslin top, use a piece of inner tube for the head. The covers must be intact. A more durable drum with a better tone will result if the box is given a coat of clear shellac after it is decorated with watercolors, crayons, or enamel paint. A cord or ribbon fastened through two holes in the long side of the box will enable the player to hang the drum around his neck while playing. Two lightweight drumsticks may be used.

3. True Indian drums can be made by covering a hollow log or other similar container with sheepskin that is bound or laced into place while wet. This is a more difficult operation than the others suggested. We recommend a book on Indian handicraft to anyone interested in this type of drum.

### Drumsticks

Sticks for drums can be made from any available cylindrical pieces of wood 10 to 12 inches long and ¼ to ½ inch thick. They should be sanded smooth and rounded at both ends, avoiding points that might be dangerous. They may be painted to match the drum. If the drum has a head on both ends, two sticks are needed; otherwise, one is sufficient, since the player holds the drum under one arm while playing.

## *Other Types of Drumsticks*

1. Tinkertoys (for muslin-top drums)
2. Wooden beads, cork fishing floats, or large spools fastened on the ends of doweling

3. Single, padded stick made by padding the end of a piece of broomstick or other round stick with cotton, felt, or wads of cloth and kept in place by means of cloth or chamois cover tied securely to the wooden handle
4. End of a wooden spoon

## Rhythm Sticks and Blocks

### *Rhythm Sticks*—Materials

1. Round sticks of varying length and thickness, doweling, chair rounds, broomsticks, etc.
2. Paint, turpentine, etc., for decoration

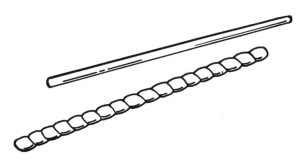

*Directions.* The sticks should be tried out by tapping them together to find the best combination for interesting tone effects. These may then be cut to convenient lengths—12 to 15 inches—and shaped with sandpaper. Points should be avoided. They may be finished by staining, varnishing, or enameling in bright colors and designs. They are especially useful for members of a large group in rhythmic play.

### *Rhythm Blocks*—Materials

1. Scraps of wood, approximately 3 to 5 inches long and at least ½ to ¾ inch thick.
2. For the handles: such things as a pair of drawer pulls, pot-cover handles, spools or small blocks of wood that can be bolted or screwed on, or pieces of an old leather belt or other material for making strap handles

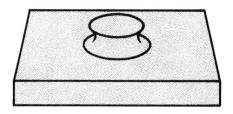

3. Small tacks, screws, or bolts, depending on type of handle
4. Paints for decorating the blocks

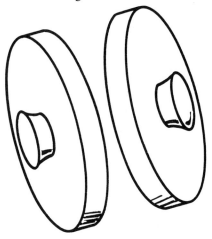

*Directions.* Two blocks the same size and shape should be cut from the wood. Oblong, round, square, and triangular shapes are interesting. Sand the blocks until smooth and then design and paint with enamel. New wood needs a coat of flat white paint first. Attach handles so that a perfectly flat surface is preserved for playing.

### *Chinese Wood Block*—Materials

1. Small, oblong, lightweight wooden box such as a cheese box, cigar box, or an old English Leather (men's shaving lotion) box
2. Braided rags, string, ribbon, or other type of cord for suspending the block
3. Walnut or dark oak varnish if desired
4. Small, round stick for beater

*Directions.* In order to get that delightful hollow sound that suggests galloping horses or tramping feet, it is necessary to cut long slits ¼ inch wide on the four long sides of the box. This may be done by boring a hole in one corner of the oblong shape to be removed and then using a keyhole saw, working slowly so the wood does not split. When all four slits are made, sand the edges smooth and even with sandpaper. Drill two holes in one end of the box for the cord, which can be fastened before the cover is nailed on or maneuvered into position with the help of a nail. Finish the wood block with one coat of dark stain (not enamel, which destroys the sound) and a coat of clear shellac or varnish if

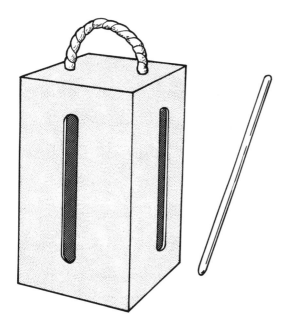

desired. This improves the appearance but not the tone. A stick similar to a drumstick can be used to strike the instrument.

### Sandpaper Blocks—Materials

1. Two oblong blocks of wood, approximately 3 × 5 inches, and at least ½ inch thick
2. Medium-grade or fine-grade sandpaper for covering bottom and sides of blocks
3. Large-headed tacks or nails
4. Materials for handles, similar to wood blocks
5. Paint for decorating the blocks

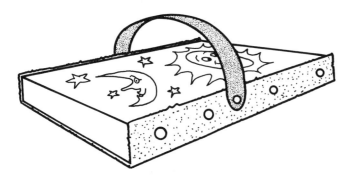

*Directions.* The sandpaper should be cut to fit the bottom of the block with enough on each side to fold up and cover the edges of the block. It should be attached to the block by sufficient thumbtacks, nails, or staples along the covered-up edges to hold it securely.

Make handles by securing the ends of a 5 × ½-inch plastic or leather strip to each side of the block. The rhythm sound may be obtained by inserting the hands through the handles and sliding the blocks back and forth.

## Rattle Sounds

### Soap Shaker Rattle—Materials

1. Wire soap shaker with wooden handle
2. Four round metal bells—miniature sleigh bell type, not the open kind with a clapper
3. Flat white and colored enamel paint

*Directions.* Give the shaker a coat of flat white paint and then two coats of enamel. When it is dry, put bells in the boxlike part of shaker and fasten securely by pushing small metal ring as far down toward the box as possible, working with a hammer and screwdriver. Pinch firmly into place with pliers.

### Gourd Rattle—Materials

1. Dry, well-shaped gourds (shells should be hard and firm)
2. Small feathers of colored yarn and beans for decoration
3. Beads, sand, small pebbles, rice, seeds, or other material for inside rattle
4. Small pieces of round wood for handles
5. Large-headed nails for fastening handles
6. Glue for fastening decorations
7. Enamel paint, shellac, and turpentine

*Directions.* Select well-shaped gourds—the larger the better. Remove a small part of the narrow neck with a coping saw or keyhole saw. The size of the hole depends on the thickness of the handle to be inserted. Remove the gourd seeds, unless they make a satisfactory rattle, and add a sufficient quantity of whatever hard substance is to be used to give the rattle the volume of tone desired. Corn or beans are good, and sand, fine gravel, or rice give a softer sound. Insert stick and push to the top of the gourd, leaving at least four inches for the handle. A single upholstery nail through the center of the top of the gourd into the end of the handle should hold it firmly. Fill the crack around the handle with glue, or plastic wood if preferred. Paint and decorate rattle if desired. Attach feathers or ribbon with glue or sealing wax.

Interesting rattles can be made of gourds that have a pleasant sound by virtue of their own dried seeds by simply decorating them and using them without handles. A coat of clear shellac often helps the tone of rattles of this kind.

### *"L'eggs" Hose Shaker*—Materials

1. One plastic "L'eggs" hose container
2. ⅜-inch dowel stick ten inches long
3. Twelve dried beans, rice, or small stones
4. Plastic glue

*Directions.* Cut ⅜-inch hole in the long end of the "L'eggs" hose container. (Use hot instrument or a drill to cut the hole. The hole can also be made with a heated darning needle.) Insert dowel through hole. Put glue on end of dowel inside of container around the ⅜-inch hole and around the center overlapping portion of the container. Place beans inside container and assemble. Make sure that the dowel is touching the inside of the container so that the glue will make the assembly rigid. Allow glue to dry overnight. Decorate. Acrylic paints work well and provide a smooth finish.

### *Hand Shaker*—Materials

1. Piece of wood 1½ to 2 inches wide, 8 inches long, ½ to ¾ inch thick
2. Four metal soft drink bottle caps
3. Two ½-inch washers

*Directions.* Flatten soft drink bottle caps. Through each center, drill or punch a hole slightly larger than the diameter of the nail. Assemble bottle cap, washer, and second bottle cap on nail and tack to wood paddle ½ inch from one end. Repeat second assembly two inches from first nail. Carve end opposite the bottle cap assemblies to fit child's hand. (See illustration at bottom of page.)

### *Coconut Shell Clappers*—Materials

1. Coconut (should not be too large for hands of young children)
2. Saw

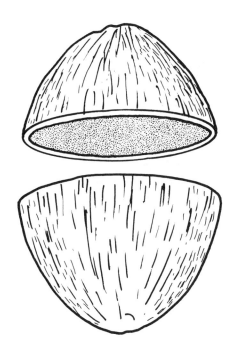

*Directions.* Select a coconut whose rounded ends will easily fit the palms of a child three to five years old. Allow the coconut to dry for several weeks to dry up the milk inside and cause the solid portion to shrink away from the sides. Then place the coconut in a vise. Take a wood saw

and saw through the middle. (Having another person hold the other side of the coconut while one person is sawing is helpful.) After the coconut is cut in two, take a knife and lift out the solid portion. Sand outsides of shell, file off pointed ends of coconut and shellac surface, if desired. When the shells are tapped together they make a hollow clip-clop sound—a good imitation of horses' hooves.

### Tin Can Rattle—Materials

1. Small tin can with cover
2. Small object for inside the rattles—corks, rice, and beans give nice tones
3. Flat white paint and enamel for decorating cans
4. Glue or plastic tape for fastening covers

*Directions.*   Select a can free from dents and sharp edges—one with a tight-fitting cover. Experiment with various kinds of material until the desired sound effect is achieved. A single small cork or nut has been found to be pleasing. Glue the cover in place if there is any possibility of its coming loose unexpectedly. Give the can a coat of flat white paint. When dry, decorate with enamel. Cardboard cans with metal ends often give interesting two-tone effects. Cardboard boxes may be used also, but they are much less durable and are not suitable for very young children.

### Wrist or Ankle Bells—Materials

1. Four to six round metal bells (not the open kind with clapper)
2. Material for making the band (may be knitted or crocheted)—colored yarn or string or heavy cloth such as denim, ticking, or canvas

3. Needles and *strong* thread (such as nylon) for fastening bells and ends of bands

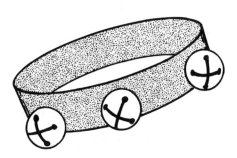

*Directions.*   Make a band seven inches long and one inch wide, fastening the ends together securely to form a circle. Sew bells firmly to the band at even distances. (Suggestion: Instead of fastening the ends together to make a circle, sew a section of Velcro on each end of the band. By using the loop-type on one end and the hook-type on the other end, this will provide for a size adjustment on the band. Velcro can generally be purchased at a store that sells fabric goods.) Bells may also be sewed on elastic to make the wrist and ankle bands.

## Orff Instruments

Use of the Orff concept of teaching music is growing very rapidly (pp. 236–237). Instruments for the Orff method are specially designed percussion instruments of excellent quality. They are rather expensive but excellent to use with young children.

# Conduit Pipe Xylophone

Conduit pipe usually comes in 10-foot lengths.
It costs about $6.00 per length.
You will also need about 3 feet of felt weather stripping.

Small set—use 10 feet of ½-inch electrical conduit pipe.
Large set—use 20 feet of ½-inch electrical conduit pipe.

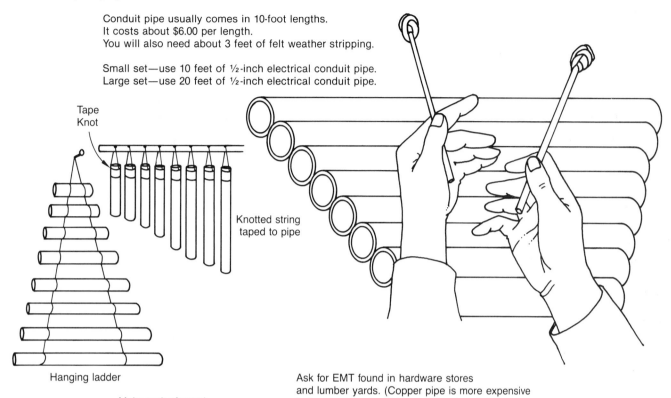

Tape
Knot

Knotted string
taped to pipe

Hanging ladder

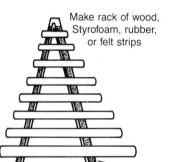

Make rack of wood,
Styrofoam, rubber,
or felt strips

Felt dividers

Table model

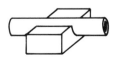

Styrofoam cradle

Individual Styrofoam
pipe cradle

Ask for EMT found in hardware stores
and lumber yards. (Copper pipe is more expensive
but easier to cut and has a richer tone.)

**1** Cut the longest pipe first. In case you lose this note by cutting the bar too short, you can use the "mistake" for the next note and nothing is wasted. Filing the pipe end heightens the note. (It helps if you have a good ear for tone.)

**2** Cut 2 one-foot lengths of felt weather stripping. Then cut 11 ½-inch felt divider pads. Glue pads between pipes so pipes don't roll. Or, you can cut ditches in Styrofoam blocks, or make each note bar an individual cradle, or you can tie the pipes into a hanging ladder. (Ditches cut in Styrofoam blocks or ½ of egg carton seem to give the best results.)

## Measurements

|  | Large | Small |
|---|---|---|
| low so | 22 7/16″ | 11 7/32″ |
| low la | 21 1/4″ | 10 5/8″ |
| low ti | 20″ | 10″ |
| do | 19 1/2″ | 9 3/4″ |
| re | 18 1/4″ | 9 1/8″ |
| mi | 17 1/8″ | 8 9/16″ |
| fa | 16 5/8″ | 8 5/16″ |
| so | 15 5/8″ | 7 13/16″ |
| la | 14 3/4″ | 7 3/8″ |
| ti | 13 3/4″ | 6 7/8″ |
| high do | 13 7/16″ | 6 23/32″ |

From Elementary Science Study, with permission of Education Development Center, Inc., Newton, MA.

# Subject Index

# Song Index

# About the Authors

**Kathleen M. Bayless** is currently Professor Emeritus, Teacher Development and Curriculum Studies at Kent State University. Since retirement she has been teaching early childhood music courses, supervising student teachers, and assisting with a class of special learners on a part-time basis. She served on the National Association for the Education of Young Children's Commission on Appropriate Education for Four- and Five-Year-Old Children. She serves as a consultant and presenter for school systems, teacher organizations, and preschool parent groups in the field of music for young children. Her current research interests involve using music with the special child.

**Marjorie E. Ramsey** currently is a freelance writer, consultant, and lecturer, having retired from the University System of Georgia. She served as Chairman, Division of Education, and Director of Teacher Education, Georgia Southwestern College until July 1988. Her experience as a classroom teacher, principal, supervisor, and college administrator has been shared in numerous publications, lectures, workshops, and professional organizations. Dr. Ramsey has traveled extensively in Europe, the Far East, the People's Republic of China, and Taiwan, as lecture tour director and liaison to educational systems. Her present research interests center on leadership, language development, and creativity.